RESULTS-DRIVEN TEACHING

Teach So Well That Every Student Learns

Keen Babbage

Rowman & Littlefield Education
Lanham, Maryland • Toronto • Plymouth, UK
2007

Published in the United States of America
by Rowman & Littlefield Education
A Division of Rowman & Littlefield Publishers, Inc.
A wholly owned subsidary of The Rowman & Littlefield Publishing Group, Inc.
4501 Forbes Boulevard, Suite 200, Lanham, Maryland 20706
www.rowmaneducation.com

Estover Road
Plymouth PL6 7PY
United Kingdom

British Library Cataloguing in Publication Information Available

Library of Congress Cataloging-in-Publication Data

Babbage, Keen J.
  Results-driven teaching : teach so well that every student learns / Keen
Babbage.
      p. cm.
  ISBN-13: 978-1-57886-548-2 (hardcover : alk. paper)
  ISBN-13: 978-1-57886-549-9 (pbk. : alk. paper)
  ISBN-10: 1-57886-548-4 (hardcover : alk. paper)
  ISBN-10: 1-57886-549-2 (pbk. : alk. paper)
  1. Motivation in education. 2. Effective teaching. 3. Teacher-student
relationships. I. Title.
  LB1065.B25 2007
  371.102—dc22   2006023607

To Robert and Mattie Johnson,
Mary Nichols Biswell, and Christine Johnson

CONTENTS

PREFACE

They spoke with unlimited hope, inspiring convictions, strong faith, confident commitment, and penetrating insights. They are results-driven teenagers who expect of themselves a persistent pursuit and absolute attainment of a life that matters.

These teenagers led the worship service today at a church I visited upon the invitation of a former student who told me last week of the upcoming youth Sunday program at his church. Of course I attended. I knew that my young friend would appreciate seeing an adult who he had invited attend the service. My other motive was quite selfish. I knew that the teenagers would present a vibrant but challenging and uplifting program. They did their job flawlessly.

The teenagers looked the congregation directly in the eye, the mind, the heart, and the soul. They shared thoughts from the depth of their beliefs and toward the height of their hopes. They made me think, wonder, reflect, conclude, awaken. They caused learning through their willingness to eagerly interact with questions, ideas, each other, the congregation. They were driven by a determination to get results.

The messages from those results-driven teenagers contrast severely with the topics I read about in the newspaper this morning. More rebellion, insurgency, death, and destruction in Iraq. The price of oil is increasing with no apparent possibility of restraint. The price of gold is increasing with alarming swiftness. The debt of the United States as a nation and the debt of individual Americans suggest a nation that is dangerously flirting with a national financial emergency. Those are real problems that demand real solutions now. It is unethical, immoral, and childish to postpone resolution of those problems so another generation is forced to solve problems its parents or grandparents created and then ignored.

The speakers I heard this morning are results-driven teenagers. They explained that they expect themselves to correct their mistakes, take initiative to help improve the lot in life of other people, put their faith into action, and live up to the standards set for them and the higher standards they eagerly set for themselves.

This book is designed to create, nurture, challenge, equip, educate, and inspire results-driven students by creating, nurturing, challenging, equipping, educating, and inspiring results-driven teachers to do results-driven teaching.

It is how the teenagers I heard this morning look at, perceive, and think about life that compels them to be results-driven.

Likewise, it is how educators look at, perceive, and think about teaching that leads to how they do their job. This book is about the perspective of teaching that compels a teacher to be a results-driven teacher whose standard is results-driven teaching.

❶

WHAT IS TEACHING?

What bonus is given to teachers whose students successfully and completely learn? What penalty is imposed on teachers whose students do not successfully and completely learn? The answer to both questions in most schools is "none." There is no official bonus for magnificent achievement, and there is no official penalty for dismal underperformance. Is this true in other professions, in other jobs, in other parts of the economy? Is this the ideal for the teaching profession?

What is teaching? If teaching is to be accurately evaluated and measured, it must be precisely identified and described. School districts create long forms with longer lists that administrators use when visiting a classroom to conduct a formal observation of a teacher. "Actively engages students," "uses a variety of questioning strategies," "effectively incorporates technology into the lesson," "quickly resolves disruptive behavior," and "efficiently makes transitions from one activity to the next activity" could be among the many items on the observation checklist.

If there are 100 items on the checklist, how many must a teacher demonstrate to merit an overall satisfactory level? Would 70 be enough? Or if a teacher does brilliant work with 10 of the items, could that compensate for not including the other 90 items in that one class? If 70 items equals satisfactory, would 80 mean that better teaching was observed? Would 90 mean near perfection or 100 mean perfection?

Perhaps bad teaching is more easily identified than good teaching. Perhaps there are more ways to teach well than there are ways to teach poorly; therefore, exact identification of every acceptable teaching action in the good range is a more complex task than exact identification of every unacceptable teaching action or inaction in the bad range. Perhaps bad teaching is a function of what is not done as much as it is a function of what is done.

The foundational concept of this book is attitudinal. Certainly there is merit in the scientific, quantifiable, precise measurement of the work that teachers do. Some attention to the best work of teachers, the work that accomplishes the purpose of teaching, which is to cause learning, will be included in this book. Still, the foundation of *Results-Driven Teaching* is a results-driven attitude about, perspective on, and understanding of teaching. The results-driven teacher expects and requires himself or herself to get results in the classroom. The essential classroom result is learning. The results-driven teacher causes learning and relentlessly finds or creates proper ways to cause learning.

Comments from results-driven teachers might include the following: "My duty is to cause learning." "I have to make sure that all students learn." "I get to work with students so everyone learns." "I know what the personnel form says, but what matters most is that all of my students learn. I'm not motivated by some observation form. My standard is much higher." "I expect myself to teach so well that every student learns. That's how I see teaching."

Those teaching ideas emerge from a results-driven attitude, perspective, and understanding. The purpose of a school is to cause learning. The duty of a teacher is to cause learning. The measure and impact of results-driven teaching is that learning is caused. What learning? The properly identified curriculum is learned by each student, and that learning is the result of actions that (a) cause the current learning and (b) establish the skills, comprehension, and mastery needed for additional learning. Plus, the current learning was caused in ways that inspired, intrigued, fascinated, and challenged students and was so personally meaningful that each student emerges with a compelling eagerness to learn more.

Results-driven teaching occurs when a teacher fully knows what students are supposed to learn, knows how current students best learn, knows how to design instructional activities that cause current students to learn the current curriculum, and is satisfied only when all students have sufficiently learned.

If 25 patients visit a medical doctor during a week when a stomach virus is rampant, will the exact same action be taken to help each person get well? No, because many variables will have to be evaluated: other medications being taken, the patient's overall health, other health conditions, allergies, and so on. In other words, several factors impact the physician's decisions about each patient. The physician does not give the patient a book about stomach viruses, a worksheet to complete with multiple-choice questions about stomach virus problems, a video about stomach virus treatments, and the odd-numbered problems on page 63 in the stomach virus statistics workbook. The results-driven physician takes action to cause healing. The results-driven teacher takes action to cause learning.

Some teachers expect themselves to cause learning. Some other teachers expect themselves to provide each student with opportunities to learn, but the students may or may not accept the opportunity. Still other teachers provide activities for students to complete so subjects are covered, not learned. All three groups will return to school year after year, although only one group is getting outstanding student achievement. What drives the results-driven teacher to answer the "what is teaching" question with the answer "to cause learning"? What drives the results-driven teacher in general?

Work ethic is one part of the answer, but it is not the dominant factor. Results-driven teachers have an honorable work ethic and often invest above average hours into their career, but they are not obsessive work addicts who work 12 hours daily, 7 days weekly. Some very ineffective, unproductive teachers spend extra hours at school, but they accomplish little even if they seem busy. Their activity just is not useful, productive, results getting, or learning causing. What else drives results-driven teachers? Some possible answers include dedication to students, an eagerness to touch lives, inspiration from a great teacher years ago, personal fascination with the subject being taught, a desire to advance in a career to other jobs within a school or a school district, integrity, a sense of honor to their employers, or promises made to themselves about the type of teacher they would be.

There is another driving force within a results-driven teacher. A results-driven teacher continues to learn every day about students, about teaching, and about the subject(s) being taught. The dynamics, the possibilities, and the adventures within the classroom of a results-driven teacher are forever vibrant, innovative, and energetic while always focusing on the purpose—causing learning. Results-driven teaching realizes that learning is infinite including what a teacher can learn about students, about <u>how</u> <u>students learn</u>, about the subject(s) being taught, and about how learning is best caused now, knowing that how learning is best caused tomorrow, next month, or next year may be quite different.

Results-driven teaching does not fit the following pattern: graduate from college at age 22, begin teaching three or four months later, endure the first year by finding some routine that at least avoids major disruptions in the classroom, repeat the routine for 29 identical years, and retire. Certainly, during those 29 rerun years, seemingly endless professional development programs will be attended, educational fads will enter and exit, and governors or superintendents will bring reforms that will be reformed by their successors. But some teachers will comfortably adjust to a routine that accomplishes little, disturbs few people, draws no attention, violates no laws, and causes little or no learning.

What attitude, perspective, and understanding are within the mind of the rerun-driven teacher whose career is 29 repeats of the same pedantic worksheet, textbook, video, and Friday test of year one? Is this person taking the easy way out, stealing a paycheck and/or intentionally denying himself and his students the wonderful learning experiences that are occurring in a classroom down the hall? Do rerun-driven teachers think they are doing great work? Do rerun teachers just do enough to avoid getting fired? Do rerun teachers see the purpose of school as passing time for young people, ages 5–18, in the most restricted, routine, superficial way? Does the rerun-driven teacher limit himself with the conclusion, "I could never do what that other teacher does?" Does a rerun teacher think there is value and virtue in imposing rigid routines on students who might otherwise think creatively or act energetically or challenge ideas?

Rerun teachers might say the following: "But it takes so much time to prepare anything different." "But I have so many bad students." "But I tried something like that once and it didn't work." "Other people get fancy in their classroom, I just keep it simple." "Teaching takes so much of my time I can't do anything other than what I always do." "Well, our school bought those textbooks and worksheets so I'm going to use them." "I do what my teachers did when I was in school. It worked then. It will work now." "I'm not changing everything because we would just change it all again in a few years. I've seen it happen too many times." "I'm just not like that other teacher. My personality just won't adjust." "Why should I have to change what I do? The students can work harder. It's their education."

Results-driven teaching does not require superhuman intellect, obsessive work hours, Hollywood star personality and charisma, or secrets revealed only to a chosen few. Results-driven teachers confront all of the challenges and difficulties that rerun-driven teachers use as excuses. What, then, is the difference? When answering the question "what is teaching," what is a results-driven teacher thinking that is different from a rerun-driven teacher?

Results. Results-driven teachers have an uncompromising conviction that they are responsible for taking the legal, ethical, and professional actions that result in each student learning. This conviction is supported by an attitude, a perspective, an understanding about teaching that accurately acknowledges that we know what works to cause learning; therefore, anything less than causing learning is unacceptable. This conviction is also supported by a devotion to students and a devotion to learning—the results-driven teacher is a student of students, a student of teaching, a student of their respective subject(s), and a lifetime lover of learning.

State governments have departments of education that publish guidelines, standards, benchmarks, testing scores, and other required data. Results-driven teachers accomplish more than any state government bureaucracy could ask or imagine.

The federal government, through the No Child Left Behind law and other constitutionally questionable coercion, establishes additional guidelines, standards, goals, formulas, requirements, and testing objectives. Results-driven teachers accomplish more than the U.S. government bureaucracy could ask or imagine.

Local school boards pass policies, set goals, endorse esoteric mission statements, and establish quantitative statistical expectations for schools. Results-driven teachers see past all these local measurements and accomplish much more.

Individual schools, school councils, principals, faculties, subject matter departments, or grade-level teaching teams may set goals, monitor test scores, pass policies, or enforce actions taken by the school board, a state government, or the national government. Results-driven teachers professionally comply with all laws, policies, regulations, and directives; however, results-driven teachers create achievements that far surpass these requirements.

Results. For results-driven teaching, what is the source of the drive to cause much more and much better learning than any governing body establishes as the standard? The attitude, perspective, and understanding of the results-driven teacher. The integrity, sense of honor, and acceptance of duty by the results-driven teacher. The drive of a results-driven teacher is from the heart, soul, and mind; it transcends law, policy, regulations, or bureaucratic reform. Results-driven teachers expect more and get more out of themselves than any law, policy, regulation, employer, or supervisor could draw out of a teacher.

Governmental bureaucracies are a reality of society. For highways systems to be developed, managed, renovated, and financed, a complex governmental system is necessary. Despite frustrations with taxes for roads, traffic delays during highway maintenance, and difficulty finding the right transportation department employee to answer a question, the governmental bureaucracy system for streets, roads, and highways usually is preferred to a system of privately owned and privately maintained pay-as-you-go toll roads.

For education to be provided to all children and teenagers, a governmental bureaucracy exists at the national, state, and local levels. This system produces laws, regulations, policies, and debates. This system establishes budgets. This system designs and implements accountability processes. This system identifies at the state and/or local level what students are to learn as itemized in comprehensive curriculum documents.

This system provides some guidance and some support for how teachers can implement the curriculum, yet much of this work—teacher certification and preparation—is more directly completed by colleges and universities where undergraduates complete teacher certification programs and where college graduates complete advanced degrees.

Results-driven teachers are not motivated to achieve greatness by this vast governmental bureaucracy. A results-driven teacher might say, "Finally, the state department of education has created a regulation to implement the law which says that every student will write a five-page short story in their sophomore year of high school as a joint venture across language arts, social studies, and humanities classes. Now, I'm going to create the most fascinating and the most productive classroom activities so my students meet this new state government regulation and requirement." Results-driven teachers already have their students doing more and better work than the new regulation requires.

Results-driven teaching surpasses all requirements of governmental bureaucratic educational systems. For that matter, results-driven teaching surpasses the policies and standards of private educational institutions or systems. Results-driven teaching lives by the cause learning standard: "I will find and/or create legal, ethical, and professional ways to cause each student to learn." The laws or policies that govern public schools do not, for many reasons, mandate a cause learning requirement. Private schools do not necessarily use a cause learning requirement or guarantee. Results-driven teachers expect themselves to cause learning because they know it is possible to cause learning, because they expect themselves to find ways to achieve the possible, because they reject excuses as personal and professional embarrassments, and because their sense of integrity requires that they complete the task as measured by results, not as measured by compliance with minimum requirements or as measured by simply going through routine motions that might provide some opportunities for some students to appear to learn some parts of the curriculum that was designed by someone, somewhere.

Results. The purpose of a school is to cause learning. The purpose, duty, and standard for a teacher is to cause learning. Results-driven teaching and results-driven teachers thrive on the pursuit and accomplishment of results. In the following passages, three teachers relate how they think about their work, their job, and their duty. While reading these perspectives, ask yourself if teaching—causing learning—is what each of these people is actually doing at work each day.

"I'm Fred Wade, high school math teacher. This is my twenty-third year of teaching. Usually I teach geometry or algebra classes. Sometimes I teach a basic math class for students who are still way behind. Throughout my career, I've sponsored the yearbook, sponsored recycling projects, coached the academic team, coached the swim team, and sponsored the senior class.

"I've served on a lot of faculty committees through the years. I worked on a curriculum revision task force in this school district about 10 years ago. I attend faculty meetings and I go to all of the required professional development programs. I do everything I am supposed to do.

"My annual evaluations are always fine. I'm not the teacher of the year or anything like that, but I don't cause any problems either. I know the rules, the regulations, the policies, and I cooperate with all of that.

"I'm not the first person to arrive at school, but I am not the last to arrive either. I do leave pretty soon after school ends each day, but that depends on whether there is a meeting to attend or an activity I sponsor. Right now I'm not sponsoring or coaching anything, but I'll start doing a lot of that next year. It will help increase my salary in the final years of my career, and that means I'll make more when I retire.

"The students and I get along fine. I do wish that the lazy students would work harder. I keep showing them exactly what they are supposed to do: what pages to read, what questions to answer, what problems to do, and what will be on the next test. I always ask them if they have any questions, but they almost never ask anything. Then they fail a test and get a bad grade on the report card. I get asked about that, and I show the details of my lesson plans. It's so obvious. If the students had just turned in all of the work I assigned right from the textbook, they could pass the class. Some students do the work and some students don't. I give everyone the same opportunity.

"The new textbooks we are using came with all kinds of electronic materials: videos, math on CD, worksheets, a quiz for each section of each chapter, a test for each chapter, and math posters that I put up all over the classroom. I'm using everything I was given—the textbook and all of the other materials. Some students do the work, some students don't. I just don't think it's my job to make people work and learn. I can't force them. I can give everyone a chance and I always do that.

"About 15 years ago, our state had a big education reform effort. Everything was supposed to change. I was in my eighth year of teaching when all of that reform started. I seriously considered quitting the job and joining my brother-in-law with his home construction company. That company has been very successful, and I do work for him in the summer. I kept teaching because the more experienced teachers told me that school reforms come and go, but they never last. They said I really would not have to change much of what I was doing and they were right. Five years after that reform started, there was not much left of it. A new governor plus a new superintendent here and a new principal at my school meant that old reform was forgotten and new reforms were started. Those lasted about five years, too. There's always some reform going on. I just keep plugging along with the textbook and the math problems and the rest of it. Some students work hard and learn a lot. Other students work an average amount and they do okay. Other students barely get by and some others fail. I do my job for all of the students, but not all of the students do their part. I guess it will always be that way because, from what I've experienced, it has always been that way.

"Sure, I'd like for every student to succeed. I'd like every student to earn an A grade in math. I know that they need to learn math. It disappoints me when students fail math class, but everyone had the same chance to learn and to pass. My principal says we have to do better. Well, she should talk to the students and their parents or guardians, too. Who tells them that they have to do better? I can't do it all. Yeah, I've talked with other teachers about this. Some of them agree with me that school gives every student the same opportunity to learn. For some students we actually give extra chances with after-school tutoring or before-school homework help. We give some students free breakfast, free lunch, free clothes, free pencils and paper, but the grade in math class is not free.

"Well, that's how I see it. I do my job. I'll keep doing my job for five more years or so. I can predict that in those five years some students will work and learn. Other students will get by and others will fail. I'll give everyone the same chance, the same textbook, the same homework, and the same tests. I'll be perfectly fair to everyone."

"I'm Catherine Cox. I teach science to 7th graders. I decided to become a teacher when I was 11 years old. Sure, I changed my plans many times. I was going to be a scientist, then a television news reporter, then a banker, then a pharmacist, then a preacher, then back to a teacher, and that never changed once I started my sophomore year of college. My 5th-grade science and math teacher gets the credit. She told us that everything in life connects with science and math. I figured that was impossible. I was really involved with soccer and I saw no science there. I was involved in Girl Scouts and we never did anything with math textbooks there. The things in life that mattered most to me in 5th grade just didn't seem to have anything to do with science or math.

"So, I very politely asked my 5th-grade teacher to show me how science and math connected with soccer and Girl Scouts. Well, about 10 minutes after I asked my question, the teacher was still showing everyone in the class how scientific and mathematical soccer is. From how the soccer ball is made to how big the soccer field is, science and math were everywhere. Then she told us all about going camping like we do in Girl Scouts, but she told us how science and math would make us better campers. She explained how a compass works and the best way to put up a tent so wind does not knock it down. I was convinced. I never forgot that day in my 5th-grade class. Even when I was considering all of those other career possibilities, I kept realizing that science fascinated me more than anything else and that if I could teach science as well as my 5th-grade teacher taught me, I could have a great career and I could get students to do better work than they ever thought of doing.

"So I majored in physics in college, minored in biology, and stayed for a fifth year to complete the master's degree program, which included teacher certification. I went to my first year of teaching with a strong foundation in science and a newly completed graduate degree. After one week, I was ready to quit. I wanted to be a banker, pharmacist, restaurant manager, sales representative—anything but a teacher. The first week was awful. I cried Friday night, but on Saturday I decided to take action. I called Ms. Phillips, my 5th-grade teacher, inspirer, mentor, and role model. She reminded me that I did not do much work in science until she showed me how science impacted soccer and Girl Scouts, my strongest interests at age 11.

"On Monday each of my 7th-grade students (I confess that I called them names other than 'students' as I cried on Friday night—'criminals' and 'heathens' were the most repeated terms, but on Monday I could again call them students) filled out a short interest survey. I warned them that everything they listed had to be G-rated, legal, proper. They cooperated. The lists ranged from skateboarding to caring for a pet snake, from snow skiing to cutting grass to making money, from working on cars to working on computers, from fashion to food, from music to movies, from space travel to basketball, from getting rich to getting in shape. I did what Ms. Phillips did for me. I made the wholesome interests of students the beginning topic of any discussion, activity, lab, or reading we did in science class. The results were amazing.

"I did cry again later that year. I cried when we got results on a 7th grade science test that all students in our school district take. My students did so well that our principal got a call to see what was going on. The central office staff had never seen such an increase in science scores.

"Here's what is best about that: the students and I almost never said anything during the year about those annual science tests. We just did science work every day that fascinated us and that made science real through connecting science and the wholesome interests of the students. The students (I started calling them scholars and they loved it) learned science, and the test scores, well sure, test scores went up. We aimed at science, and by hitting science, we also hit test scores.

"So, teaching to me is much more than those tests every year. The school district gives tests. The state government and the national government require more tests every year. My scholars can do so much more than those tests require that they should be exempt. Teaching is so much more than what those tests measure. Science is so much more than those tests measure. Teaching and science are infinite. I never place limits on what the students—the scholars that is—and I can accomplish together.

"In case you are wondering how long and how hard I work, here's my answer: I work as long and as hard as it takes to make sure that my students learn. I'm no workaholic. I'm at school about 9 hours each day. I have about an hour of school work to do each night at home. I do about

5 hours of school work each weekend. That adds up to 55 hours weekly. I know plenty of teachers who work fewer hours and some who work more hours. I measure myself by results. Doing the job well requires a certain amount of work, a certain amount of hours.

"One reason I don't have to work more than 55 hours each week is that the way I teach works. Ms. Phillips knew it worked for her. I know it works for me. Textbook science, worksheet science, and video science are not real science. Investigating the science of soccer, the science of making candy, the science of cooking pizza, the science of sending photographs through computers, the science of physical fitness, the science of skateboarding will fascinate students, plus I get excited when they get fascinated and learn. I almost never have to reteach anything because my scholars learn the first time we work on something.

"One other thought: I love science. I learn more about science every year I teach it. I learn about how students learn science. I read scientific journals. Science changes every day. Students change all the time. My classroom keeps up with all of that change. I can't imagine doing the same thing in the classroom year after year, class after class, for an entire career. That isn't scientific and that sure isn't good teaching.

"I know some teachers at this school who do the same thing, year after year. The students hate it except for some students who realize how easy it is, and they just go along. Some students hate it because it is so dull, and other students hate it because they would really like to learn something worthwhile.

"I've noticed that some of the teachers who are so monotonous in their teaching are often the people who complain the most. They complain about lazy students, about coming to school when it snows, about the building being too hot, about custodians not sweeping their classroom, about the principal, about so much work to do, about a new law or about a tight budget. The only thing they can personally and directly do much about is what happens in their classroom. I concentrate on getting great results in my classroom. That's why I am here. My only real complaint is if my scholars are not learning as much or as well as they can and should. When that happens, I fix it. My students can learn in a classroom that was not swept yesterday. They cannot learn in a classroom where the teaching activity yesterday was the same boring, "when-will-we-ever-use-this-waste-of-time" crossword puzzle of science words as the day before, and the year before that.

"That's all I intended to say. I'm a teacher. I'm a scientist. As my young scholars learn science, I learn about the scholars and about science. There is no other job like this. I belong right here."

"My name is George Richmond. I taught elementary school for 17 years. Then I got a job in another school district as the director of elementary schools, special education, gifted and talented education, federal government programs, and school district communications or public relations. I left that job after two years and became an elementary school principal. I did that job for three years and then started wondering why it was worth it to work at school 13 hours per day and still never get caught up. My school district expects elementary school principals to do two or three full-time jobs, from school security officer to personnel director, from building manager to social services coordinator, from mediator to instructional leader and more.

"So with eight years to go before I can retire, I wondered what job would make sense. My wife suggested that I either go back to teaching or become a school district superintendent. Neither option sounded very appealing. I refused to work the 14-hour days that superintendents work and deal with every impossible financial, educational, political, or bureaucratic problem they are responsible for. What else was there to do?

"Then I heard about a job at the state's department of education. People who work at schools wonder what most state education people do all day. They almost never work with students. They apparently send a lot of emails, attend a lot of meetings, and do a lot of paperwork, but how tough can it be to do that? So I applied for the position of assistant commissioner of elementary school, middle school, and high school reforms, transitions, and evaluations. Our state is seeking the perfect solutions to how schools are organized by grades. Should elementary school be grades K–4, K–5, or K–6? Is middle school best with grades 6–8, or different grades? Was junior high a better idea than middle school? And what about high school? What is best for 9th graders? What's best for seniors? What alternative schools, vocational schools, or gifted and talented programs are needed? What high school extracurricular issues need to be resolved?

"I got the job, but I quit after one year. The state government bureaucracy has a very limited idea about what reality is in schools or in school districts. People who cannot teach should not make or influence policies, regulations, or laws about teaching. People who cannot lead or manage a school should not tell people who do lead and manage schools how to do their job.

"I went back to teaching elementary school. I was not thrilled about it, but it had to be better than central office jobs, the principal job, or the state bureaucracy job. I had 4th graders for reading and social studies in the morning. I had a reading tutorial program for any student in 3rd, 4th, or 5th grade who was not reading on grade level. Then in the last part of the day, I had 5th graders for reading and social studies. It really was not much better than those other jobs because, well, so many things had changed since I started teaching. So many students were lazy. So many parents were apathetic. The school district expected miracles. The principal expected the impossible. What could I do? I selected an option to try for a one-year experiment. I would do the least that would avoid problems. I just decided to do what nobody could claim was unprofessional, insubordinate, illegal, or unethical.

"My students quickly mastered the routine. We had a plan for each day of the week. Every Monday was like every other Monday. On Mondays, the students opened their book to a new chapter and silently read it. This worked for every class, whether it was reading, reading tutorial, or social studies. If you finished reading and there was time left, you were supposed to read it again.

"Tuesday was our day to outline the chapter. Wednesday was our day to define the keywords in boldfaced print. On Thursday, we would answer all of the questions at the end of the chapter. On Friday we would take a short test or quiz and then watch a video about the next chapter. On Monday the process would begin all over again.

"The grades were always—I mean always—a bell-shaped curve. In a class of 28 students, there would be three As, five Bs, twelve Cs, five Ds, and three Fs. Some reading skills improved for about one third of the students. Another third of the students maintained their reading level. The other third fluctuated, sometimes showing improvement, sometimes showing decline, and sometimes showing no change.

"In April, the principal visited my classroom right before annual evaluations were due. He told me after class how impressed he was that every student knew exactly what to do with minimal directions given. In May, the principal called me into his office to ask what could be done about students whose reading level had not improved. I was ready.

"I said, 'I do wish their reading level was higher. As the scores show, some of my students have made significant gains in their reading level, so I know my approach can work. We just need the other students to be here every day, to work harder, and to have their parents to follow through at home more. The students who are not doing well seem to be absent more, and it seems to be difficult to reach their families or to get much response from their families.'"

"The principal encouraged me to work with the school district's literacy specialist. I emailed that person immediately. She invited me to a one-day literacy workshop to be held in June. I signed up to go thinking it would be pointless but wanting to say I went, I listened, I read the materials, I did what the principal and the literacy specialist told me to do.

"I think I'll keep this system going for three or four more years, and then I'll become a principal again for a few years to get my salary up and to increase what I'll be paid in retirement. I do wonder about one question: When I'm a principal again, how will I deal with teachers who do their job the way I currently do my job?"

There is one other teacher to hear from. This teacher worked in other jobs for 11 years before becoming a teacher. She was a stay-at-home mother for six years until her sons began 1st grade. Then she managed a daycare center at her church. Then she was a business manager of a for-profit tutoring program that worked with elementary, middle, and high school students who had academic problems in school. She decided to update her teaching certificate, and with the right graduate school program, she finished a master's degree as she also updated and expanded her teaching certification. She found a teaching job, two 11th-grade U.S. history classes, two 9th-grade civics classes, and two 12th-grade advanced placement U.S. government classes made up her block rotation schedule at Emerson High School.

"I'm Katie Jefferson. I've taught high school for six years. I love it. I absolutely love it. I have three different subjects each day with 9th graders, 11th graders, and seniors. Most teachers tell me they would never accept three different preparations, you know, having to do three different lesson plans because of three different classes. I tell them that if I taught the same subject to the same grade all day I'd still have three different lesson plans, because different students and different groups of students learn in various ways. Most other teachers just shake their heads or roll their eyes, figuring that eventually I'll conform to the ordinary procedures and processes. Not a chance.

"I always intended to teach, but my husband and I were eager to start a family early in our marriage. I stayed at home with our twins until they were in 1st grade. I've had jobs outside of school teaching. Customers at my daycare center demanded superior results for their children. The same was true for customers at the tutoring center where I worked. Each family insisted on and deserved what was best for their child. We got results or we lost customers. I think of teaching in the same way. I get results or I lose the wonderful possibility I had to very effectively educate a student.

"So, I bring a business perspective to my classroom. In business, products have to be improved, customer service has to be exemplary, and results must be achieved. A car company will go out of business if it tells the customer 'we know that our cars are not great. We know our cars never change from year to year. We know that our cars do not have all of the features or performance levels you expect. We know a lot about cars. All of the changes that other companies make in their cars don't interest us. We offer a reliable, old-fashioned, basic car. It's been good enough for years, so don't tell us how to make cars, and we won't tell you how to do your job.'

"The parents and guardians who send children to the tutoring center where I worked expected a program to be designed to help their child reach goals uniquely identified for that child. If we gave everyone there the same instructions, we would have failed. Sure, schools have lots of students, and tutoring businesses have fewer students, but when a teacher has a group of students for 90 minutes every other day as I do, you can get to know them, and with a little investment of time, you can create classroom activities that build on strengths of your students or that address their needs.

"Successful businesses listen closely to customers. I listen closely to students. I cannot give them everything they ask for or want, but I can give them experiences that connect with their interests, their personalities, their goals, their talents, their ambitions, and their real lives right now. They want that. They want school to be interesting and active and real. I give them experiences like that, and they give me their total effort, concentration, and cooperation. We work together. We learn together. We're in the business of learning. The students and I are great business partners.

"I don't mean to imply that what I do is easy. It's hard work, but it is so rewarding that it creates energy instead of absorbing all of my energy. I hear other teachers complain a lot. While they sit in the teachers' lounge and tell each other how difficult or unreasonable their workload is, I grade papers, prepare new lessons, visit classrooms of great teachers to get new ideas, make phone calls to families to say how well students did or to say what improvements students need to make, check out a library book, or do some Internet research for an upcoming class discussion. It's better to get the work done than complain about the work. Action gets results. Complaints get, well, more complaints.

"Those two businesses I worked for made our job descriptions very clear, and our work performance was measured against precise standards. Measured is the keyword. At both jobs, each employee had very specific records to keep about actions they took each day in compliance with their job description, with company policy and with any applicable legal regulations. Some actions were unacceptable. Some actions were legally acceptable, but better performance was required. Both businesses were about getting results that fully satisfied customers, that therefore produced profits, and that gave employees rewards in terms of accomplishments and in terms of career and financial progress.

"Some teachers tell me that they will get paid the same if all of their students learn or not. That really is not true. Sure, they get a paycheck, but they never get the pay that is available from students who tell you that yours was the best class they ever took or that you have inspired them to become more than they ever thought they could be. Some teachers make more dollars than I do because they have more years of experience or they have a more advanced graduate degree than I do. Our monetary pay is based on years of teaching and extent of graduate degrees. But our human pay—the pay that cannot be spent, but can be felt in our heart, mind, and soul—is unlimited. When the students and

I have brilliant discussions in class, that is priceless to me. When students who used to barely pass move up to make a better grade, because in my class they became fascinated with learning, or at least willing to work harder, I am paid in what I call conscience currency. In my conscience—my inner sense of right and wrong, ethical and unethical, proper and improper—I know that the students deserve my best effort. My employer does not demand from me as much as my conscience demands from me.

"So, doing my teaching job to get fantastic results is good for the students, plus it is a little bit selfish. A classroom of energetic learning means that I am learning, too. A classroom of successful students means that I have given students what they deserve and what my integrity, my conscience, my ethics all require of me. I just cannot imagine doing less when doing so much more is possible. I can't imagine denying the students and denying myself the very best learning experiences."

These four varied perspectives on teaching return us to the important question, "what is teaching?" One answer could be, "Teaching is the total of all classroom instructional activities that teachers do to implement the curriculum." That answer raises an immediate problem—actions done by a person who is employed to be a teacher may or may not teach anything to any student. If learning was not caused, teaching was not done.

These four varied perspectives on teaching indicate a concern, if not a problem. How can people employed to be teachers have such vastly different ideas about what they are supposed to accomplish and about how they are supposed to accomplish that? Do people employed in other careers—police officers, medical doctors, automobile assembly line workers, restaurant managers, nurses, computer technicians, lawyers, farmers, radio broadcasters, bankers, and more—have such a wide range of perspectives about what their job description is and how they are to do it?

Imagine four different restaurants managed separately by four different people who see the job of restaurant manager as Fred Wade, Catherine Cox, George Richmond, and Katie Jefferson see their job as teachers. What would be different in these four restaurants in terms of hospitality, eagerness to satisfy customers, willingness to do whatever it takes to give each customer a good dining experience, willingness to correct any problem or dissatisfaction regardless of how it happened, employee training, career opportunities for employees, and treatment of employees.

It is likely that Fred Wade would say to customers who exit the restaurant complaining about unacceptable service and substandard food, "Well, that waitress has been here for 10 years and she knows her job. The food is from the same supplier we always use. I wish you liked it better. Maybe you just aren't feeling well today. I think we did everything we were supposed to. I don't hear complaints from other people. Maybe you will like the food better next time." These customers will not return for a next time.

Katie Jefferson would offer a different response, but, more than that, she would never let the problem reach the point where dissatisfied customers were leaving with loud complaints. Katie would be very visible throughout the restaurant. She would be informed by employees of any problem. The employees would be empowered to do whatever is needed to solve the problem. Katie would personally confirm with each customer who made any complaint that the situation was resolved.

Fred Wade's restaurant is a place where Fred and his employees provide an opportunity for customers to get an acceptable meal. Katie Jefferson's restaurant is a place where Katie and her employees assure that each customer is fully satisfied with their meal.

When a customer takes a car to the automobile repair shop, the expectation is that for a set cost, the car will be repaired. The expectation is not that an effort will be made to repair the car, that it might work or it might not work once the effort has been made. I once had concerns about a car I had recently purchased. I returned to the car dealer to discuss my concerns. One of the repair technicians went with me as I drove the car and he asked me questions. Every issue, concern, problem, and question was resolved. I have done business with that car dealer for 15 years, and I will continue to do business with them. They are committed to results. They think and work like Katie Jefferson.

A television I purchased quit working after about eight months. I returned to the retailer and asked about options. I was told that it would be repaired or replaced. I left it to be repaired. Four weeks later, they called to say it was ready and the cost was $82. I reminded them I had been told that they promised to repair it or replace it. "Well," the person replied, "whoever told you that was wrong." They stubbornly refused to offer any solution other than my paying them $82. They money was not paid, and that business lost a loyal customer who had purchased four other major appliances from them throughout the years. They think and work like Fred Wade.

Where did Fred Wade get his ideas about teaching? How did he become satisfied with an approach to his job that produces minimal achievement by students? What causes Fred to think that merely giving all students a very superficial, ordinary, prepackaged routine of simplistic tasks is sufficient? Is Fred aware that there are better ways to teach? Is Fred aware of how eagerly his students work in other classes and in other parts of their lives outside of school? Is Fred aware that some other teachers are having absolutely fascinating learning experiences with students every day? How did Fred Wade miss the understanding about teaching that Catherine Cox and Katie Jefferson have? Why has Fred been allowed to do such minimal work and get such limited results throughout his career? Why has Fred Wade not been told that his answer to the question "what is teaching?" is wrong?

Is it possible that when Fred was in college, studying to become a teacher, all of his education classes and professors told him that textbooks, worksheets, videos, and Friday tests were the most productive, instructional methods to use? Or did Fred settle for the ordinary on his own? Has Fred decided that it does not matter what he does because some students will learn a lot, some students will learn a little, and some students will learn nothing despite the instructional activities used?

What is teaching? Teaching is the series of legal, professional, ethical activities that are designed for and experienced by students so that the intended learning is caused. Teaching causes learning. Fred Wade is not a teacher because what he does in his classroom does not cause learning. Fred Wade is a classroom clerk who distributes books and worksheets and then collects them, who pushes the play button on a VCR and who later pushes the same button to cue up the same video for the next class. Fred does not cause learning. Fred is not a teacher. What Fred does is not teaching.

Catherine Cox and Katie Jefferson are teachers. They cause learning. They get results. They are driven by the pursuit of results and the attainment of results. They do not begin with textbooks. They begin with students—with what today's students need to know; with the wholesome knowledge, talents, and interest of today's students; with an eagerness to design instructional activities that will cause today's students to fully learn the curriculum content while also learning about learning.

Is George Richmond a teacher? Is what he does with students worthy of the term teaching? He knows, after his experiences in several different jobs within education, that something just is not working well. He finds fault with the state education bureaucracy, locally provided professional development, the minimal effort of some students and their families, and school administrators, yet he left a job as a school principal. George has observed education and found many imperfections in the educational system. He has tried a variety of jobs and was not satisfied with any of the jobs. He has looked everywhere except deeply into his understanding of teaching, his perception of teaching, his dedication to teaching, his work ethic in teaching, his methods used in teaching, and what he could do in his classroom to get better results. What could happen if George Richmond profoundly pondered the question "what is teaching?" Has he done that since he was a junior in college and had to write a lofty, esoteric, pithy paper about his philosophy of education? Let's imagine how George Richmond might have written such a paper well over 20 years ago when he was a junior in college.

"Learning is the gateway to tomorrow. Knowledge is the pathway to potential. Education is a one-way ticket to a brighter future, because an educated person cannot become uneducated. An athlete may get out of shape. A beauty queen may lose her Hollywood radiance. The educated person cannot lose his or her education.

"School is the best place to get the best education. In school, each student can develop an interest in learning, pursue ideas, and imagine a wonderful life.

"Teachers must give every student the opportunity to develop to the highest potential. Teachers cannot predict what each student will become later in life, so every student must learn the basics and much more."

We could continue with more of George's weak attempt to persuade his college professor that he had given some real thought to education, learning, and teaching. George probably wrote that paper the night before it was due and hoped to get a B on it. He deserved a more useful assignment, but he also deserved less than a grade of B on his banal, empty, ordinary statement of platitudes.

George has just gone through the motions of his teacher preparation in college and his career in education. He may have been evaluated as "meeting the standards" on annual performance reviews based on two observations of George's work. If a teacher teaches five classes per day in a school year of 175 days and is observed twice for one class period, that means 2 out of 875 classes taught by the teacher were the direct basis for conclusions about how the teacher's work was done. George had no trouble doing acceptable work on those two observation days. He had no trouble staying employed because while he never did anything great, he also never did anything illegal or insubordinate. His goal is now to maximize his income during his final career years so his retirement payments will be higher. George, similar to his students, just goes through the motions in a classroom. Time is passed. Material is covered. Chapters are read. Blanks are filled in on worksheets. Learning does not occur. Teaching is not happening.

Here's an example of causing learning. I absolutely insist that students in my 8th-grade economics class earn a grade of A or B. I honestly tell them that grades of C, D, or F will get them nowhere. C means average, and doing average work is unacceptable. D is a phoney grade which merits elimination. F is disaster.

For the final homework project in one section of the economics class, I tried something different. Most students were exempt from doing the project because they had already earned an A or B for the class. Everyone else had to do the project, which, as with all projects in the class, gave students choices of activities. I told the students what grade they had to earn on this homework project to improve their grade to B level. Some students had to do both choices, because they needed extra work to cause extra learning to earn extra points.

On the due date, all but one student turned in the work. I thought at first that there was no reason on my part to make any additional effort. If he could not respond to this opportunity, there was nothing further that he or I could or should do about it. I quickly deleted that thought. My job is to cause learning. This student needed to learn more about economics, responsibility, and work, and he also needed to learn more about a teacher, boss, or supervisor who demands excellence.

I called the student's mother on Friday. "He turned in the extra credit, yesterday didn't he?" she asked. I explained that he had not. She said, "He told me he did. Well, what should we do now?"

We agreed that by Monday he would turn in the extra credit work. We also agreed that for him to earn the opportunity to still turn in the original extra credit work, he would have to do an additional project, which would also be due on Monday immediately after he arrived at school.

On Monday morning, the student walked up to me and politely handed me all of the work. He was eager for me to read it right then, even though we were in the gymnasium where two teachers and I supervise about 200 students as we wait until it is time for everyone to go to their lockers and then to first-period classes.

I read the work he had done for the original extra credit project. He showed high-quality thinking and clever creativity. I then read the additional work he had done, which was a brilliantly inventive, lyrical poem that accurately included the 17 core content economic vocabulary terms, such as supply and demand, competition, opportunity cost, productivity, and money.

The student had learned about economics. He had learned also that there was no escape—"I don't have it" was unacceptable. He had learned that accepting responsibility is important. He had learned that his mother and his teacher were not going to tolerate any excuses. He had learned that it was easier to do what is right and what is required from the outset, rather than hoping that duties will just evaporate or that people who impose demands on you will get tired of requiring you to do what you are supposed to do. He also learned how good it felt to succeed and achieve, as he was quite proud of the impressive work that he eventually completed.

I called his mother to confirm that her son had completed all the work and had turned it in exactly as we had agreed he would. She assured me that he had done all of the work himself and that his weekend schedule was based on doing this work first before any other weekend activities could be considered.

Results. The mother, the student, and the teacher teamed up to get results. Sure, I could have concluded at one point that I had made enough effort to get this student to work. I could have decided that if the student was not going to respond to the opportunity I offered, then he could just not learn, not pass the class, or barely pass the class with a low grade. Those options were unacceptable to this results-driven teacher.

Is it ethical for a medical doctor to say, "I tried two different types of medication, plus some physical therapy, and then we involved a specialist for out-patient surgery. This patient just is not getting better." No, the physician is expected to persist in the search for additional actions that can help the patient.

Is it acceptable for a high school basketball coach to say to a player's parent, "We gave her 10 chances in practice to hit free throws. She made five of them and missed five of them. This was one day after we worked on free throws for most of practice. This was after my assistant coached worked directly with your daughter. We give up." No, the coach is expected to continue working with the athlete. The athlete is expected to do extra practice on her own. The parent will make sure that the personal practice happens.

Physicians are expected to be results-driven. Coaches are expected to be results-driven. The best teachers require themselves to be results-driven. Those teachers are relentlessly determined to find ways to cause learning. Results-driven teachers understand that their duty is to cause learning. Results-driven teachers are not quixotic, work-obsessed employees who have no life outside of school. Results-driven teachers are aware of effective teaching methods and use those methods rather than using activities that are just what is available or typical. Results-driven teachers know how their students learn; know their students' talents and interests; know how to create activities that make connections between what students know and what they need to know.

Results-driven teaching answers the question "what is teaching" with the following confident response:

"Teaching is causing learning. We know what works in classrooms, so I do what works. I know my subject, but I keep learning about it. I know about students, but I keep learning about each student each year because everyone is unique. Teaching is never exactly the same day after day, year after year. Sure, I occasionally use some tried and true teaching methods, but I also find or create new activities. I get to cause learning. I am obligated to cause learning. I require myself to cause learning.

"I did not become a teacher to go through ordinary, repetitive motions of worksheets and textbooks, to watch students lose interest and to watch passively as group after group of students maintain a pattern of bell-shaped curve grades. I went into teaching to get results, to cause learning, to convince students that learning is unlimited and to experience unlimited learning with them. I went into teaching to get students to achieve learning results that otherwise would not happen without my work and the work I inspire students to do."

What is teaching? One answer could be that teaching is the set of daily activities that teachers do. Imagine it is 8:00 A.M. on a Tuesday morning, and two high school teachers walk into the teacher work area adjacent to the office. First-period class begins at 8:15 A.M. One teacher just arrived at school moments before the 8:00 A.M. required arrival time. This teacher, Mr. Borders, is immediately frustrated by the lines at both copy machines. He has to make copies of three worksheets from the supplemental materials that came with the psychology textbook. His juniors and seniors have been reading about various theories of childhood development. The worksheets are a way to review the ideas of prominent psychologists or cognitive theorists. At 8:04 A.M., Mr. Borders finally gets to the front of a copy machine line only to realize that it is out of paper. He finds a nearby box filled with reams of paper and he quickly resupplies the machine. He silently wonders why the person who just made copies left the machine with no paper.

As the copies are being made, Vickie Simpson cordially greets Mr. Borders. Ms. Simpson also teaches social studies classes. Today her students will thoroughly analyze the Declaration of Independence, the Preamble to the U.S. Constitution, and the Gettysburg Address. In recent days, the students and Ms. Simpson read these vital documents. They then worked individually and in groups to paraphrase the documents in search of the essential concepts and meanings. Today the goal is to search for ideas that are common across the three documents. Students will also analyze how thinking about government in this country changed from the 1770s to the 1860s.

In a few days, Ms. Simpson and her students will evaluate five major national news stories to see if political leaders today are abiding by the fundamental principles of American democracy. After conclusions are reached, each student will write and send a letter to his or her local member of the U.S. House of Representatives or to one of the two U.S. senators from their state.

What chapter in the U.S. government textbook is Ms. Simpson using for this assignment? None. The textbook had the U.S. Constitution in the appendix. One chapter had two sentences from the Declaration of Independence. Another chapter had the concluding sentence of the Gettysburg Address. Ms. Simpson obtained copies of the documents from a local civic organization that eagerly provides such materials free to teachers and students.

What supplemental materials—similar to those being copied by Mr. Borders for his psychology class—is Ms. Simpson using? None that were part of the package of materials that the U.S. government textbook publishers provided. Ms. Simpson occasionally glances at those printed materials, but she rarely uses them. She did use one audio CD that the publisher provided. It had campaign songs from presidential election campaigns throughout U.S. history. The students were fascinated by the musical styles across the decades and by the humorous or critical lyrics. Of course, Ms. Simpson then had the students go farther than listening to the songs, as each student then wrote a campaign song that a current candidate could use.

At 8:15 A.M., Mr. Borders distributes worksheets to 27 compliant high school juniors and seniors who know the routine. One sarcastic, "Cool, another worksheet. There's nothing I'd rather do," comment was heard. One honest, "Again? Isn't there more to psychology than worksheets?" was also heard. If Mr. Borders heard the comments, he paid no real attention. The school bought the textbooks because the curriculum committee decided those textbooks were the best match with the psychology curriculum. The textbooks come with supplemental materials. The supplemental materials could be copied so each student had a worksheet. The worksheets kept everyone busy. That's how the system is set up, as Mr. Borders understands it.

In Ms. Simpson's class, a few students are discussing school sports, others are talking about their plans for the weekend, and a few students are asking each other about some television news or newspaper stories that relate to the topics in class today. At 8:15 A.M., Ms. Simpson hits the PLAY button on a CD player, and the voice of a very popular local radio announcer is heard repeating the Preamble to the U.S. Constitution. The students are captivated. The radio announcer is a graduate of their high school and has told the teachers that she is always available to help.

Is Mr. Borders teaching? Is Ms. Simpson teaching? How do their perceptions and understandings of teaching differ? Is there a minimal amount of time, work, and thought that must be included in lesson planning for that effort to be seen as part of teaching? Is there a minimal amount of original thought—versus copy machine action and supplemental material repetition—that must go into lesson planning for that effort to be seen as part of teaching? How wide is the range of acceptable classroom activities within the description of teaching, of actual learning-causing, of results-driven teaching?

Mr. Borders' students and Ms. Simpson's students are having significantly different experiences in class. They are at the same school, which has policies, procedures, and practices established for everyone. Are Mr. Borders and Ms. Simpson both fully consistent with the requirements of those policies, procedures, and practices? Are Mr. Borders and Ms. Simpson both teaching? Are Mr. Borders and Ms. Simpson both teachers? Are Mr. Borders and Ms. Simpson both results-driven teachers?

One important distinction between Mr. Borders and Ms. Simpson is the extent to which they are diagnostic and prescriptive. When a teacher is diagnostic and prescriptive, she is continually identifying what students know, what they need to learn, what they are having trouble learning, what they are learning rather easily, which teaching methods are most effective in causing learning, which teaching methods are not effective for causing learning, and how the life experiences of students can connect with the curriculum.

Mr. Borders is not diagnostic or prescriptive. He does not evaluate the knowledge status of students and then prescribe/design instructional activities that are consistent with the diagnosis/evaluation. He automatically selects the textbook and the supplemental materials that came with the expensive textbook. Mr. Borders expects students to conform to the textbook. Mr. Borders could be much more productive if he designed instructional activities that conform to the needs and the strengths of students.

How could Mr. Borders learn to be more diagnostic and prescriptive? He could talk to Ms. Simpson and observe her teaching. He does not need to travel to a costly education conference or listen to a costly guest speaker who is brought to his school district at a price of $10,000 and with no certainty of results. That same costly guest speaker will make the same speech tomorrow in another school district where a search for solutions is overlooking the success stories within the schools of the district itself.

Mr. Borders' understanding of teaching and/or his default method of teaching limits his students to what can be learned from textbooks and worksheets. Such "learning" is closer to memorizing or to recall of information. This barely, if at all, goes beyond training. Ms. Simpson's understanding of teaching and her resulting method of teaching opens minds—hers and the students—to unlimited learning, real learning that uses recall of information but that also advances into analyzing, explaining, creating, knowing, and understanding.

Answering textbook questions is finite and matches a perception that what students can achieve or what teachers can inspire in students are finite units of information compressed neatly and superficially into textbook pages. Analyzing the Declaration of Independence, the Preamble to the U.S. Constitution, and the Gettysburg Address is an unlimited intellectual journey through information into thinking, imagining, evaluating, researching, listening, reflecting, debating, knowing, and understanding. Which approach gets more results and better results? Which approach is used by results-driven teachers? Which approach is teaching? Which approach is mere schooling—the routine of going through the very limited and very ordinary activities that fill the hours at school but that do not challenge or develop the minds of students?

Does Ms. Simpson just have a different, more creative personality than Mr. Borders? No. Results-driven teaching is not a function of personality, disposition, or inherent creative flair. Results-driven teaching is a function of knowing the students you teach, the subject you teach, and which instructional methods cause your students to fully master the curriculum. Results-driven teachers also have a lively work ethic and a personal sense of professional duty that compels them to find ways to cause each student to learn.

Is Mr. Borders motivated by money? Is Ms. Simpson motivated by money? Are they paid the same salary for doing their jobs in very different ways? Often, teachers' salaries are determined by which cell on a spreadsheet grid chart matches their highest earned academic degree and their years of teaching experience. A teacher in her first year of teaching right out of college might be paid $30,421. That teacher's pay would be $32,176 if she had a master's degree. If she had five years of teaching experience plus a master's degree, the pay would be $36,437.

Although Mr. Borders is doing minimal work and getting minimal results, his pay is not a function of work or results. Although Ms. Simpson is doing superior work and is causing outstanding results, her pay is not a function of work or results. This might seem to be unfair; however, teachers know what their salary will be before they accept a teaching job. Teachers know how their salary will be calculated before they begin a teaching career.

Ms. Simpson does not make calculations based on the teacher pay spreadsheet grid. Her calculations are based on ethics, integrity, professionalism, and honor. Her calculations also have a bit of selfishness included. Ms. Simpson would never put herself through the mundane, repetitive, and unproductive routine of assigning worksheet after worksheet, textbook question after textbook question, textbook chapter after textbook chapter, and publisher-provided, Friday multiple-choice test after publisher-provided, Friday multiple-choice test.

Ms. Simpson perceives teaching as a vibrantly interactive adventure in which learning is caused as learning-causing experiences are created and implemented. Passively completing worksheets or rapidly scanning textbook pages for boldfaced keywords will not cause learning. Energetically interacting with students, ideas, knowledge, and activities that inspire thinking will cause learning.

Mr. Borders does not perceive teaching as an adventure through which learning is caused or created. Mr. Borders' perception of teaching reduces himself and his students to copy machines. Copy the key terms from the book, copy the questions at the end of each section of the chapter from the book, and copy the correct answer from the book. Copy the right answer from the book onto the worksheet. Copy the 10 words from the overhead projector, because they will be highlighted on the video and you will need to copy their definitions when it is shown during the video. Copy what you copied Monday through Thursday when you get your copy of the test on Friday.

The experiences students have in Mr. Borders' class are the opposite of experiences students have in Ms. Simpson's class. Although it is easy to make an A grade in Mr. Borders' room by merely copying, week after tedious week, few students earn that easy A. Most students pay little attention to Mr. Borders, because he pays such little attention to students. Mr. Borders' perception of teaching is identical to his perception of students. Mr. Borders sees students as people who must be limited, restrained, regulated, kept busy through routines, and silenced. Students may cause few problems when they are sedated with worksheets and textbooks. Mr. Borders does not seek to cause learning. Mr. Borders merely manages the minutes of each class and systematizes the students. The minutes pass, the system endures, and the students exit no different than when they entered.

Ms. Simpson perceives learning as an emerging, renewing, inventive, expanding, fascinating, and unpredictable yet still orderly adventure, which she and her students experience together. Ms. Simpson rereads the Declaration of Independence, the Preamble to the U.S. Constitution, and the Gettysburg Address whenever those topics are part of a lesson. She does not rely on her memory of those documents when she originally read them. Plus, she continues to read about and to think about events in U.S. history rather than limit her knowledge of that topic to what she knew the day she graduated from college.

Ms. Simpson knows that when her mind, brain, knowledge, experiences, interests, talents, and ideas interact with her students' minds, brains, knowledge, experiences, interests, talents, and ideas, the classroom will be a vibrant place where learning is caused and where results are produced. Because Ms. Simpson is a learning-driven teacher and a student-driven teacher, she is also a results-driven teacher. Part of the pay she gets when her students learn and when she learns with them cannot go into a bank account, but it does make a deposit into the account of promises that Ms. Simpson made to herself when she became a teacher. Ms. Simpson accepts her salary as the reality of what teaching currently pays. Her salary is finite, but is sufficient. The results she can get with her students are infinite. Each day's new and better learning results are sufficient evidence that Ms. Simpson is doing the work she is most suited to do. Perhaps she could make more money in a different job, but she is not driven to cause results in another job. She is a results-driven teacher, so she thrives in a classroom where she creates, challenges, develops, encourages, and nurtures results-driven students.

Ms. Simpson's students work, think, accomplish, and learn more in her classroom than students who are in a Mr. Borders' classroom. Ms. Simpson's students, fully aware of the demanding and challenging work they are required to do, never ask for worksheets and textbook chapters. The students know how easy worksheets are to complete and how simple textbook chapters are to finish, so how does Ms. Simpson convince them to do more demanding work?

First, Ms. Simpson designs instructional activities that fascinate students. People who are fascinated become inherently motivated to work. Second, Ms. Simpson designs instructional activities that are real, meaningful, and related to the students' lives. Third, Ms. Simpson listens to students, uses their ideas whenever possible, takes their input seriously, and includes students' ideas in designing instructional activities. Ms. Simpson knows what students must learn according to the curriculum. As a results-driven teacher, she is quite willing to vary, and she expects to vary the method of instruction based on what works best with her current students. Ms. Simpson creates a classroom community in which teacher and students are results-driven through a mutual, symbiotic commitment.

Why is Mr. Borders entrenched in the textbook and worksheet habit? Why does Mr. Borders deny himself and his students the available adventures of learning? Does Mr. Borders think that Ms. Simpson's teaching methods are more entertainment than they are education? Does Mr. Borders equate school and drudgery? Is Mr. Borders convinced that his methods are the most effective, or does he think in terms of "good enough" rather than terms of effectiveness?

What could energize Mr. Borders' teaching? Would a new law passed by the national government or the state government cause Mr. Borders to change his mind about how to teach? No. Would a school board policy requiring use of a variety of resources cause Mr. Borders to teach differently? Minimally, as he might begin to use publisher-provided materials other than the worksheets he typically uses. Publisher-provided "think and remember" advanced worksheets often require little thinking and are rarely worth remembering.

Perhaps students could ask for different activities in Mr. Borders' class, but Mr. Borders does not perceive students as being a resource for instructional ideas. Perhaps observing colleagues teach could be a source of ideas, but that would take time away from Mr. Borders daily afternoon session at the copy machine during planning period. Perhaps the school principal could revisit Mr. Borders' classroom, observe a lesson, and issue a directive to Mr. Borders on using different teaching methods. Mr. Borders can then have the teacher union or association representative join him and the principal for a follow-up meeting, in which Mr. Borders and the representative show that the worksheet and textbook approach is in violation of no law or policy, thus it will endure and prevail.

When the principal begins to visit Mr. Borders' classroom weekly in search of different teaching activities, he sees no change. He does get an email from the union representative about "excessive, atypical supervision that is approaching the confrontational level." The principal has other issues to deal with, so he ends the weekly observations in Mr. Borders' room. The principal does request that the chair of the school's curriculum and instruction committee have her committee discuss the importance of using a variety of teaching activities in each classroom. Perhaps a school policy of, by, and for the school could be useful. To disobey a policy could put a teacher in the insubordinate category, and that can have career impact. Must the process to improve Mr. Borders' teaching become a show of force?

Let's hope not. Maybe Mr. Borders sincerely thinks that he is teaching. Maybe Mr. Borders long ago concluded that textbook authors and publishers know more about social studies than he does, so unquestioned use of their materials was merely polite deference to experts. Perhaps Mr. Borders sees life as a bell-shaped curve—for example, some families are wealthy, some families are in poverty, and most families are in the middle—so the bell-shaped curve of grades in his classes is just reality. Perhaps Mr. Borders wishes that more students did better, but at least only a few fail in each class and even those students were given the same chances as everyone else. Those "maybes" and "perhapses" sound like excuse-driven teaching and unprofessional rationalization.

Let's try something else. The principal meets with Mr. Borders, and together they design some creative, interactive lessons for one week of classes. The principal joins Mr. Borders for first-period class each day for one week and plays a supportive role in the teaching. The students keep looking for the textbook and worksheets, but that does not happen. Discussions, case studies, current events, historical mysteries, and social issues are the agenda for the week. Mr. Borders and the principal evaluate the productivity at the end of the week in terms of student attention, learning as measured by class participation and the quiz on Thursday, unpredictable but very impressive ideas from students, and three minor misbehaviors that happened on Tuesday and Wednesday. Overall, the results for the week were very encouraging.

The next Monday, Mr. Borders led the students through the textbook chapter that related to topics and activities of the prior week. Every class sailed through the bold print words, the end-of-the-section questions, and the end-of-the-chapter sections. The content already made sense to them from the activities of the prior week. On Tuesday, the students were given three days of worksheets from the chapter. Students completed these quickly, easily, and accurately, because they had already learned and thought about the topics the week before.

Mr. Borders may not radically transform overnight into a results-driven teacher, but his thinking could be changing. Why? He saw the results, he experienced the results, he knows that his students learned more and learned better than they would have. He also knows that his teaching caused more and better learning to occur. Mr. Borders feels personal pride and professional satisfaction. His students feel the invigoration of real thinking and of meaningful learning. Mr. Borders had taken an essential step toward becoming a results-driven teacher or, at least, realizing that there is a better way than his regular routine-driven classroom system.

What new skills does Mr. Borders have? What skills did Mr. Borders have originally? How were all of these skills obtained? Ms. Simpson began her teaching career with certain skills and has steadily increased her skills. How were all of her skills obtained? Is there a basic set of essential skills for teachers? What causes some teachers to obtain more and better skills than other teachers? Is that imbalance correctable?

The exact procedures and terminology used for teacher preparation programs will vary from college to college, from university to university; however, at some point, probably in the freshman or sophomore year, a college student who intends to become a teacher completes an official application and acceptance process. For successful candidates, some evaluation of the application and perhaps an interview by a screening committee leads to acceptance into the teacher preparation program.

Each state has established requirements for teachers who wish to apply for an official teaching certification. Requirements could relate to the number of and/or the content of college classes taken in the subject areas a person will teach, plus college classes taken in the areas of education. Time spent observing teachers in schools may be included. Time spent as a student teacher is a common requirement and could be the emphasis of one college semester.

During the teacher preparation program in a college or university, what skills are participants supposed to master? State governments, local school districts, and educational professional groups have published standards that list many indicators of effective teaching. Mastery of these standards and indicators—such as "designs instruction," "maintains a proper learning environment," or "makes real-life applications of subject matter"—could be one measurement of skill development by prospective teachers. Grades in college classes and scores on standardized tests could also be useful measurements. Still, what are the essential skills that teacher preparation programs should emphasize to assure future success for teachers in the programs?

Results-driven teaching places the highest emphasis on causing this result: each student learns. The purpose of a school is to cause learning. The purpose of a teacher is to cause learning. What skills are essential for a person who causes learning? We could use a long list of standards and indicators similar to those mentioned above; however, some of these lists approach as many as 100 different items. Such lists can be cumbersome, confusing, bureaucratic, and awkward. Let's be more human, real, practical, and genuine.

Based on research that I have done for a decade involving over 4,000 participants and that graduate school students of mine have repeated and confirmed, there are four essential characteristics of highly effective teachers who get results. These teachers:

✓ 1. Use a variety of instructional activities and methods
2. Are enthusiastic about teaching, about students, about learning
3. Challenge their students
4. Make connections between what is being taught and the real lives that students are living now

How is Mr. Borders doing in terms of this list? Variety? No. Enthusiasm? No evidence of that. Challenging students? No, again. Making connections? None. Mr. Borders is zero for four.

How is Ms. Simpson doing in terms of this list? Variety? Yes. Enthusiasm? Much evidence, as her interest in students and in learning emerges from the creative activities she has designed. Challenging students? Yes, again. Making connections? Many. Ms. Simpson is four for four. Are these four characteristics skills that college students could learn in their teacher education programs? Yes. Could current teachers also acquire, develop, or master these skills through some version of professional development or continuing career education? Yes. The next question is, how? Current teachers can master these skills by thinking, working, and writing together. I will offer an idea for each of the skills, and the reader will add another idea, although you do not need to stop at one idea.

1. Results-driven teachers use a variety of instructional activities and methods.
   a. Observe a variety of great teachers; observe and analyze closely what instructional activities and methods they use; create ways that these activities and methods could be applied in your classroom with your students.
   b.
2. Results-driven teachers are enthusiastic about teaching, about students, and about learning.
   a. Take a class in theater, drama, or speech or get instruction from a teacher of theater, drama, or speech. This can help you communicate your enthusiasm about teaching, about students, and about learning as you acquire additional communication skills that actors and public speakers use.
   b.

3. Results-driven teachers challenge their students.
   a. Divide a demanding academic task into small steps. For example, a teacher challenges her students to master the multiplication tables through 12 times 12. Each student in the class creates relevant word problems such as "If 12 students each eat two slices of pizza, how many slices of pizza did all 12 students eat together?"
   b.
4. Results-driven teachers make connections between what is being taught and the real lives that students are living now.
   a. Go to the school cafeteria and stand in the serving line areas. Listen closely to what students discuss as they select food, as they discuss the past weekend, as they comment on upcoming events at school, as they evaluate a new movie, as they just talk about real life. Use these topics in your classroom. For example, say, "At lunch yesterday, some of you were talking about soft drinks no longer being sold at school. There is a new law about that. Who made that law? How was that law made? Did anyone ask you or me our opinion before that law was approved? Should anyone have asked us, or do we need to make the effort to be heard?"
   b.

   Notice that you and I created different ways to implement the four characteristics of results-driven teachers. There are many more ways we could observe, read about, think of, or learn about to help implement the four characteristics. These are skills that can be observed, acquired, improved, and perfected. Great teachers do not secretly protect their successful teaching methods. Great teachers very publicly present those teaching methods in their classrooms daily. We know what works in classrooms. Results-driven teachers do what works. Every teacher can do what works and can avoid what does not work.

   Within the category of "what works" are many instructional activities. Two teachers in adjacent rooms at the same school could involve their separate classes in dramatically different activities on Monday morning to begin the new week at school. Both teachers are abiding by and effectively exemplifying the four characteristics of results-driven teachers.

Neither teacher is using yet another set of simplistic worksheets to go along with another superficial section from an ordinary chapter of a typical textbook. Sure, there are various ways to cause learning, but only the instructional activities that do cause learning are worthy of the term "teaching."

We know what works; we can identify precise instructional activities that are consistent with what works; and we can implement a series of classroom activities that are based on the research about what great teachers do. So what prevents magnificent teaching from happening daily in every classroom?

One difficulty may be the human complexity of working directly with classes of 25–30 students hour after hour, day after day. Fatigue is a realistic possibility, along with frustration or disappointment. Some educators may increasingly descend to using the textbook and worksheet system, because it takes less energy and it has low expectations, which means fewer frustrations or disappointments. That is flawed reasoning. It is much more rewarding, fulfilling, honorable, and productive to teach effectively, yet need a nap on Saturday, than to be a teacher who is never tired because she never invests her heart, mind, body, and soul in the adventure of teaching.

Another difficulty may be the human dynamic of people changing over time. A results-driven teacher could design fascinating math problems in September for her students who are very interested in cars. In fact, the entire class catches car math fever, and the calculations about miles per gallon or monthly car payments are done with complete commitment by the students. Then, for some reason, the students lose interest in cars. A teacher might, in a moment of frustration and disappointment, wonder if all the car math work had been worth the effort. Of course it was. The students did learn math. Now the teacher has to learn what new wholesome interests captivate the students and design new instructional connections to cause the intended learning today.

What results-driven teachers do is not a secret, highly complicated, or excessively time consuming. What results-driven teachers do is intellectually demanding and can tax their hearts, minds, bodies, and souls; however, it is so productive and so intellectually energizing that it also replenishes the heart, mind, body, and soul.

How much time and effort must a results-driven teacher invest beyond the hours spent daily in the classroom? It takes time to grade papers, tests, quizzes, homework, and projects for any teacher who uses one or more of those activities. Mr. Borders spends time grading each week's Friday test on the chapter of the week. He spent no time creating the tests, because every week, he used the tests provided by the textbook publisher. Grading the tests will be a repetitive, mechanical, mind-numbing ordeal of seeing if, paper after paper, the multiple-choice blanks were filled in correctly.

Ms. Simpson will spend time grading tests. She will write comments on each paper as a way to personalize and individualize the feedback for each student. She actually thinks and learns as she grades the answer, ideas, creations, and writing of her students. It may take some more time than the grading Mr. Borders does, but it gets better results, as Ms. Simpson actually obtains a qualitative and quantitative understanding of what her students know or still need to know.

While Mr. Borders spends time at the copy machine building stacks of worksheets to distribute, Ms. Simpson reflects on insights gained about students with whom she talked at lunch and on classroom activities that could apply those insights. By the time Mr. Borders has his final pile of worksheets copied, Ms. Simpson has set up her room for today's activity: a White House press conference with Ms. Simpson as the president, the students as the reporters, and two students who talked to her about their interest in journalism as the cohosts of a simulated call-in cable television program to discuss the press conference. The students who had earlier been the reporters would now become the callers to the television instant analysis program.

Ms. Simpson spent some time talking to students, some time arranging her classroom, and some time designing the format and content of the questions all students would answer on paper at the conclusion of the press conference and call-in program. While Ms. Simpson reads and grades the original, clever, and insightful ideas of her students, Mr. Borders will check yet another worksheet to see if a student found all of the hidden words in the pointless, time-filling word search.

On the weekend, Ms. Simpson does read the Sunday *New York Times*, *The Economist*, *Foreign Affairs*, and the local newspaper and she checks some websites about topics that relate to the classes she teaches.

She personally enjoys this reading. She professionally applies this reading to developing upcoming lesson plans. Mr. Borders turns the pages to chapter 14, remembers it from last year, marks the worksheet book at the 14-A activity, and is ready for another meaningless Monday.

So, to be honest, results-driven teachers do invest more time in preparing lessons. These teachers are intrigued by the process of learning, so they find meaning in designing new, unique lessons. Investing this time is not required by law, regulation, policy, or directive. Investing this time is required by the integrity, honor, professionalism, curiosity, standards, and conscience of a results-driven teacher. The time is meaningful and is willingly invested.

Results-driven teachers sufficiently use experiences away from school to gain ideas for teaching activities that can be used at school. While eating supper at a restaurant, a results-driven teacher takes a moment to look at the menu, how it is organized, how pictures are used, how different sizes or styles of typefaces are used, and how the menu is designed to be customer friendly. How could this apply in my science class? the results-driven teacher wonders. How about taking the periodic table of elements and having the students organize that peculiar looking array into a menu of elements? She makes a mental note about the idea, but then thinks to ask the restaurant manger if she could take a menu with her to use at school. "Sure. I have a box of old menus we don't use anymore. You are welcome to all of those." Results. All the teacher had to do was think and ask.

Many professions require continuing education. Lawyers, doctors, dentists, accountants, police officers, firefighters, and many other workers are regularly updated on skills, laws, ideas, or procedures. Automobile mechanics must learn about the new cars with each year's model changes. Pharmacists must learn about new laws or guidelines that impact prescription medications. What can results-driven teachers learn from these professions' continuing educations?

The next time you have an appointment with your doctor or dentist, ask how people in their profession are kept informed of and skilled with innovations that work. The process of creating the innovations and of successfully teaching people about use of the innovations could provide ideas that can be adapted to the school setting.

Middle schools and high schools have many extracurricular activities. From student council to marching band, from academic team to soccer team, from school newspaper to student technology club, sponsors and coaches involved with these groups may be using teaching methods that can be adapted for classroom use. It is quite likely that some sponsors and coaches do this supplemental, extracurricular work without textbooks or worksheets. Sponsors and coaches probably approach their clubs or teams like Ms. Simpson teaches. How can the expected energy and the "whatever-it-takes" attitude of extracurricular activities also become the norm with classroom activities?

One part of the answer is to avoid the "not-invented-here" blockade. Certainly, some of the best ideas about teaching can come from successful schools, great teachers, effective principals, well-informed college or university professors in education programs, books written by educators, and educational websites. Some additional teaching ideas can come from other sources.

Toy companies invest much time, effort, and money to understand a lot about children. Companies that make and sell sporting goods, fashion apparel, music, video games, video game systems, and fast food do a lot of research to learn how to most effectively communicate to children and teenagers. Teachers could apply insights from publications that serve these industries.

Closer to home and school, attentive and observant teachers listen to and watch students. It becomes very genuine, natural, and productive to them to interact with students about what they heard or noticed. These teachers might say, "I heard you mention that movie you saw last weekend. I heard it's pretty good. Tell me about it." The teacher who asks that question now listens to a student talk about a movie, but also hears a student unintentionally suggest teaching ideas. A language arts teacher can now use the plot, characters, drama, humor, unexpected events, and predictable ending as resources for a class discussion about literary devices and their cinematic equivalent. That thinking adventure does not occur with worksheets and textbooks.

This chapter has not given much attention to the "d" word—discipline. Whether the term used is classroom management, discipline, structure, or rewards and punishments, the concept is similar in bottom-line reality. College students who are anticipating a teaching career, first-year teachers who are just starting their careers, and experienced teachers all encounter students who misbehave. However, some teachers seem to have very little difficulty with misbehavior. What do those teachers know and do to inspire cooperation?

They know that students cooperate with, work for, learn from, obey, and appreciate teachers who fascinate them, intrigue them, relate to them, and demand the best from them. Those teachers know that effective teaching is the best discipline and classroom management system. Students who are fascinated, intrigued, involved, challenged, acknowledged, encouraged, listened to, and taken seriously will commit themselves to learning with such dedication that misbehaving is not an option to the student. The extra time Ms. Simpson invests to design fascinating lessons or to write individualized comments on papers she grades can significantly reduce time spent on discipline procedures. While Mr. Borders takes time to write a discipline referral about a defiant student, Ms. Simpson keeps teaching because her students are fascinated, involved, taken seriously, challenged, and encouraged.

How do teachers make this happen? How do results-driven teachers evoke this mutual commitment as they create and nurture results-driven students? Check the list of the four characteristics of results-driven teachers for the answer. What does that tell us? It tells us that great teaching is the best classroom discipline plan. Captivate the mind and you also manage the behavior. Teaching in ways that do not captivate the mind is a certainty of misbehavior to come. Separating teaching and discipline is almost schizophrenic. The student who is eagerly learning is a student who is also willingly obeying.

Yes, a system for dealing with misbehavior is needed in every classroom. Yes, a discipline system is needed within every school and throughout every school district. There are many books about, programs for, and examples of such systems. Still, some teachers create classroom communities that transcend these legal codes by building a mutual commitment to learning and to each other. Those teachers are results-driven teachers.

What wisdom could results-driven teachers offer to college students who are preparing for a teaching career? First, if you are cut out for teaching, no other work will satisfy you. You have to be with students in the grand adventure of causing learning.

Second, if teaching is of limited interest to you and you are getting certified as a teacher just to have something to fall back on, change your plans. Why put yourself and students through the mutually agonizing or-deal of you attempting to do work you are not fully dedicated to, and them attempting to get through each ordinary day in your superficial classroom without failing or getting in trouble?

Third, teaching well is very demanding work and will increase in com-plexity as (a) society continues to expect more of schools, (b) families have more nontraditional or even dysfunctional aspects, and (c) students have more disorders, syndromes, phobias, medications, court involve-ment, mandatory accommodations, and/or excuses. In those moments of deepest discouragement, remember that you are doing the work you are best suited to do.

Fourth, we know what works. Educational books and periodicals, ex-perienced teachers and school administrators, young but already suc-cessful teachers, educational websites, your former teachers, and, yes, your current students are all resources. Use those resources rather than trying to answer every question by yourself or solve every problem alone.

Fifth, take great care of heart, mind, body, and soul. Results-driven teaching is a very rewarding approach to work at school, but teaching will drain your energy. Renew yourself often.

In this chapter, the question "what is teaching?" has been considered along with some related topics. Some attention was directed to teachers as individual workers, but the emphasis was on the overall work of teaching. The next chapter specifically applies to individuals as the topic moves to "what is a teacher?"

②

WHAT IS A TEACHER?

Television program host: Ms. Simpson, you are known as a highly effective teacher. Parents and guardians make extra efforts to have their children in your classes. Your students consistently do very well in your classes and on the state tests in the subject areas you teach. You have been quoted as saying that your classroom approach can be best called results-driven teaching. Please tell us what that means.

Simpson: Thank you for your kind words and for inviting me to be a guest on your program. I'm not used to being on television, so please be patient with me. You asked about results-driven teaching. That is my way of saying that I understand my job description and my professional responsibility are to make sure that every student completely learns the curriculum for any class a student has with me.

Host: Every student completely learns the curriculum. Does that mean no student ever fails your classes? Do all of your students always make an A grade?

Simpson: No student has failed a class I taught during the past three years. I intend to keep it that way. In the past year, no student had a D grade on a report card either. I tell the students that a D means nothing; it is unacceptable and they are required to do much better. I hope to eliminate C grades, because C means average and being average just is not good enough.

Host: The school district you work for would accept the results if some students made C, D, or F grades, right? You are not required to get every student up to B or A grades, are you?

Simpson: Good question. I require myself to get all students up to a grade of A or B. My employer does not mandate that of me. I am driven by results and to results. I'm similar to coaches of athletic teams at our school. Their ideal is to win every game, to be undefeated. When students do not learn, I see that as a failure on my part. I expect to be undefeated each year. I expect all of my students to learn, to master the curriculum of any class they have with me. I am in the business of causing learning. I expect myself to do exactly that. I was hired to teach, which means I was hired to figure out ways to make each student successful in my classes.

Host: How did you develop your ideas about teaching? Is this what you were taught in college?

Simpson: It all goes back to 7th grade. I had been a fairly good student in elementary school, but I sure wasn't a superstar student then. In 7th grade, I had two teachers who got my attention more completely than any teacher ever had. They were different in what they did in their classes, but one thing sure was similar: they got more work out of me than I had ever done before.

Host: What did they do to motivate all of that work from you? Did they give rewards? Did they scare you into working hard? Or was it something else?

Simpson: My 7th-grade math teacher, Mr. James, had a system. There was a problem on the board waiting for us every day. Mr. James explained the system once and that was that, walk in, sit down, begin solving the math problem, remain silent. Then Mr. James would call on one student to explain the problem. He would call on another student to explain how to solve the problem. He would call on a third student to have that person explain why what had been said was correct or could be improved. Mr. James kept score. We could earn three points daily as a class—one point for each answer from the three students. For every week that we earned 15 points, every student in they class automatically earned 15 extra credit points. It worked. The rest of each class was also part of his system. He was a big basketball fan, plus he had played baseball in college. He was convinced that his knowledge of math was what made him a good baseball player. He used statistics to figure out everything in baseball. The same was true for basketball. No matter what the math concept or skill was, Mr. James made it fit in with baseball or basketball. It made sense that way.

Host: Did Mr. James do anything for students who were not very interested in baseball and basketball?

Simpson: One day a student in our class asked a question about that. The student was a very talented musician. Drums, guitar, violin, piano, and singing—she could do it all. So she asked in class if Mr. James could show if math had anything to do with music. The room was silent. Would Mr. James resent the question? Would he be glad to hear a question that showed good thinking? I can remember it to this day. He walked over to a radio he kept in his room. He turned it on. The station was from a local university and was playing classical music, maybe Beethoven. Mr. James asked us, "Any math in this music?" Hands went up. Students were called on. Answers about quarter notes or the number of instruments in an orchestra or why there are still people paying money to go to concerts of old, classical music. I had never seen any math in music until then. I promised myself that if I ever became a teacher, I would show my students how what they learn in school relates to real life.

Host: You mentioned that there was a second teacher in 7th grade who also got your attention, but in different ways.

Simpson: Ms. Paulus. I remember her just as clearly as Mr. James. They were so different in personality and in how they taught, but they were both great teachers. Ms. Paulus taught 7th- and 8th-grade science. She was my teacher for those two consecutive years. I had never been interested in science, but that changed on the first day of 7th grade. Ms. Paulus wore Rollerblades that day. She checked attendance, she gave us a writing task to complete and she rollerbladed throughout the room while we did our writing.

Host: What was the purpose of the Rollerblades?

Simpson: She told us that science makes Rollerblades possible. We discussed everything from friction to the chemicals or elements used to manufacture Rollerblades. She asked us what our hobbies were. We told her basketball, soccer, shopping, movies, swimming, music, dancing, softball, piano, singing, television, video games, amusement parks, concerts, and everything else 7th graders like. The next few days we researched how science helps make all of our hobbies possible. From then on science made sense and seemed to be worth knowing. Ms. Paulus made us do lots of work, but it was so interesting and so personal that it never felt like work.

Host: It sounds as if you had other classes where the work was not as interesting or personal.

Simpson: There were so many classes like that. In those classes, I learned how not to teach. In 9th-grade language arts, we had a literature book with 894 pages. Every day in class was exactly the same. We would read six pages, answer whatever questions came up during those six pages, and turn in our work at the end of class. Our school had 180 school days, so by reading six pages per day, the teacher kept us busy for 149 days. The other 31 days were tests on Fridays or days when the school schedule changed and language arts class did not meet. I hated that class. The work was easy, but it was so dull. Every year in middle school and high school, I had two or three classes that were taught that textbook way. I promised myself then that if I ever became a teacher, I would be a lot like Mr. James and Ms. Paulus. That's exactly what I have done, and it works.

Host: Any other ideas or experiences you would like to share with our audience?

Simpson: Just this: parents and guardians need to visit school as often as possible. When your children enter middle school and high school, you attend their athletic events or their concert performances, but not their math class. Please come visit some classes, have lunch in the cafeteria, get to know the teachers and your child's friends. Your involvement says so much to your children.

Host: Thanks for those wise words. Our guest today has been Ms. Vickie Simpson, outstanding social studies teacher at Matthew M. Johnson High School.

What is a teacher? The interview with Ms. Simpson provides some of her thoughts and convictions about what a teacher is. Take a few moments, and consider your answer to the question "what is a teacher?" You may want to write your ideas on other paper or, if this book is yours, you could write in the margin on this page, but please, take a few minutes to reflect and to write.

Teachers cause learning. How is this done? Teachers create, design, and/or find instructional activities and experiences that cause students to learn. Teachers have already learned what the students need to learn. Teachers have also learned how to cause learning to occur in the brains of students, whether by their experience as a student when they had a great teacher, in their college preparation for teaching, or through their career successes. Teachers must thoroughly know what they are teaching and must, with equal thoroughness, know how to cause students to learn. For example, a math teacher must thoroughly know math and how to design and find instructional activities and experiences that cause students to learn math.

The goal of a teacher—the purpose of a teacher—is to cause students to learn. There is good news about this seemingly daunting task: all students have learned. From infancy to childhood, from childhood through the teenage years, all young people learn. Before coming to school at age four or five, a child has learned. Upon leaving school for the weekend on a Friday afternoon, a 16-year-old will continue to learn while away from school.

Properly organized schools help arrange a learning process and a learning sequence so an approved curriculum of essential, high-priority information, knowledge, and skills can be presented to students who need to master that curriculum. That's the overall plan, but does it always work for each student? It works for students whose teachers truly teach—that is, truly cause learning. Some teachers do cause learning, so we know how to do that. Some teachers do not cause learning, cause only a small amount of learning, or cause only some students to learn. If you work in a classroom at a school and have the title of teacher, you are supposed to do what it takes legally, professionally, and ethically to make sure that all students learn. That perception of teaching is well known to Ms. Simpson. That perception of teaching is confusing to Mr. Borders. How can two people be in the same profession, have the same job title, perceive the job with completely different insights, and still both claim to be doing the job?

They cannot if they're being fully honest. That is, unless Mr. Borders was never required to cause learning. Maybe his college's teacher preparation program introduced him to many conceptual interpretations of human cognition; made him aware of a long list of societal, family, childhood, or adolescent issues, crises, problems, disorders, and syndromes; and paid more attention overall to educational psychology, sociology, history, and concepts, so his papers could be written about various philosophies of education. Mr. Borders could have emerged from such an esoteric undergraduate experience with little preparation for the realistic nuts and bolts of causing learning in a high school classroom. Meanwhile, students are sitting in their desks at 8:20 A.M. on Monday morning, ready to learn.

Of course, Mr. Borders may have been informed during his college years of many very specific methods of classroom instruction. His teaching certification may have been earned only after he demonstrated awareness of, skill in, and mastery of a generous variety of instructional methods. Mr. Borders may know how to cause learning, but as his career progressed and certain experiences occurred or some priorities changed, he settled into the textbook and worksheet approach because, well, because it's simple to do and it causes no problems.

It also causes no learning. If textbooks, worksheets, videos, and other prepackaged, generic, superficial, limited, ordinary materials are imposed on every student in Mr. Borders' classes every year, the operating assumption is that learning fits into those packages and that each student must conform to that package.

A results-driven teacher is not textbook driven, worksheet driven, or Friday test driven. A teacher is driven by results, the most important of which is that all students learn completely what the approved curriculum requires and what the school permits through deeper, challenging enrichment.

A teacher thinks first of students, second of what students need to learn, and third of the most effective instructional activities that will cause students to learn.

A teacher does not think of covering material or finishing the textbook. Academic material is not designed to be merely covered; rather, academic material—subjects, curriculum, knowledge, wisdom, skills, information—is to be understood, experienced, interacted with, mastered, made real, analyzed, explained, applied, expanded, and uncovered.

It is possible that a teacher and a class of students could complete the final chapter of the textbook in the final week of the school year, but the material was simply covered—the teacher and the students went over the material. They did not get into, uncover the ideas within, make sense out of, or relate to the material. They quickly covered and then quickly forgot much of the material.

The activities that cause students to learn the current curriculum may need to differ from activities used in other school years with other students. A teacher is all about learning, which is an incredibly fascinating, unlimited, invigorating, demanding, inspiring, interpersonal, meaningful, and rewarding experience.

A teacher causes students to learn. A teacher is dedicated to students and to learning. A teacher is fascinated with students and with learning. A teacher is intrigued with the creation, discovery, finding, and identification of the instructional activities that will cause current students to learn the current curriculum.

Teachers continue to learn about the subject or subjects they teach. They continue to learn about the students they teach. Teachers continue to learn about learning. Teachers are not obsessed; rather, teachers are dedicated. Results-driven teachers are deeply dedicated to causing each student to learn. Results-driven teachers do not possess and hide secrets of great teaching; in fact, results-driven teachers continually seek to learn more about how to be better teachers. Results-driven teachers know what works best to cause learning, and they do only what works best to cause learning. That knowledge of what works best is available to any teacher. Doing only what works best is an option available to any teacher, but is an option not applied by every teacher. It could be.

Is Mr. Borders doing only what works best as his instructional methods? No. Let's hear from him to find out what he is thinking.

"Teaching is so much more difficult today than it ever was before. I get so frustrated with all of the people who keep complaining about teachers not doing their jobs well enough or about schools not perfectly educating every student, including the young criminals who come to school to steal and destroy.

"I do my job. I know that other teachers are more innovative and more creative than I am. That is their style of teaching, and maybe it works for them. My style of teaching is very orderly. I don't have to send students to the office for some misbehavior. My classroom is quiet and under control. The students know the routine we use, and that routine never changes.

"The school paid $58 apiece for the textbooks my students use. I'm not going to waste that money. We use those textbooks every day. The people who wrote the textbook are experts, so we can learn from them.

"These textbooks came with more materials than I have ever seen with any other textbook. Why would I just ignore all of those free worksheets, tests, quizzes, videos, and pictures? Why should I spend time making new materials when the professionals at the textbook company have already done that?

"Do you have any idea what it is like to teach now? I get so tired of what I read in the newspaper. The president, the governor, other politicians, school board members, superintendents, and community leaders keep telling us that we have to teach better. I challenge them to come teach for one year, one month, or even one week. They would never last a day. Have them deal with a classroom of 28 students, some of whom are taking powerful medications for their mental conditions. Have them get cussed out by some out-of-control child whose mother tells us that she cannot be reached by phone, but who comes to school yelling whenever she feels people at school are being unfair to her child.

"Speaking of calling, I'm sick of cell phones. Students are allowed to bring them to school. They have to be turned off and kept away during the school day. That does not happen. Some students use their phones all day. They take pictures of each other. They download television shows. So I confiscate the phone like the policy tells me to. Then the parent goes crazy. I don't deserve some verbal abuse or threats from that parent after I did what I was supposed to do.

"Grades. If some of my students make an F grade, I get criticized. I did my job. The student was lazy, but I get the criticism. So I'm expected to make every student a brilliant scholar who earns a college scholarship? Nobody can do that, including the people who expect me to do that.

"Families. How many parents or guardians have told me that they can't control their children? But they expect us to control, teach, discipline, feed, medicate, and counsel them, give them second chances, make sure they don't bully anyone, and show them the difference between right and wrong. Come on. This is a school. We are not a social services super agency, where every possible problem that a student or the student's family can have is our total responsibility to resolve.

"At least I show up. Maybe I miss one day each year. What about those lazy teachers who miss 10 or 15 days every year? Who believes that they are really sick on all of those Fridays? I've talked to substitute teachers. They tell me about teachers who leave absolutely no information, no materials, no lesson plan. They tell me about teachers who leave an awful video with a note attached saying, 'Show this. Tell them to be quiet. Tell them they will have a test on the video when I get back.' That's teaching? At least I show up.

"So, now you know what I think. I teach the way I teach because it can be managed. Amid all of the distractions and problems and very difficult people I have to put up with, my way of teaching lets me keep the classroom under control. I deserve credit for that. Before anyone tells me how to do my job better, I challenge them to come do my job."

Challenge accepted. There are outstanding teachers who accept Mr. Borders' challenge daily and who, despite working in the same difficult circumstances, effectively cause learning. Those teachers can list the same problems that Mr. Borders mentioned, but those teachers do not admit defeat merely because teaching today has complexities and difficulties that surpass the school problems in earlier years. What do those persistent, determined, and successful teachers think, know, understand, or do differently than Mr. Borders?

It begins with how and what those effective teachers think about their job, about teaching. Results-driven teachers are not unfounded optimists who simply hope that problems will go away or who expect that tomorrow will be better just because positive thinking magically assures positive results.

Results-driven teachers think—realistically and aggressively with a certainty of conviction—that to every problem, there is a solution. Results-driven teachers are fully aware that teaching today is much more complex and demanding than ever. Results-driven teachers are fully aware that schools are expected to achieve more and deal with more today than ever before. Results-driven teachers express ideas, concerns, and frustrations, but results-driven teachers do not let those frustrating problems define the whole of teaching.

Despite the current and unprecedented complexities of teaching today, results-driven teachers concentrate their efforts on doing what works in the classroom. Results-driven teachers know that despite a school's guidance office having to dispense potent medication each day to an increasing number of students, despite the school social worker having to get state authorities to intervene with negligent parents or guardians, despite the juvenile justice system sending young offenders right back to school, there are endless opportunities in the classroom to work very productively with students, most of whom are quite willing to learn.

An effective teacher thinks of what he or she can do within the realm of a teacher's authority to cause learning. This results-driven teacher is aware of the realistic problems that impact schools, but is also convinced that superior teaching can overcome many of those problems, at least during a class period. Because learning can be so compelling, results-driven teachers use the power of learning and the commitment-building potential of teaching in effective ways to create a classroom community in which problems are overcome as learning dominates.

A teacher, a results-driven teacher, is a person who makes learning dominate in the classroom. Despite societal changes that complicate the work of teachers, despite endless complaints about schools from community leaders who could not do the job of teaching, despite some belligerent parents or guardians who blame everyone but themselves, despite some incorrigible students, results-driven teachers know that almost all students are willing to think, listen, work, cooperate, and learn when the combination of what is taught and how it is taught is so fascinating that it transcends the problems or excuses that might limit learning.

Because schools face so many unprecedented problems and because so many old problems have worsened, it is now more important than ever that teachers fully utilize their most effective resources—the inherent eagerness of students to be fascinated, learn something real, do something interesting, be involved, be challenged, be relevant, be taken seriously, and be part of something that is immediately worthwhile and applicable to real life.

If a person thinks that she can run a marathon, she investigates the recommended training programs, selects a training program, begins and completes the training, while also registering for the upcoming race. She arrives on race day, begins the marathon run, and four hours later, completes the very challenging and very rewarding adventure. The starting point in this process was her thinking that she could run a marathon. Had her thoughts been otherwise, she would not have started completing the series of actions that eventually took her to the marathon's finish line. Actions followed thinking.

If a teacher thinks that her duty is to cause learning, she will take the necessary actions to cause learning. If a teacher thinks that his duty is to give everyone the opportunity to learn, yet assumes that some students will learn and other students will not, he will take actions that provide the opportunity for learning, but he will not ensure that everyone learned.

If a teacher thinks that her duty is to keep the classroom quiet, orderly, and controlled at all times, she will take actions to maintain that quiet, orderly, controlled classroom. Learning experiences that include some noise, unpredictable creativity, and spontaneous moments of innovation will not occur. Learning will be limited to what can occur within quiet, orderly, and controlled activities. How sad, because there is no limit to thought unless limits are imposed. For details of such activities, ask Mr. Borders.

Classroom management is important. Designing and implementing effective instructional activities are more important. The teacher is in charge. The teacher is the responsible adult who must cause learning. Seeking, applying, and building upon interaction with students expands the learning experience for everyone. When I gave students a list of 10 companies to buy stock in for their hypothetical $100,000 investment portfolio, I selected only blue chip Dow Jones 30 stocks. Several students asked if they could include Apple computer company in their portfolios. If quiet, order, and control were my top priorities, their question would not be considered. If causing learning is the top priority, their idea becomes a new resource for everyone to consider. During the time period of our class, Apple stock nearly doubled in value, and those students who invested in it had the most successful investment portfolios.

Results-driven teachers take student input seriously. Students who are taught by results-driven teachers offer serious input, because they know they are taken seriously as real participants in the learning endeavor.

Another student in a different economics class I taught was eager to invest in a company he selected from the comprehensive list of stocks in the newspaper. His reason? He liked the name of the company. I advised against the investments, because no facts about the company were known; however, I allowed him to invest in it as part of his diversified portfolio. We did research about the company. The investment did nothing during the duration of the project, while other investments he made or other students made generally did well. Learning was caused. A results-driven teacher can guide, shape, and apply student input to cause the intended learning. Results-driven teachers know that.

Excuses are different than reasons. Excuses can come from students, parents/guardians, teachers, or school administrators. Reasons can come from different people in those same groups. Excuses seek ways to get out of work responsibility and results. Reasons seek ways to identify and solve problems so results can be obtained. Results-driven teachers deal with reasons and solutions, not with excuses.

The following are examples of excuses: "My students just won't do homework. I tried giving them less homework. I tried giving them less time and more time. It never changed. Some students did the work well. Some just barely completed something to turn in. Other students did nothing. Since they won't do the homework I'm not assigning any more homework."

Some homework should not be assigned. "Complete these worksheets for homework and turn them in tomorrow. Complete all of the odd-numbered problems, 1–71, for homework. Turn it in tomorrow." Why? What good will the worksheets do? What's the irrefutable evidence that doing all of the odd-numbered problems will enhance learning? What happens if the teacher selects 10 of the best problems for practicing and developing mastery of the skill? Better yet, what happens if the teacher creates 10 math problems that practice skills, develop mastery, and make relevant, meaningful connections between math and real life? An example of one such problem might be the following: "Jason works at a fast food restaurant that a local family owns. One of the owners has created a new food item for the menu. He needs to determine the right price for the item. The cost of the food ingredients, according to the industry norm, is about 30% of the retail price customers pay. So, if the food cost for this new menu item, a breakfast pizza, is $0.90, what should customers be charged?"

Jason is a student in Ms. Simpson's class. It is a social studies class, not a math class, but her curriculum includes economics. She knows that Jason works part time at a restaurant. She knows that other students have similar jobs. She intrigues the class with this economics math problem to begin the lesson. A few more economics math problems like that could be done in math class, with others assigned for math class homework. Jason and the other students would see that math and social studies connect as school subjects and that math, social studies, and the real-life experience of a part-time job also connect. Class activities and homework that purposefully connect with real life are more productive, because they build upon wholesome knowledge, talents, interests, and commitments of students.

There is no need to fight the homework battle, which everyone loses. There is no need to make excuses about homework. There are reasons to make homework meaningful and worthwhile. Most students will eagerly do work that is real. Fast food math is real. The odd-numbered problems on any page of any math book are rarely real. Sometimes all of the problems on a math book page are odd.

More excuses are heard in schools such as, "I gave them the work to do in class. They still flunked. What else am I supposed to do? It's the same work I've had students do for years. It's not that hard for any student who will try to get it done. Is it my fault they are lazy? This happens every year. Actually, it gets worse each year. More and more students just refuse to do the work. What can I do about that?"

This last question raises the essential issue. Of all the variables and reasons involved with a student lazily, defiantly, or irresponsibly not doing assigned work at school, what can a teacher do? Can a teacher change the family situation of the student? No. Can a teacher make sure that the student has a quiet place at home to study? No. Can a teacher make sure that the student ate breakfast and got enough sleep? No.

A teacher can decide what work a student will be assigned to do. A teacher has almost total control on this aspect of the school work. Students who make excuses about not understanding math—"I'm no good in math," "I never pass math," "I hate math," "My mom said she was bad in math, and I just got my math weakness from her"—are the same students who absolutely understand the math involved in the costs of a movie and popcorn at the theater, baseball batting averages, miles between cities they have visited, points scored by players in a basketball game, cell phone prices, the cost for an extra slice of pizza at lunch, and much more real-life math.

The goal is to learn math. Part of reaching that goal requires that students do math work. Doing typical textbook math work is not the only way to learn math and is not necessarily the best way to learn math. A math teacher causes learning of math using the most effective instructional methods and activities. A results-driven math teacher does not complain about students who refuse to do the math work and does not make excuses by saying the students were given the opportunity to learn, but they were too lazy. A results-driven math teacher confidently, realistically, and creatively analyzes this situation, perhaps by saying the following: "Okay. About one third of the students do little or no work on these textbook assignments and worksheets. Another third does just enough to get by, but they are not fully mastering any of this. The other third, bless them, do all of the work and understand everything we do, but I have to admit, they never are very energetic about it. They just make themselves do it. So what can I do to improve the situation for everyone?"

The exact answer may vary from class to class, from student to student, from year to year; however, the overriding principle guiding the answer is to connect math with what the student's brain is already familiar with, committed to, interested in, knowledgeable about, talented in, successful with, and motivated by. For example, which car purchasing deal is best: 0% financing for 36 months, 1.9% financing for 48 months, 3.9% financing for 60 months, or no financing at all but a $3,000 rebate on the price? Use a real newspaper advertisement from a real local car dealer to do real math. Unless and until a teacher has used this connection—a real-life application approach that works—the teacher does not yet know how well and how much the students could work and could learn, nor does the teacher know how effective and rewarding the instructional experience could be for him or her.

A teacher does not make excuses when student achievement is below acceptable levels. A teacher does make a realistic evaluation of everything she is doing and of everything else she could do. A teacher diagnoses the problem and prescribes a solution based on the facts and realities of the current problem. A results-driven teacher knows that the desired result is to cause learning, not to cover the pages of the textbook or the workbook. Thinking in terms of causing learning leads teachers to different actions than thinking in terms of covering material.

If people who work in classrooms at schools are merely covering material, that does not make them teachers. If they are causing learning, they are teachers.

Imagine a doctor saying the following: "You have to keep taking this medication. It is the best medication for your condition. You have taken it for two years. I know you are still sick. I realize that you have not improved. I realize that the truth is that you are worse than before, but this is good medicine. You have to keep taking it."

If your physician said that to you, wouldn't you be interested in a second opinion, in trying some other action, medication, treatment, therapy, or surgery that could help? Apply that reasoning to the classroom. Just as a physician must be willing to try different treatments when facts show that the current treatment is not working and probably will not work, a teacher must be willing to try different instructional activities when facts show that the current approach is not working sufficiently and probably will not work sufficiently. Great teachers have learned throughout their careers that the goal is to cause learning, and how that is done must be adjusted whenever needed so learning is caused with current students in the ways that current students most productively learn.

For results-driven teachers, part of the job's duty and reward is the discovery, creation, finding, identification, and then implementation of the instructional activities that most productively cause learning by current students. Results-driven teachers find much personal and professional satisfaction in learning about learning, about how different students learn, and about the best ways to cause learning. Throughout a 25–30 year career, results-driven teachers thrive on the perennial adventure of increasing their effectiveness, knowledge, and skills. Their twenty-fifth year of teaching is not the twenty-fourth rerun of their first year of teaching; rather, it is their twenty-fifth new and improved year of teaching better than they have ever taught.

What convinces a teacher to remain a teacher for 25–30 years, despite all of the difficulties, frustrations, disappointments, and the constantly increasing demands of the job? For some determined teachers, it is the personal and professional challenge of continuing to cause more and better learning each year while overcoming those difficulties and increased demands. These teachers knew the trends that complicate teaching would continue; however, that truth merely strengthened their resolve to find, create, or identify ways to cause learning.

If what primarily motivates a person to continue working at a school for 25–30 years is the possibility of retirement at age 50 with a fairly reasonable pension, that person is not a teacher and is certainly not a results-driven teacher. Of course, salary and retirement pay are important; however, higher salaries and better retirement plans exist outside of education.

Teaching students full time in elementary, middle, or high school does not exist outside of education. Real teachers stay in teaching because teaching is a significant part of who they are and what they do. To do otherwise would be to deny truth, self, ethics, and the moral imperative to do the life's work you are called to do.

Can anyone become a teacher? Let the debate begin. Are teachers made or born? Let the debate advance. Teachers cause learning. If you work in a classroom at a school but you do not cause learning, you did not teach and you are not a teacher.

Some might argue the following: "Yeah, well, what about physicians? Their patients eventually die. Does that mean they aren't real doctors?" Death is inevitable. Academic failure or academic underachievement is not inevitable.

On the day my father died, I said to the doctors—who were honorably searching for additional heroic actions to take two hours prior to my father's death—"You have done all you could to help. Dad lived a great life. There is nothing more to do than be thankful for the life he lived. You really have done everything possible that could help."

Unless and until a results-driven teacher has <u>done everything possible</u> <u>that could help cause learning</u>, there is more that could be done to help the students.

So, are results-driven teachers made or born? This is an ancient question with modern impact. Plato pondered in his *Republic* about an ideal society in which people did the work for which they were inherently most suited to do. Plato included an ethical element for people who have the ability to do the very difficult task of governing; they must accept the responsibility to govern lest society be governed by someone of lesser ability. Doing the job a person is most suited to do also harmonizes that person's skills with his or her duties. Some religious thoughts include guidance for people to discover the talents they have been given and how to apply those talents in honorable ways. Philosophical ideas and religious thoughts provide conceptual support that the inherent nature of an individual may include an inclination toward and a calling to particular work. A person must still master the skills associated with successfully doing the work and cannot hope that life itself will supernaturally provide competence to go along with inclination toward, aptitude for, or an inherent gift in certain work. An undeveloped inclination, aptitude, or gift is a promise unfulfilled.

So, are results-driven teachers made or born? Made. When students and I are together causing learning in a classroom, my heart, mind, body, and soul are perfectly united in a glorious harmony, and I am quite certain that I was born to teach. But even with this disposition toward teaching and an ethical imperative that life itself expects me to be a teacher, many teaching skills had to be acquired through the years to be able to cause learning. More skills and ideas will be needed to teach better tomorrow than I am teaching today. I expect myself to continually improve as a teacher, because I expect myself to continuously cause more and better learning, more and better results.

Can anyone be a teacher? No. Some people say, "I would never do your job. I could never put up with those students all day." That is important to know, and the person who reached that conclusion should never spend a day as a teacher—the students and that person would be miserable and would be unproductive.

Others say, "I could never be a teacher. All of your authority has been taken away. You can't paddle the students. The parents don't believe what teachers tell them. Parents and students threaten to sue any teacher who dares to impose any real discipline or who gives a student the F he deserves if it means losing athletic eligibility."

Teachers have clear authority and need to use their authority to the maximum legal level. Most parents and guardians can be reasoned with. Because of the parents and guardians who are often intentionally unreasonable, it may be helpful to obtain some legal liability insurance coverage to protect yourself from the vultures. Know the laws, know the school district policies, know your school policies, follow laws and policies, document anything that may need future reference, keep your supervisor informed of any possible student or parent issue, and confidently do your job.

To be a public school teacher, a person must attend college, apply to and be accepted into the teacher preparation program at their college or university, complete all teacher preparation program requirements, graduate from college, apply for teaching jobs, get selected, accept the job, and then effectively do the job. Many people have not and will not complete those steps so they—unless they use an alternative, nontraditional route to teacher certification and employment—cannot be hired as teachers in public schools.

As we contemplate results-driven teachers, a different question emerges: Can everyone who is hired into a teaching job become an effective teacher, a learning-causing educator, a results-driven teacher? The optimistic answer is yes, because we know what works to cause learning, to get results in the classroom.

Identifying or creating the instructional activities that get results is not the more complicated part of the endeavor—making sure that teachers do only what works best to cause learning is the greater task. How is that done? Perhaps the most efficient way is to instill the conviction that teachers are responsible for results, with the highest priority result being to cause learning. When teachers accept the duty to get results, especially to cause learning, they will insist that they and their students do in the classroom only those instructional activities that most effectively cause learning.

I've heard some teachers say, "But I do everything you tell me to do. I borrow great teaching ideas from colleagues. I visit other classrooms to see what works there. I know the wholesome knowledge, interests, and talents of my students, and we make connections in the classroom all the time between what they know and what they need to learn. We absolutely never use any of the plain vanilla materials that textbook publishers provide. I would be embarrassed to give my students some generic word search or other time- and brain cell–killing worksheet. We use the textbook as a reference, but we use other resources that are much better. I still have three or four defiant, impossible students who refuse to work, cooperate, or follow instructions. I have done everything one human can do with those incorrigible students. Can't they be educated in some alternative program? I know they cause similar problems in most of their other classes."

Those are the words of a results-driven teacher who truly has done everything one person could do. The school and the school district need to intervene. A small percentage of students, probably 5%–10% based on data I have been shown, need to be educated in alternative schools. Being a results-driven teacher does mean doing the difficult tasks. It does not mean endless efforts to do the impossible. The incorrigible students can and must be educated, but that will be done in a results-driven alternative school that is designed as a unique program, with a curriculum, with a structure, and with a faculty/staff that are uniquely prepared for that work and for causing learning with those students.

One teacher cannot create an alternative educational program. One teacher cannot unilaterally assign a student to an alternative educational program. One teacher certainly can request that her school district begin or expand an alternative education program.

A teacher's authority in the classroom is nearly exclusive. The principal and the assistant principal may visit the classroom, formally observe, review lesson plans, offer ideas, and suggest resources, but given the staffing reality in most schools, administrators spend very little time directly observing the classroom work of most teachers. Unless a serious problem is noticed, such as a high number of students failing in a particular teacher's classes, or unless one or more serious complaints about a teacher are expressed, the teacher's authority in the classroom is often close to 100% on how teaching is done. Even when teachers are told they must use specific, scripted materials, how they talk to students, interact with students, energize the classroom, and add a human style to the classroom work everyone does is within the teacher's control.

For issues that go beyond the work done in one classroom—issues such as school policies or procedures, school district policies, or state/national public laws about education—a teacher's impact could come through providing ideas, opinions, information, or research. Some teachers may become frequently involved in committees that review school procedures or school district policies. Other teachers may rarely if ever have such involvement for a variety of reasons.

The results-driven teacher cannot ethically ignore policies, procedures, laws, or concerns that go beyond the classroom because those matters can impact the people in the classroom. The results-driven teacher knows how the organization works and knows where she fits in the overall organization chart. Serving on a committee; sending ideas through representatives; writing polite, constructive letters or emails; and attending meetings can be productive and diplomatic ways to impact results beyond the classroom, but it is in the classroom that the results-driven teacher can have the most important and direct impact, the impact for which she is uniquely qualified.

Imagine two musicians who each play the violin. Both are talented, have taken lessons for years, practice daily, work hard, and are very accomplished musicians. When the musicians performed a duet, one member of the audience commented, "Isn't it amazing how much they get out of those violins?" The reality is that they get much from the violin because they put so much into the violin.

An aspiring musician who is in her first year of violin lessons does not get as much out of the violin as the more experienced musicians do, but with sufficient, proper teaching and practice, the novice musician can become as accomplished as the two more experienced violinists.

A results-driven teacher gets the most thinking, working, studying, asking, answering, and learning out of her students. In the classroom, this teacher is devoted to getting the most out of each student. The teacher puts so much into the classroom, so much of what causes learning, that he gets so many results from students.

The two accomplished violinists join dozens of other experienced musicians to form a symphony orchestra. The orchestra conductor is dedicated to get the most out of each musician and to get the most out of the total orchestra. The orchestra does not cover music. The orchestra does not do worksheets about music. The orchestra does not read textbooks about music. Sure, there may be some academic instruction about the history of the selected music, the idea or the story behind the selected music, the life of the composer, and the various interpretations of the selected music by other orchestras and their conductors. The orchestra is results-driven. The conductor of the orchestra is results-driven. The desired result is a flawless performance of the music.

A results-driven teacher has some similarities with the orchestra conductor. Each musician needs to get the most out of his or her instrument. Each student needs to get the most out of his or her brain and mind—the brain adds 2 + 2 and gets 4; the mind understands addition, thinks about addition, and can explain the idea of addition. The conductor teaches, guides, inspires, challenges, and nurtures musicians. The individual musicians and the conductor become a united orchestra, which is greater than the sum of its parts. The individual students and the results-driven teacher become a classroom community, which is greater than the sum of its parts.

If the question, "what is a teacher?" had been asked at the start of an educator's 30-year career and then was asked again at the conclusion of that educator's career, would the answers be similar, or would the passage of time plus the changes in society and school during that time mean that the answers would be quite different?

No doubt, circumstances would have changed during that 30-year career. Societal changes can impact schools. During any recent 30-year time period, a teacher could have noticed more students being reared by grandparents, more students needing to take prescriptions during the school day, more students identified as having mental illnesses, more court-involved students, more students whose mothers consumed drugs while pregnant, more students of all ages who have minimal or no social skills or manners, more students who use vulgar language, more students whose parent is court involved, and more students whose experience with the juvenile justice system convinced them that crime pays.

During that same recent 30-year time period, a teacher could also have noticed more students who eagerly mastered a second language, more students whose computer skills made them an unofficial employee of the school as a technology advisor, more students able to take an accelerated curriculum at younger ages, more students ready to graduate from high school after three years, more students actively involved in community volunteer work with significant leadership responsibilities, more honorable students impatient with juvenile criminals at school, more students bored with ordinary classes and ordinary teaching methods, more students having educational experiences in the summer that surpass their school educational experiences, and more students increasingly reluctant to wait for other students to catch up before the entire class can move on to new learning.

The range is expanding. The troubled students are bringing more severe problems to school with them. The successful students are ready for more demanding academic challenges. The juvenile criminals are committing more serious crimes. The teenage scholars are ready for college classes at younger ages. In the midst of this growing range, what is a teacher? Can one teacher have every solution to every problem of every troubled student who enters her classroom while simultaneously having every challenge for every academically advanced scholar who enters her classroom? No. Schools, school districts, and school systems can collectively, as comprehensive organizations, address the range of student needs and student abilities. And the question "what is a teacher?" cannot be realistically answered with the solution that one person flawlessly provides all necessary interventions, accommodations, solutions, challenges, opportunities, and guidance to every possible set of circumstances brought to school within each classroom's group of students.

Consider two settings that are not classrooms: First, imagine a large grocery store with thousands of products, hundreds of shelves, many aisles, and many check-out lanes. No two customers at the grocery store follow exactly the same route through the store. No two customers compile the exact same assortment of products into their grocery carts. Customers would be perplexed and resentful of a grocery store system with a one-way route through the entire shop that required every customer to travel through the complete store, passing by every product, going past every shelf, and walking through every aisle.

Second, imagine a basketball coach whose high school team of 18 players has a midseason record of six wins and six losses. Every day at basketball practice, every player follows the exact same procedure from start to finish. From stretching and warm-up drills, through skill stations, to three-on-three activities, to five-on-five scrimmages, to conditioning running, and back to individual skill stations, such as free throws or three-point shots. By the time practice ends each day, every player has spent exactly the same number of minutes on each task as every other player. An athlete who averages hitting 90% of free throws and 10% of three-point shots spent the same time working on those two skills as the athlete who averages 40% of free throws and 30% of three-point shots.

What observations can be made about the grocery store and the basketball team that apply to the question, "what is a teacher?"

A large grocery store makes available a wide range of products that can satisfy the shopping list of many customers; however, no one grocery store will have every possible size, shape, flavor, scent, and brand of every possible product. The emphasis will be on the most commonly purchased sizes, shapes, flavors, scents, and brands because that efficiently addresses the wants and needs of most customers based on sales data and consumer research.

The marketplace includes specialty grocery stores for neighborhood convenience, for a particular cultural or demographic customer base, or for unique needs of customers in a particular niche. Supersized grocery stores may offer more varieties than a merely large store, but no one store sells every possible product in the ever-widening grocery product category.

The basketball team could quite easily end the season with a record of 12 wins and 12 losses. What might happen if instructional and coaching effort at basketball practice allocated some time to specific needs. Any basketball player who is hitting 70% or lower of free throws will take extra time today to work on free throws. Simultaneously, the other players will work on the statistically measured aspect of basketball that they need to improve most or that they have the most likely possibility of becoming superior in if they are already very good.

One teacher simply cannot provide every possible educational product to every possible student consumer of education.

One method of teaching cannot fully develop the academic abilities of each and every individual student, but results-driven teachers, results-driven schools, and results-driven school districts can reach that goal together.

In order for a teacher to successfully cause learning today, schools, school districts, and school systems must keep up with the realities of today. Simply telling teachers to solve every new problem and maximize every new potential of each student without organizing the school to fully support that directive is unrealistic. The grocery store manager who seeks to provide the widest possible range of products and services today is supported by a corporate structure, distribution system, and technology and human resources to get the job done. The successful business enterprise of today does not use decades-old organization charts, distribution systems, technology, or staffing levels. Schools often are not as adequately updated in organizational terms as businesses.

The answer to the question "what is a teacher?" cannot be "a person who miraculously resolves all issues brought into the classroom by all students and who also maximizes the academic potential of all students." The answer can be "a person who causes learning," especially if sufficient school, school district, community, and society attention is given to the student realities teachers deal with daily.

I would make this offer to a society that is concerned about how productive schools are: the standard for a teacher is to cause learning, and the standard for the community is to realistically support, staff, and co-operate with schools based on the facts of today.

Results-driven teachers cannot and do not wait for society to realize that schools today are asked to do more than ever before while dealing with problems that are more complicated and numerous than those of earlier decades, without realistic, up-to-date organizational structures and supports to address current realities. Results-driven teachers require themselves to get all possible classroom learning results anyway. Not all teachers think that way or perceive teaching as a results-driven endeavor yet. The question "what is a teacher?" can be approached by considering a variety of teacher types as follows:

1. *The Bell-Shaped Curve Rules:* This person is convinced that student achievement will always follow a normal distribution with a few failures, a larger group of students who nearly fail but pass, a very large group of students in the middle with fair or ordinary grades, a small group with good grades, and a few superstars with great grades. Mr. or Ms. Bell-Shaped Curve regrets that some students fail, but concludes that too many factors are beyond his or her control to reverse the failure. This person is pleased to see the scholars do so well and wishes that more students did what those scholars do. This person accepts that the large group in the middle is just how it always has been and always will be. At least everyone was given the opportunity to come to school and to learn. What more can you do than provide the opportunity?

2. *The Routine Rules:* This person established a classroom routine very early in his or her career as an educator. There is no variation. Every day of every week in every school year follows the same routine that that day of that week followed last year. There is a high reliance on textbooks and supplemental materials provided by textbook publishers. Chapters and worksheets are repeated throughout the year. One chapter per week. Four worksheets per week. One test per week on Fridays. Leave for the weekend, return Monday, and repeat. Why? This sort of teacher will say, "Students need a routine. My students know how our system works. We never have to waste time doing anything different or learning a new way. I can tell you exactly what we will be doing on any day. My classroom is quiet and controlled." The educator forgot to include that the classroom quiet is the sound of no meaningful learning taking place.

3. *Information Director and Task Manager:* This educator perceives his or her work as conveying information to students. Textbooks and worksheets are used. Lectures and videos are used. Additional readings are copied and distributed. Tests are used to measure how accurately and how much students can repeat what they have read, heard, or seen. All classroom tasks are information delivery driven. Minimal attention is given to analysis, thinking, creativity, wonder, interaction, research, or questions. The supreme task is to cover material. Cover means to go over. Often, after students go over the material and complete the test, the material evaporates from their memory, except maybe for a few pieces of trivia that stick in their brains like a bad song. Cover material, then cover more material is the predictable repetition in this treadmill classroom.

4. *Is It Summer Yet?:* This educator remains employed by never violating law, policy, or procedures. The absolute minimal level of work that can keep a person employed is what this person does. Absences on Mondays and Fridays are common. Lesson plans are copies of some introductory pages from the teacher edition of a textbook. This educator might take some field trips, show some videos, have some guest speakers, or take classes to the library. These activities are designed to easily pass time. Little or no academic work is done in relation to these activities. This educator has excuses for everything. This educator also can show that the instructional materials that the school provided are being used in the classroom. The approved curriculum is posted in the classroom. Student work is graded and returned. Nothing illegal is happening. The educator and the students go through the motions of playing school, but learning is not occurring. On any day, this person can tell you how many school days remain until summer vacation. In May, this person can tell you how many days, hours, and minutes remain until summer vacation.

5. *Willing and Trying:* This educator agrees that all students need to learn and that if the old ways do not work, new actions are needed. This person willingly attends professional development programs to hear about teaching innovations. This educator returns to school and is seen each day trying to implement every method, activity,

and innovation he or she has been told about. This person experiences some successes, some frustrations, some accomplishments, some disappointments. Occasionally this educator thinks, "You know, every year we try something new. Then we try something new the year after that. I do what I'm told to do. I'm loyal, I'm willing to work hard, and I'm trying to do my job well. I just wish that we would stick with something long enough to really get some benefits. Our school district changes everything so often that we never know what worked or didn't work. I'll still do what I'm told. What else can I do?"

6. *We Can Do Better:* This educator takes school seriously. This educator follows laws, policies, and procedures. This educator uses the instructional materials that the school provides yet also brings other equally good or better materials into the classroom. This educator has a classroom structure or routine but realizes the potential of an unexpected learning moment that requires taking steps off the beaten path. This educator attends all required professional development programs and implements all required activities, but always with a conviction that "In my classroom, we can do better. I'll take what I learned in our training program, and I'll make it even better for my students." This educator is capable, reliable, and dedicated. This person asks some important questions to colleagues, but is always diplomatic. Most students do fairly good to very good work with this educator. Few students fail or barely get by in this classroom. This educator knows that those students can do better, that they have been given chances after chances, and she will keep working with them persistently.

7. *Results-Driven Teachers:* Restricted only by the boundaries of what is legal, ethical, and professional, this teacher causes learning in the brain of each student. This teacher is driven by the result of causing learning for, with, and from students. This person is not obsessed. This person is not a workaholic. This person does not have delusions. This teacher knows what works in the classroom to cause learning. This teacher thoroughly knows the subject matter he or she teaches with expertise, yet continues to read, study, think, and learn more about the subject matter. This teacher thoroughly knows how to design instructional activities that cause students to learn, yet

continues to analyze, reflect on, and get colleagues to evaluate his or her teaching. This teacher thoroughly knows students—their wholesome knowledge, interests, talents, prior achievements, goals, difficulties, personalities—and updates that knowledge continuously. This teacher energetically interacts with knowledge and with students to gain the result of causing learning. This teacher is driven to and by results. The pursuit of results is fascinating to this teacher. The attainment of results is inspiring to this teacher. What is a teacher in the most honorable sense of the word "teacher"? Results driven. A teacher is driven to and by causing learning for, with, and from students. Relentlessly seeking, finding, creating, and effectively implementing ways to cause learning makes an educator a teacher. The best teachers, the genuine teachers, the teachers who touch lives, are results driven. The results-driven perspective and performance elevate an educator to the status of teacher, a results-driven teacher, a person who causes the intended learning.

What causes an educator to be a results-driven teacher? Are there insurmountable factors that prevent an educator from becoming a results-driven teacher?

If more money were spent on schools, education, resources, salaries for educators, or school buildings, would there be more results-driven teachers? Maybe, but would a 10% increase in educational spending be followed by a 10% increase in teaching effectiveness and then a 10% increase in student achievement? It is unlikely that any such series of changes would provide a series of mathematically precise increases.

If there is not necessarily a direct relationship between money and more effective teaching, how then could more teachers become results-driven teachers? Should schools seek to increase the number of results-driven teachers, or is the wide range of perceptions about a teacher's job just a reality that is part of the human condition?

Of all the types of teachers listed earlier in this chapter, the results-driven teacher stands out as the teacher a parent would prefer to teach his or her child, principals would prefer to have as a faculty member, and students would most favorably respond to, knowing they will have to work hard yet also knowing that the work will be very worthwhile and fascinating.

Of all the types of teachers listed earlier in this chapter, the results-driven teacher's experiences in the classroom stand out as the most likely to cause learning by students and the most likely to provide a meaningful, satisfying, rewarding career for teachers. Later chapters in this book will provide more detail about increasing the number of results-driven teachers, but it is useful here to explore initial thoughts about the matter.

Expect from yourself as a teacher more than you expect from your students. You expect your students to be on time to class, so make sure you are early. You expect students to be prepared for class, so make sure you are overprepared with more high-quality instructional activities than could ever be used in one class period. You expect students to turn in work on time, done completely and correctly, so grade all papers thoroughly and promptly, and return them to students within two days of when they were turned in. Yes, returning papers within one day really does impress students.

You expect students to complete all homework, so make homework assignments worth doing by making them useful, meaningful, and essential to fully learning the subject. Also, make sure assignments are reasonable amounts of work that can be done within a reasonable amount of time. Avoid homework that is mere busywork.

You expect students to take school seriously, so you always take students seriously. You know that students are real people living real lives right now, so you make classroom learning experiences real, not generic, prefabricated, superficial, textbook controlled, or worksheet dominated. Make sure the classroom experiences don't result in your silence when students ask, "When will we ever use this? Why do we have to learn this?"

You expect faculty meetings to be worth your time. You expect teacher training sessions or professional development programs to relate to you and your work. Give students classroom instructional activities and learning experiences that are worth their time, that relate to them and to their real lives right now.

You expect every student to not cheat, so you never cheat your students. You would take action against a student who copied the work of another student and sought credit for that fabrication. You do not copy instructional materials and present them to students as your own best effort to maximize the learning of all students. You expect students to do their own work, so you do your own work, knowing that the results will be far superior if you design instruction that uniquely addresses the needs, abilities, interests, personalities, and goals of your students rather than imposing some ordinary tasks provided by an anonymous expert in the mechanics of superficial, mundane, limited, generic, pointless, prepackaged, instructional nadirs that copy machines obediently reproduce and that students resent, reject, or return with superficial answers to match the superficial questions.

You expect your students to pay total attention, think, properly respond with questions or answers or ideas, read, study, and learn. So you provide classroom instructional experiences that captivate the full attention of students, that so intrigue students that their questions or answers or ideas are unlimited, that motivate students to read, that energize students to study, that challenge students to fully and eagerly learn.

You expect your students to produce results at school, so you require yourself to get results with, for, and from your students. You decide to be a results-driven teacher and you do the work to be a results-driven teacher because it is right, it is honorable, it is best for your students' education and for your career. You surpass what is required by law, by policy, or by directive. Your standard is results.

The attitude and perception of the work of a results-driven teacher is a total attitude, a perception, a work ethic and teaching method that is available to every educator. To do less is to limit students despite learning itself being unlimited. To do less is to limit yourself as a teacher, despite teacher effectiveness being unlimited. How do we get more results-driven teachers? We expect and accept nothing less of ourselves as teachers. This is not imposed on us by law, policy, or directive. This is a gift we give our students and ourselves. The price tag and the value of this gift is not measured in dollars; rather, the price is measured in quality of work experienced, and the value is measured in students' and teachers' lives that are touched.

This gift cannot be purchased with donated dollars, tax dollars, endowment dollars, or fund-raising dollars. This gift may have monetary impact, but it does not have a monetary foundation, source, or origin. This gift is from the human mind, brain, heart, integrity, and senses of honor, purpose, duty, meaning, and responsibility. This gift is from the human longing to matter. Results-driven teachers get to live a professional life that matters profoundly.

Is it good or not, productive or not, helpful or not that different people who work as teachers may have very different answers to the question, "what is a teacher?" When does healthy debate combined with different ways of teaching become counterproductive and beyond the range of acceptable work?

Acceptable work gets the desired results. Unacceptable work does not get the desired results. One of the research-confirmed characteristics of great teachers is that they use a variety of teaching methods and activities, but they use that variety to get results. Their success is not measured by the variety of instructional methods used, but in the results gained. Because teachers teach a variety of students who can change from day to day and who certainly do change from year to year, various instructional methods are needed. The bottom line—was learning caused?—does not change. The desired result is to cause learning. Acceptable ways of teaching are those that get the desired result in legal, ethical, professional, G-rated ways.

It is unacceptable for an educator to know about effective teaching methods but never or rarely use those methods due to stubborn resistance or personal inconvenience. If a teaching method can more effectively cause your students to learn, use that teaching method even if it is not the teaching method you are most experienced or comfortable with. It's not about your experience, your comfort, or your schedule. It's about student achievement. It's about students learning. It's about causing learning. It's about results, not excuses.

Some teachers knew from an early age that their career would be as a classroom teacher. The classroom called those people, and they eagerly answered the call.

Some people went through childhood and teenage years with a succession of career interests but eventually decided on teaching and felt a confident certainty that their skills and the work of teaching would be a good match.

Some people went to college and moved from one major to another before finally deciding to study one or two subjects, take education classes, and earn teacher certification while earning a college degree.

Some people went to college and earned teacher certification in case graduate school plans or other career plans just did not work out. Teaching was (the backup plan.)

Some people would like to be professional musicians, professional actors, a college athletic coach, but the chances of making any of those become a full-time career seem limited, so teaching music, teaching drama, or coaching high school sports while also having a teaching job is a more stable approach.

Some people become teachers with little intention to remain in the classroom for long. A different job, a family situation—marriage, the birth of a child, a spouse's job requiring relocation—or graduate school can permanently end the temporary teaching work.

How do results-driven teachers realize that they should be teachers? Do they select teaching, does teaching select them, or do they select each other in a symbiotic match? That selection process is driven by the unequaled power of symbiosis. The results-driven teacher must work in a classroom with students because the results that concern and drive that person can be produced only by direct work with students. The experience of, the setting of, the unlimited possibilities in, and the importance of classroom teaching are compelling to the results-driven teacher.

Education matters profoundly. Results-driven teachers have a professional life that matters profoundly. To fully be who they are, results-driven teachers must teach. For education to fully be all it can be, students must be taught by results-driven teachers. If the match of teacher and teaching is less than total, mutual commitment, the outcome declines.

Are you a teacher simply because you completed a college degree that included the requirements of your state for teacher certification? You have in your possession a document that confirms that you have met the state's requirements to seek and be selected for a job as a teacher. You are certified to teach, you have met the requirements, and you have been reviewed favorably by a governing authority. Are you a teacher yet?

You interview for a teaching job. You are selected for the job. The school year starts, and students enter your classroom throughout the day on schedule. Are you a teacher yet? You were hired to teach. Are you teaching? More information is needed. What experiences and activities are you providing for your students? What, how much, and how well are the students learning through those experiences and activities? If all students are fully mastering the desired learning just as you are also fully mastering how to most effectively teach your current students, then you are a teacher worthy of the highest regard, because you are a results-driven teacher.

If you are relentlessly devoted to making every minute count, causing every student to fully learn and continually creating, finding, discovering, and effectively implementing better ways to cause learning, you are a results-driven teacher.

As a concluding idea for this chapter and as an introductory idea for the next chapter, it is useful to note the difference between teaching and training.

When we need for everyone to be identical in some capacity, training is used. A fast food company needs for every hamburger to be cooked and served exactly alike, so the employees are trained in the one, exact way to cook and to serve hamburgers. Training provides uniformity and efficiency. Some of what is done in some classrooms is training—every student doing the same type of task over and over. Even if some training is acceptable for some classroom work, most classroom work needs to far surpass the restricted benefits of training. If the journey toward learning involves 100 steps, the first few steps could involve training, but the other steps require—for unlimited learning—results-driven teaching.

When we need for everyone to be different or when we acknowledge and apply the reality that everyone is different, we teach. The required curriculum must be learned by everyone, but how it is best learned varies from student to student, from class to class, and from year to year if a teacher opens the learning process to a variety of instructional activities. Worksheets and textbooks train students. When students draw a picture that represents the idea of a fraction—one slice of an eight-slice pizza, a dime next to a dollar, 15 minutes out of an hour, six months marked off a calendar—the drawings are different, yet each one presents an aspect of the idea of a fraction. Each student drew something of interest, worth, meaning, curiosity, or importance to him or her. Each student learned, but no two students learned in exactly the same way. After presenting their drawings to the class, the students now had heard, seen, and thought about fractions more and better than ever. Training does not accomplish that. Teaching does accomplish that. Results-driven teachers make that happen.

It is likely that far too much of what is done in too many classrooms today is training, not teaching; is compliance-driven redundancy, not results-driven teaching; is time-filling laborious chores, not mind-filling academic adventures. Training is not teaching. Teaching is not training. Teaching is causing learning. Results-driven teachers are satisfied only when all students have learned at a significant and profound level.

Should training be forbidden in schools? No. Having every student memorize the multiplication tables through 12 times 12 could be done through training activities that emphasize recall. A trainer would stop at the point of almost every student passing a 144-question multiplication test. A results-driven teacher would take the students from mastering the multiplication table to an explanation of what multiplication is, to application of multiplication in real life, to identifying mnemonic devices, to evaluating how division undoes multiplication. A trainer imposes limits. A teacher removes limits. A trainer is satisfied with giving everyone a chance and with student achievement that ranges from low to high. A teacher is only satisfied with every student fully learning.

Students need results-driven teachers. A results-driven teacher is a person who students need to lead them to unlimited learning. Doing that with students means that results-driven teachers have professional lives that matter profoundly. That is what a results-driven teacher is. That is what a results-driven teacher does.

WHAT IS THE IDEA AND THE IDEAL OF A TEACHER?

"What is the idea of a fraction?" That question intrigued the 6th graders who I faced in a first-period math class. Traffic problems had delayed their teacher's arrival, so I gladly taught the class until she arrived.

"It's part of something." "It means you split something into pieces." "It's less than a whole." "It's, you know, it's when you divide something up." Their answers revealed important insights into what a fraction is, into the idea of a fraction, into how those students could be taught about fractions.

The idea of a fraction is a bigger mental consideration than any one fraction or than any one mathematical calculation involving a fraction. Exploring and understanding the idea of a fraction can enhance subsequent math work done with fraction calculations.

The idea of a teacher is a larger mental consideration than any one specific activity that a teacher does. The ideal of a teacher—or put differently, the ideal teacher—is a further expansion of our mental consideration that began with idea and now ascends to ideal. For our purposes, a results-driven teacher is one manifestation of the ideal teacher.

The ideal of teaching is the idea of causing learning. Teaching is more than training and is different from training. Training in classrooms emphasizes repetitive recall of limited information and/or repetitive application of

limited skills. Learning is unlimited. Training is limited. Teaching is unlimited. The results a teacher can create are unlimited. The results a trainer
can get are limited.

People need to learn; therefore, people need to be taught. Yes,
through the process of trial and error, a person can acquire some conclusions about what works or what does not work in certain parts of life.
A person could develop an interest in cooking and decide to experiment
with certain foods, seasonings, cooking temperatures, cooking times,
and various types of cooking supplies, appliances, ingredients, and combinations of ingredients. The trial-and-error process will produce some
inedible concoctions and, eventually, some tastier menu items.

Is there a better way to learn how to cook? An eager student of food
preparation could read a cookbook and precisely follow each step in a
recipe. The trial-and-error inefficiency would have been replaced by
cookbook efficiency. The apprentice cook may follow a recipe precisely,
but the food item could still not be very appetizing. Perhaps this new
cook prefers more spice, less salt, meats that are closer to well done than
medium, or, due to health concern, less sugar. The cookbook was designed for the typical cook with recipes for the typical consumer.

So the determined apprentice cook takes a cooking class offered by a
local neighborhood, owner-operated, customer-friendly grocery store.
The class begins with this statement: "Aristotle was right when he said
that 'The diner, not the chef, is the best judge of a feast.' The same food
can taste differently to various people. Your tastes differ from mine. In
this class, I will teach you about cooking. You will have some choices
with each recipe. For the parts of cooking that allow no variation, I will
train everyone in the same techniques. For the parts of cooking that allow variation, indeed thrive on variation, I will teach you many options
and you will create others. There is no limit to the number of ways that
foods can be prepared, cooked, and served, so we will not limit ourselves."

A person whose cooking ability is limited to conclusions reached
through the trial-and-error process may stumble across a few cooking
methods and recipes that work; however, the person may default to simple sandwiches and bowls of cereal because errors are eliminated. Trial
and error can be a very inefficient, frustrating, and limiting way to gain
information, skill, knowledge, or insight.

A person whose cooking ability is limited to cookbook processes being imitated will be able to prepare more foods in more ways than before using the cookbook; however, the ability gained goes no further than the information in the cookbook. The cookbook trained the person to follow recipes, but did not enable the person to analyze options, to evaluate information, to explain reasons, to understand cooking, to know food. Training is inherently limited. Results-driven teaching—ideal teaching—is unlimited.

A person whose cooking ability is developed, encouraged, guided, nurtured, challenged, disciplined, and applied by a teacher is a cook whose experiences with food can be unlimited. This person knows everything the cookbook can tell anyone, because the teacher and the student read and discussed the book. This aspiring chef has every skill that training can provide, because the teacher required mastery of all cooking fundamentals. This aspiring culinary master fully understands the science, art, history, and business of food preparation and presentation. With this depth of understanding, unlimited results can occur. New recipes will be created. A restaurant could be opened by this person someday. Years of healthy, enjoyable food await this person who was taught, who learned, who learned how to learn, and who created new knowledge. Teaching and teachers make all of that possible. Training and trainers do not seek or reach such ideal levels.

The 6th grader was sitting at his desk looking at a math worksheet with total bewilderment. He was going from math problem to math problem with absolutely no understanding of what the problems were about, what he was supposed to do, what could get him to the right answer, and what the right answer really means. I had been called to the classroom to help resolve a discipline matter. I remained to rescue a 6th grader who was stuck in a math quagmire of trial, error, and worksheet.

For the math problem $1/3 + 2/9$, the student had written $9/6$. I asked him to explain how he had solved the problem. He said, "Well, we were told to multiply the numbers across top to bottom. I know 9 times 1 is 9, and 2 times 3 is 6. So, 9/6 is the answer." As I paused to think of what to say, the student spoke. "No. It's 3/12, isn't it? Because 1 plus 2 is 3, and 3 plus 9 is 12. I had to add across, not multiply up and down." Trial-and-error math complicated, by worksheet math, had completely confused, misled, mistrained, or misinformed this student.

I began to ask questions, and the student eagerly answered. Now I knew more about how much he had learned regarding adding fractions. Very little. I took out a few coins and soon he added dimes and quarters, pennies and dimes, quarters and nickels. Money made sense to him, so money math made sense to him. No trial and error was used. Some training through repetition of questions was used. Now it was time to teach.

We went to the marker board at the front of the class. I drew two circles.

"Do you like pizza?"

"Yes, sir. Are those pizzas?" he asked politely.

"Yes, they are. If we had a big, round pizza here, how much of it could you eat?"

He eagerly said, "Half. I know I could eat half of one pizza."

I drew a diameter in one circle to show half of the pizza. He assured me that he could eat that much. I probed further. "Well, if we cut the pizza into your half and my half, would you pick up your half and start eating it? Half of a pizza would be one giant slice."

He thought silently and seriously, and then said, "No, that's too much to hold. I'd cut it up." Success.

I replied, "Great idea. That makes it easy to hold." So on the other circle I drew four diameters to create eight slices of pizza. Now his half of a pizza was shown as 4/8 of a pizza. We drew, discussed, shaded in, and colored the circles.

"So if you ate half of the pizza with that one giant slice or if you ate four of these smaller slices, which is more?"

"You mean which piece is bigger?"

I clarified, "No, which meal would be bigger, more to eat? The one big slice that is half of a pizza or the four smaller slices that add up to 4/8 of a pizza?"

He smiled and said, "I understand. I get it. They are the same. That's really neat." We worked a few more problems. He grew in confidence and in competence. I did mention that because 1/2 is equal to 4/8, you can multiply 2 times 4 and 1 times 8 to check if the fractions are equal. Now up, down, and across multiplying made sense, as did adding fractions, as did denominators and numerators.

Originally, he was working on his own in the maze of trial and error. Every trial was producing another error. He and I did some basic math computation training to establish a foundation upon which teaching could be built. Then we interacted. I learned what he knew. He thought about fractions in terms of money and pizza and could then learn about fractions in terms of math. I was driven by the importance of, the possibility of, and the need for results. He was driven by connections, progress, fascination, and success. Such experiences help reveal the idea of and the ideal of a teacher.

The student was quite eager to learn. Until teaching happened, he was comfortable repeating his computational errors, because he thought he was doing the math correctly or at least doing something to fill in the blanks of a worksheet. His teacher-assigned task was to complete the worksheet, not understand the math. What he was doing made no sense mathematically, but it worked for him in terms of process, procedure, coming up with an answer, being able to explain how that answer was created, and finishing the worksheet.

When the student understood the idea of a fraction, the idea of adding fractions, and the application of fractions to pizza, he had a basis for determining whether his math work and his answers to the math problems were correct. He could reason that 1/2 of the pizza plus 1/2 of the pizza would not equal the 2/4 of a pizza that the adding across method gives. Training does not give the student the ability to reason. Training gives the student the ability to repeat a task. This student never asked himself, "Do the answers I am getting make sense?" because such reasoning had not been part of his worksheet math training.

As I worked with the student, we moved from the limited but necessary benefits of training to the unlimited and essential benefits of results-driven teaching. His goal with worksheet math was to finish the worksheet. Accuracy and understanding did not matter. Finishing the worksheet mattered. His goals with money math and with pizza math were to "get it," answer correctly, know why that was the right answer, and understand the idea of adding fractions, not merely to use some process of mixing the numbers together to produce some answer that, although incorrect, at least was consistent with some computational system that enabled him to finish the worksheet.

Why did the student's teacher permit him to sit at his desk and inaccurately continue the worksheet math? Perhaps because that teacher is a classroom trainer? No, even the training was unsuccessful.

The computational tasks that effective training could enable a student to use repetitively and accurately were not part of this student's skills. He had not been taught. The training he had been given had not worked. The teacher was sitting at a desk doing routine paperwork. The student was sitting at a desk doing worksheet math inaccurately. All of this was unacceptable. All of this falls far short of a proper idea of teaching and an honorable ideal of teaching.

When classroom instruction declines to training only, the emphasis day after ordinary day is the routine, the procedure, the recall of bits of information, the limited, the superficial parts of education. Students hear, "Study this because it will be on the quiz. We covered it yesterday and will review it today." Training can be a useful first instructional step toward more meaningful learning. Training should not be the only in-structional step taken in classrooms and repeated as if more training could ever equal any teaching.

When classroom instruction ascends to the idea and ideal of the ex-perience of teaching, then the fascinating, creative, profound, unlim-ited, and meaningful parts of education are emphasized. A teacher who has moved beyond training might say, "Now that everyone has mastered the fundamental vocabulary, let's create a real-life application of those words. Imagine that you are at a shopping mall. You have $20, but the products that appeal most to you cost much more than $20. Using 10 of the 15 vocabulary words, write your explanation of what you will do. Of course, your ideas must be G-rated, legal, and ethical." That task goes far beyond training into the learning zone of teaching.

What would a job description of a results-driven teacher include and exclude? How does that description express the idea and the ideal of su-perior teaching?

Stating my job description requires a sentence, a paragraph, or an itemized list. Doing the work contained within that job description takes a lifetime. I truly expect to do my best teaching during the final year of my teaching career. I require myself to improve annually, continually, daily. I acknowledge my successes and achievements, but then I evalu-ate what can improve and I create improvements.

A results-driven teacher's job is to put the most into and get the most out of each student's mind. Then a teacher is a brain surgeon who oper-ates in a classroom, who has 150 patients daily, and whose surgical pro-cedures include profound questions, fascinating projects, creative homework, intriguing tests, lively discussions, and a relentless drive to get results of the academic learning kind.

Athletes, actors, politicians, entertainers, movie stars, television reporters, college coaches, and corporate executives are among the people in our society who obtain fame. Results-driven teachers live a very different life. Each day I walk into a classroom and encounter the brains, minds, personalities, hopes, problems, failures, successes, struggles, fears, dreams, tears, anger, kindness, and reality of my students. They are real people living real lives right now. Their lives are greatly enhanced when I do my job well, when I put the most into and get the most out of the brain and the mind of each student.

In the grand scheme of life, I am one out of the planet's six billion inhabitants. I am not on the evening news. I am rarely in the newspaper. I am not acquiring great wealth. I own little property, but my house is just fine. I did not seek fame or fortune. I do not desire a mansion or a multimillionaire's income. I expect myself to put the most into and get the most out of each student's brain and mind in each class I teach every day. To me, accomplishing that is wealth, fame, joy, who I am, and what I do. To me, it is ideal.

My idea of a teacher and my ideal of or for a teacher are very similar. Teachers exist because brains and minds can be developed, exercised, nurtured, strengthened, activated, challenged, amazed. When a teacher does that to the brain and the mind of a student, the teacher is doing that to, with, and for the person who that brain and mind live within and to the life that person lives now and forever.

Each day in my classroom, I get to create masterpieces, invent new products, discover new ideas, inspire the apathetic student, challenge the motivated student, encourage the fascinated student, and applaud the successful student, all while learning with and about all students.

College students who are preparing for a career in teaching are often asked to write a statement about their philosophy of education. The thinking for such statements can be charming but closer to fantasy than reality. Grand dreams are worthy of consideration and pursuit. Impossibly lofty or fictional fantasy statements of educational philosophy provide minimal benefits on the job.

Pondering the idea of teaching and reflecting on the ideal of teaching include sufficient elements of dreams to stretch our thoughts and our work to new levels of achievements without being mere exercises of illusion.

When a person says, "I have an idea," what does that statement communicate? It indicates that a person has used his or her brain and mind to create a new thought. The brain and mind can be used to further explain, analyze, evaluate, develop, improve, refine, test, and implement the new idea. Old ideas may have helped establish a foundation for creating the new idea; however, existing information and thoughts have now been expanded, invigorated, improved, revised, or questioned in a way that adds to a person's intellect. The new idea may or may not actually function well, but it is still a productive result of thinking, learning, reflecting without limits.

Such is the opportunity when we ponder the idea of teaching. Some might say, "I know some teachers. I hear them talk about their work. I have a mental picture of what they do each day. I remember my teachers. So, sure, I have a fairly good feel for what a teacher does." Many people could make that statement, but so much is missing when a perception and description of a teacher is limited in that way.

The idea of a teacher is the life-giving wholesomeness of developing the mind and the brain with no limits. The reality of teaching—the moment-to-moment, day-to-day work of a teacher—can cause such development of mind and brain if one is true to the idea and ideal of a teacher, but not if one accepts less.

There is another possible obstacle: "There is so much paperwork to keep up with. Plus all the meetings to attend. Then we always have some order coming down from higher up about mandated changes because the federal government or the state government or the school board or some loud, local interest group decided to tell us what to do and has managed to impose its will on everyone. How do I find the time and the freedom to teach when all of these annoyances and disruptions keep demanding my time?"

Schools do have to endure some of the political and societal pressures inherent within democracy. Educators must maintain documentation for various governmental or policy regulations. The administrative or political hierarchy may still think that some school program, initiative, process or system that got favorable publicity elsewhere could be the long-awaited, perfect educational approach, so it must be implemented in their schools immediately, no matter what else is being done and no matter what other people think.

Even if what a teacher must teach is precisely identified, usually there are options available for how the teaching can be done. The how of teaching can liberate an otherwise frustrated teacher. Laws and policies do not regulate the level of enthusiasm a teacher brings to the class-room. Laws and policies do not regulate how interactive a teacher is with students in the classroom. Laws and policies, mandates, and directives do not limit how thoroughly a teacher can get to know the whole-some knowledge, interests, and talents of students, so those insights are used as a resource to make learning connections between what students know and what students need to learn.

Because a vital part of the idea of a teacher and of teaching is to cause learning, part of the ideal of a teacher and of teaching is to outsmart, re-sist, circumvent, and simply not be limited, controlled, frustrated, or de-feated by forces that could otherwise negatively impact learning. The bottom line is results, not excuses. Anyone can make excuses. Teachers who are true to the idea of teaching and to the ideal of teaching make results happen.

The idea of art is greater than the materials used by an artist. The idea of music is more substantial and more magnificent than a mere collec-tion of notes. The idea of baseball is more compelling than the required supplies of bats, balls, gloves, and bases. The idea of math is within the numbers, not limited to the tangible numbers themselves, to the literal functions of numbers, or to the mechanics of numbers. The idea of a business is more than a collection of products or services.

The ideal art is greater than the idea of art. The ideal is the ultimate expression and experience of the idea. Similarly, the ideal teacher is greater than the idea of a teacher. The ideal is the ultimate expression of, experience of, benefit from, and wholesome, enduring impression from the idea.

To understand the idea of teaching and to implement ideal teaching is to be a results-driven teacher. To become a results-driven teacher, one must understand the idea of teaching and then implement ideal teaching.

The ideal coach maximizes the physical performance of athletes. The ideal teacher maximizes the mental performance of students. At the age of 51, I decided to once again take tennis lessons. Two prior series of tennis lessons in recent years had been helpful, but I was not satisfied with my performance. I had progressed from bad to below average, then from below average to fair; however, my goal was to become very good.

At the conclusion of a recent lesson, my very capable instructor said, "That is the best you have ever played." I had already told myself that at long last, I had played real tennis, not some simulated or modified version for people in the "over 50" category.

What made the difference? Recent lessons had been results-driven. We did not cover tennis shots; we thoroughly identified the actions that result in a perfectly hit tennis shot. We completed drills that build skill in those actions, and we discussed what causes success and what causes failure. The combination of knowledge and work, understanding and effort, concentration and commitment, connection and persistence, and various instructional techniques and progressively more demanding tasks had resulted in a new level of achievement. A little training followed by a lot of teaching got superior results.

A few weeks ago, the instructor and I might have agreed that very little progress was being made, so there was no reason to continue. In fact we did the opposite. We became much more precise in our work. We used drills that exactly addressed my errors, weaknesses, and needs. We analyzed honestly and thoroughly what I did well and what I did incorrectly. There was a harmonious merger of (a) analysis or study of how I played tennis and (b) actions that corrected my errors. This led me to an understanding of the idea behind correct execution of each stroke in tennis and to success in completing—even if only occasionally at first— the ideal execution of each stroke.

Yes, my tennis instruction has an inherently motivated student. I get to my lessons on time. I willingly work. I push myself. I challenge myself. I ask that my instructor overlook my age and work me as if I were a teenager. Still, a few weeks ago, I questioned whether any progress would be made. Now my question is how soon I get to play tennis again. Now I understand the idea, the concept, the image of each tennis fundamental. The mind and the body are in harmony, the idea and the ideal are united. A taste of success created a hunger for more success. I have been taught effectively. We were driven by results, so we were driven to results. Now there are no limits. The idea of an ideal is matched by the commitment to experience—both the idea and the ideal. Having played tennis better than I ever played, I understand tennis better; I comprehend the idea of the game, and I now know something about the ideal of the game. Such understanding, comprehension, knowledge, and results are permanently energizing. The same is true when teachers fully understand the complete idea of teaching and then experience with students the ideal achievements of teaching.

It was when I understood the idea within each shot in tennis that I began hitting each shot more in accord with the ideal execution. My brain was fully aware of and comfortable with the idea of how to hit a tennis shot correctly. My mind understood why that was the way to hit the tennis shot correctly. My brain and my mind guided my body to implement the idea. When that implementation was done correctly, the result was an ideal shot. Until I fully understood and accepted the idea, my results were very limited, and the ideal was elusive.

Fully understanding the complete idea of teaching is a similar essential step toward reaching the results-driven ideal of teaching. The complete idea of teaching parallels the totality of learning. That which can be learned can be taught. That which is truly taught is genuinely learned.

The ideal of teaching expands the current totality of learning as new knowledge is created, new insights are established, new questions are asked, new discoveries are made, and new ways of learning are identified.

During the past decade, I have asked more than 4,000 people to tell me about the best teacher they ever had. That question always stirs meaningful memories of a person who touched a mind, a heart, a life. The answers are always deeply personal, and some answers are punctuated with emotion as a teacher whose vital imprint endures is recalled perhaps for the first time in years. Such memories help confirm what the idea of a teacher is and what the ideal of a teacher is.

Purely pedantic, ordinary, superficial, routine classroom activities are not remembered by those 4,000 people I have surveyed. "Schoolish" worksheets with their generic, formula-driven plainness are quickly forgotten. Those worksheets and their partners in the ordinary—including but not limited to textbook chapter questions, word searches, videos, massive literature textbooks filled with stories that never answer the "when will we ever need to know this?" question, common math books filled with odd-numbered questions that do more to pass the time or consume pencils than they do to create learning—are not remembered. Those classroom supplies and activities are not part of the idea of teaching. Of course, a results-driven teacher could occasionally use one of those resources as an academic warm-up for a minute or two in class to establish a fundamental foundation, but little more of real worth could be accomplished with those routine, ordinary, superficial, and limited resources.

The idea of teaching is not implemented with 175 or so consecutive school days of generic worksheets, common textbook pages, word searches, videos, or outlines of chapters relying on words printed in bold type. The idea of teaching is implemented with an initial perspective about learning that realizes that the human brain can think, can be taught, and can learn without limits.

When the question "what career are you preparing for?" is answered by a college student with the response, "I'm going to be a teacher," what exactly does that indicate that the person will do once they obtain their first teaching job? If the answer had been that the person would become an accountant, a police officer, a dentist, a banker, a lawyer, a computer systems manager, a news reporter, or a preacher, the person hearing the answer and the person giving the answer may both have a generally clear and similar view of what the stated career would involve.

When the answer is "I'm going to be a teacher," the person hearing the answer may recall many different teachers who did their work in quite varied ways, so there is not necessarily a clear view of what one particular aspiring teacher will actually do once the teaching career begins.

That seems to leave much that is unresolved, unknown, and uncertain about the acceptable work done by teachers. Would the teaching profession, students, parents/guardians of students, and community be served well if a certain amount and quality of instructional tasks and instructional effectiveness were a required standard performance level by all teachers? Could this standard performance level also serve as the initial description and implementation of the idea of a teacher and the idea of teaching?

Let's imagine that the answer "I'm going to be a teacher" is followed by a second question: "What will you and your students do each day?" The answers could vary widely, but each answer would reveal some important truth about how the prospective teacher understands the idea of teaching. What would the following answers reveal about the potential teachers perspectives on the idea of teaching?

One future teacher might respond, "Well, I guess everyone will have a textbook and we'll do textbook work. I really had not thought that much about what we would actually do. I just always thought that teaching would be a good job for me."

Another future teacher might respond, "That's an interesting question. I haven't thought much about that. My education classes have been about, well, about theories of learning, philosophies of education, psychology about children and teenagers, but not much on the actual activity students and I will do every day. I'll probably work on that when I'm a student teacher."

A third future teacher might respond, "My sophomore year practicum took me to six different schools to observe twelve different teachers. I visited two elementary schools, two middle schools, and two high schools. I observed two different teachers in each school. Most of what I saw was pretty typical, you know, textbooks, lecture, notes, worksheets, and tests in the middle schools and high schools. The elementary schools had more variety, but still most of the time the students were at desks listening to teachers or doing tasks the teacher assigned. Some elementary reading classes were really lively, and one high school teacher had a big variety of activities. I pretty much thought I would try to be like that one high school teacher and do a lot of active learning projects with my students."

Still another future teacher might respond, "From what I can tell, that really is not up to me. The state and the school district seem to set up the curriculum. The school district has their evaluation system, so you need to do what they expect you to do as a teacher. We've had some guest speakers in our education classes. They pretty much said that most people follow the processes the state and the school district tell you to follow. I guess I'll do what everyone else does."

Another response from a future teacher might be, "I think about that a lot because my mother is a teacher, and we talk a lot about her work. I've always wanted to be a teacher. I used to listen to my mother and her teacher friends when they got together and talked about school. I never understood why some of them were teachers, because they complained about everything. Mom told me that they were good teachers years ago, but all of the difficulties of the job as it changed just became too much for them. I hope that does not happen to me. I want to be the teacher that every student remembers for all the right reasons, especially because my class was never boring."

Some future teacher might say, "The students and I will work in the classroom like we are at a camp in the summer. I've always gone to Girl Scout camp as a camper and then as a counselor. My summer job in college is as a camp counselor. Camp is great. The campers do so much and learn so much. School should be more like camp. That's what my classroom will be like. Why should the best teaching happen at camp? School can be like camp, too."

Another might answer the question by saying, "I'll teach math and coach football. The math book will show us exactly what to do. Most math books are about 500 or 600 pages long, so I'll make sure that we get through three or four pages each day. As a football coach, I'll do everything it takes to make our team win. I've had great coaches, and I'll use their best methods, plus a few techniques of my own. My team will win."

Still another future teacher could say, "We've really concentrated on human growth and development in my education classes, plus many of the cognitive theories about learning. We read a few books by child psychologists and other behavioral experts. Philosophy of education was a good class. So I am comfortable with the big concepts. I think I know my subject matter well. My emphasis in elementary school teaching will be literacy. I'll teach every subject, but reading interests me most. I hope to work with the youngest elementary students and teach them to read. I've studied the concepts and theories of language, literacy, linguistics, and communication. I'm sure I'll know exactly what to do by the time I graduate."

A final response from a future teacher could be, "That's easy. My college classes in education emphasize instructional design. I can show you a perfect lesson plan for any age group and for any subject. By the time I start teaching, I'll have a collection of lesson plans to get me through the first semester. I've read about teaching, and I've observed in classrooms in several school districts. One professor even took us to the police academy nearby so we could see how they are trained and taught. I'm ready to go. I have hundreds of activities to use with my students. Just give me a job and watch the teaching begin."

What differences would there be if experienced teachers are asked a similar question: "What do you and your students do all day?" Will the range of answers begin with a fundamental standard of basic satisfactory work and build to the exemplary? What will these answers tell us about how the teachers perceive the idea of teaching and the ideal of teaching?

A current teacher might respond, "What do the students and I do all day? We battle each other. What's wrong with this younger generation? My students used to listen, behave, cooperate, and work. Not anymore. They complain. They make excuses. They blame other people. They seem to think that absolutely everything should be given to them free of charge and with no work or responsibility on their part. Free meals, free clothes, free pencils, free grades. Students who have never been told 'no' or who have been given everything free are becoming the biggest problem I deal with."

Another teacher provides this thought: "I spend so much time each day monitoring and documenting. Whether they are real or made up, the number of syndromes, conditions, disorders, or other semimedical or pseudopsychological conditions take more and more of my time. I know that some students have an accurate diagnosis of a genuine illness or condition. Those students need and deserve all the support and opportunities possible. But how does one teacher in a classroom do the work of a nurse, medical doctor, psychiatrist, psychologist, social worker, pharmacist, parent, and teacher? My career began with an emphasis on academic work in the classroom. Now the emphasis seems to be on the students' mental health, social skills, behavior, time management, and organization of school materials. I'm a teacher, not a therapist."

Is there hope? Let's keep asking. A third teacher might say, "After 13 years of teaching, I knew that there were two options: quit or stand up and be heard. I stood up. I talked to PTA groups. I talked to other teachers. I talked to administrators at schools. Everyone agreed that schools just were not staffed or organized for the realities of today. Then I talked to administrators at the central office. I challenged them to come be a substitute teacher one day per week for a month. Get out of their comfortable offices and come deal with reality face-to-face. Don't just observe in schools. Work in schools. They accepted the challenge.

"The results were amazing. They honestly admitted that because it had been years since they worked in school, they had not kept up with current realities is schools. Now our school district is taking some overdue actions. School law enforcement officers, surveillance cameras, social

workers, school/court liaison staff, more counselors, and staffing for be-
fore- and after-school programs are all being added. Plus, those school
district leaders will keep substitute teaching one day each month. It's
amazing what can happen when everyone is accurately aware of truth
and has recently experienced reality."

Another seasoned teacher had this reply: "School is all about teaching.
It has always been about teaching. School will always be about teaching.
There are political issues, bureaucratic mazes of paperwork and meetings, angry or unreasonable parents or guardians, defiant students, successful students, helpful families, tight budgets, caring volunteers, and
everything else. Still, school is about teaching more than it is about anything else. I put my highest priority on how effective my teaching is.
Great teaching prevents many problems. When students are taught in
ways that meaningfully fascinate them, they get to class on time, they cooperate, they bring a pencil and paper, they don't use some syndrome as
an excuse—that is, they manage their condition or their condition seems
to subside—because doing the work is so worthwhile that they control
themselves rather than having to be controlled. It's the teaching."

One more thought from one more teacher is needed. A final response
might be, "I think often about teaching. I expect myself to be a magnificent teacher every class, every day. I loved school when I was a student.
Truth is, I'm still a student. I learn each day about teaching, students,
and the subjects I teach.

"Sure, I get frustrated. I get angry. I get fed up. Why are 15-year-old
criminals allowed to return to school when they are just going to commit more crimes? Put them in a highly secured, totally structured, zero-
freedom facility so they can make some progress and so everyone at
school can work without fear or turmoil. Why are negligent parents or
guardians not held accountable, but teachers are? Well, I could complain forever or I could take action. I decided long ago to take all the action I could in the areas I have authority over. My most important authority is not over what my students are taught. The curriculum is given
to me. Sure, I have some input when the curriculum is revised, but that
is not very often. My most important authority is over how my students
are taught. As long as I can design instruction that fascinates, intrigues,
motivates, and challenges students, that makes students learn and learn
eagerly, I'll persist despite any difficulties. I know how to teach.

"I forget most conferences or professional development workshops quickly. But there was one teacher conference that I'll remember forever. The main guest speaker was a teacher. Not some expensive consultant or out-of-touch official who had not seen a classroom for years. The teacher began his presentation with this question: 'what is the biggest idea in teaching?' I'm sure I have paraphrased the words a bit, but my version captures the meaning accurately.

"I thought and thought. I'd never wondered about the idea of teaching. I always got caught up in the activities, schedules, new ways of doing things every year, meetings, textbooks, and all of the other procedures, processes, and materials. So the speaker's question shocked me. What is the big idea behind everything I do at and for school? It's easy to get so busy with the tasks that you overlook the idea.

"The speaker had people walk up to microphones and say what they thought was the biggest idea in teaching. Imagine that. The guest speaker had the audience get involved. Everyone listened. Everyone paid attention. After 14 people spoke, the quest speaker asked us to write one word that was the most dominant theme across those 14 comments. It was so obvious. About half of the audience stood up when the speaker asked, 'How many of you wrote the word learning or an equivalent word?' Everyone started applauding. Everyone cheered.

"When everyone sat down the speaker said, 'You are absolutely right. The biggest idea in teaching is students learning. We are the people who get to make that happen, to cause learning, to cause students to learn. That's the biggest idea in teaching.'

"So I remind myself to concentrate on causing learning. I do what causes learning, and I avoid anything else. The results are spectacular. Sure there are difficulties, and it takes a lot of work, but it can be done. Every student has some wholesome interest or talent or curiosity. Every student can be shown how their interest or talent or curiosity connects with the school curriculum. You won't find that in textbooks or other ordinary materials. You find that in people, their imaginations, goals, dreams, and real-life experiences. Connect what students know with what they need to learn. That's how I make the big idea actually happen in my classroom."

At a recent professional development program for middle school teachers and high school teachers, I spoke about experiences my students and

I have had. I also asked the participants to tell us about the best teacher they ever had. I shared results from my research based on asking more than 4,000 people to tell me about their best teachers. This discussion was vivid, touching, amazing, inspiring, practical, and genuine.

After we concluded the program, one participant said these words to me as she smiled and expressed true joy: "Thank you for reminding me of what I have always known but sometimes let myself get way from. It's all about doing what works. It's all about teaching so students learn. I knew that; I just needed to be reminded."

It is important to note that the teacher did not ask for an automatic formula or perfectly prepackaged program to implement in her class-room. The teacher did not expect those to exist because the human variable, the imagination variable, the innovation variable, the spontaneous variable, and the dynamic of human development all confirm that the most effective way to teach today's curriculum to today's students never fits into a formula and never should be limited to existing prepackaged programs.

The ideal teacher continually learns about students, about how students learn, and about the subject he or she teaches to students. The ideal teacher is organized—creativity is not chaotic. The ideal teacher manages time well—this enhances productivity—but uses the spontaneous question, answer, or moment to more effectively teach the intended learning when it could work better than what was originally planned.

The ideal teacher is true to the idea of teaching. The ideal teacher is devoted to, dedicated to, energized by, and measured by the idea of teaching. The ideal teacher lives a life of learning, does the work of causing learning, and gets the results of maximizing the academic achievement of each student. One way to describe the ideal teacher is to say that the ideal teacher fully implements the idea of teaching.

The idea of real teaching has always been to cause learning. The idea of true teaching continues to be to cause learning. The idea of true teaching, of results-driven teaching, will continue to be to cause learning. The idea and ideal of teaching and of a teacher are enduring. The specific actions taken today with today's students to cause learning of today's curriculum will properly address the strengths, needs, life experiences, wholesome interests, talents, and knowledge of students by designing instructional activities that cause learning.

Today's ideal teacher knows that students must master the curriculum. Ideal teachers have always known that and have made that happen using the proper, legal, ethical, effective, instructional activities that cause learning. The ideal teacher knows that the curriculum this year may be identical to last year's curriculum; however, this year's students are not identical to last year's students. What needs to be learned changes slowly. How that learning is caused changes often, sometimes constantly. The ideal teacher embraces the reality and adventure of constantly innovating, connecting, and discovering ways to cause learning. The ideal teacher does not change the teaching methods or activities merely to change; rather, the ideal teacher does what causes learning. What caused learning yesterday may cause learning today, but it may not. The guiding factor is results. The ideal, results-driven teacher is true to students and to their learning results.

Our consideration of the idea of a teacher and of the ideal teacher prepares us well for a thorough exploration of the purpose of teaching. Yes, the purpose of teaching is to cause learning as has been clearly identified. What does that mean? Chapter 4 answers that question.

4

WHAT IS THE PURPOSE OF TEACHING?

The conviction, the perspective, and the work ethic that collectively say that the purpose of teaching is to cause learning compel an educator to be a results-driven teacher. The required result is to cause learning. Nothing less is acceptable. The results-driven teacher begins with the conviction, the perspective, and the work ethic that teaching means to cause learning. If learning was not caused, teaching did not occur; therefore, different instructional activities must be designed and implemented to properly cause the intended learning. Thinking this way leads to working with results-driven determination, urgency, and standards.

Actions follow thoughts. Determined actions follow thoughts that have become personal convictions, commitments, and ethical imperatives. Thinking, believing, and committing to the standard that the purpose of teaching is to cause learning ethically mandates that a teacher finds or creates proper ways to cause the intended learning.

If educators think that the purpose of teaching is to merely offer educational programs and opportunities, the work that follows such thinking is quantitatively and qualitatively less than when educators dedicate themselves to the results-driven standard of causing learning.

The best actions follow the best thoughts. The best thoughts I know about teaching come from two sources. First, the thoughts from more than 4,000 people who, during the past decade, have answered my questions about the best teacher they ever had. That research has clearly identified characteristics of superior teachers. When those characteristics are implemented, learning is caused, and results are obtained. As stated in earlier books—including *High-Impact Teaching*, *Extreme Teaching*, and *Extreme Learning*—and earlier in this book, those characteristics of highly effective teachers are:

1. Use a variety of instructional activities and methods.
2. Challenge students.
3. Be enthusiastic about students, teaching, and learning.
4. Make connections between what is being learned and the real lives that students are living today.

My second source for the best thoughts on teaching is my daily interaction with students who I teach. During the past four years of teaching 8th-grade economics, every student in those classes has made an A or B grade. The As far outnumber the Bs. Grades of C or below are simply unacceptable. The students master economics. I learn about how they learn. The class is never the same two times in a row, because we are results-driven, not procedure-driven, process-driven, textbook-driven, or schedule-driven. We do what works to cause learning, to get results. I am driven by results, the ultimate being for this teacher to cause learning. The students join me on this demanding adventure, because the teaching method fascinates them and therefore gains their commitment. The students team up with me because the class, the discussions, the projects, the tests, and the homework assignments are powered by real thinking that relates to real life now.

The actions in my classroom follow the best thinking available to me about teaching. From the best thinking comes the best actions. From the best actions come the best results. The way we think—about teaching in general and the purpose of teaching in particular—does impact how we teach and what results we find to be acceptable.

Expanding that idea indicates that the collective way of thinking by the administration, faculty, and staff of a school impacts the overall work done and results achieved at a school. If everyone at a school has a different idea about the purpose of teaching, it is likely that results are limited because the teachers move in different directions toward different goals and because the educational experiences for students vary so much from classroom to classroom.

Teachers are not expected to be robotic duplicates of each other. Teachers are not expected to be scripted clones of each other. Teachers are—for the maximum benefit of the educational experiences of students and for the maximum career benefit of teachers—personally, professionally, and ethically obligated to do what works to cause learning.

With that in mind, it can be very insightful to probe a range of thoughts about the purpose of teaching. Ken Johnson is a high school principal. After years of being a high school teacher and middle school assistant principal and principal, Mr. Johnson decided two years ago to seek a high school principal job. After four unsuccessful interviews, Mr. Johnson almost gave up, but he decided to try one more time. A high school in a neighboring county had a job opening for a principal at Daniel Hunter High School. Their interim principal for the past year was ready to retire. Mr. Johnson applied and was selected for the job. His first priority was to accurately identify what reality was at the school. Mr. Johnson explored every topic—from curriculum to discipline, from involvement of parents or guardians to athletics, from test scores to budgets, from special education to faculty morale, from gifted and talented education to the extracurricular clubs, from the school's mission statement to the menu in the cafeteria, from technology to the dropout rate—because he needed to know the reality of what he faced.

Mr. Johnson was not a big fan of educational theories or philosophies. He knew that those concepts had merit, but too often the theories or philosophies never came down to earth, to classrooms, to hallways. Big ideas still have to be implemented Monday morning when the teacher and the students are face-to-face. Mr. Johnson appreciated the big ideas, but a big idea without proper implementation was of little worth or impact. Still, Mr. Johnson sought to understand the big ideas and the implementation efforts and all other realities at Daniel Hunter High School. Mr. Johnson was meeting with faculty and staff members in small groups on late afternoons in May. He was finishing his duties as middle school principal, so his time at Hunter High School was scheduled after school hours. At this meeting, Mr. Johnson heard from four Hunter High School educators:

Becky Woodford, counselor
Katherine Burlington, 11th-grade U.S. history teacher
Danielle Boyle, 9th and 10th-grade Spanish teacher
Mitchell Ashcroft, 9th–11th-grade physical education and health
    teacher

Johnson: Thanks for taking the time to join me today. I'm very eager to hear your ideas, concerns, questions, frustrations, hopes, and issues. Who would like to start?

Woodford: I will. Thank you, Mr. Johnson, for taking time on so many days to meet with people at Hunter High School. We appreciate being heard. I've been here for 21 years. I taught 11th- and 12th-grade English classes for eight years. I've been a school counselor for 13 years. Everyone here knows where I stand on most topics, but everyone also knows that I think one topic matters more than anything else. Fewer and fewer students take school seriously. Sure, we have some serious students who do great work, but more and more, year after year, I see the grades of so many students drop. Some just quit school. Others stay and barely pass. If you make Ds in every subject, you pass and you graduate, but you are not educated.

We've tried every possible program to get more students to work hard and succeed. It's tempting to say that if some students are determined to fail, then that's their problem, but we have to keep trying. I mention that because I know that some teachers just accept that some students will fail. The teachers can't do everything for the students. I do know of a few teachers who demand that every one of their students pass. Actually, a few teachers tried to eliminate the grade of D because it is so low. If you pass with a 67% in a class, you do not know 33% of the material from that class. Why do we call such low performance passing?

So I'm concerned about a long list of issues at this school, but my biggest concern is that out of every 9th-grade class, we know that 25% or so will not finish high school. We also know that some or many of the students who graduate could have accomplished much more at school and done much better at school. Too many teachers and students seem to accept good enough as good enough. I mean, they are satisfied with C averages. We can do better, but if so many people accept average results, we'll never improve much. I just think we have to accomplish more than that. Why exist if we're just going to be average? The whole reason for school must be more than bell-shaped curve results. I know that if we rank students, we get a top-to-bottom list, but there has to be a way to get every student above an acceptable minimal standard.

Burlington: Ms. Woodford and I have worked together for years. We have big philosophical discussions about school once or twice a year. Usually our day-to-day chats are about particular students and how to challenge or motivate them. I have a very strong concern about our best students and about the students who could be in the best category. High school seems to be very easy for a lot of students. We make sure they take advanced placement classes, but sometimes the differences between those classes and regular classes are just more books to read and longer papers to write. There is so much more that can be done to challenge students and to energize learning. I really believe that we are short sighted, because we figure that smart students will be fine since they are smart.

We do not think that way with the best athletes or the best musicians. The coaches design specific practice activities so the best players become even better. Coaches don't say, 'Well she's a superstar, so she will be fine without any practice.' No, they increase the demands at practice. Then they schedule games against the very best teams. The band director takes the marching band to the competitions, where the best bands in the state or the nation perform. They increase the challenge. They find the most demanding and rewarding experiences for the band. We just don't always do that in the classroom.

Johnson: What keeps us from teaching classes with the same level of challenge that coaches and band directors use?

Burlington: There are so many reasons, but I'll tell you the two reasons that I am most aware of. First, textbooks seem to rule the curriculum and the classrooms. Too many teachers seem to think that the purpose of teaching is to cover every page in the textbook. Students may or may not learn, but on the last school day, they got to the last page in the textbook, so everything is wonderful.

What's just as bad is that some classes do little or nothing besides page after page of textbook activities. You know, do the odd-numbered problems on page 117. Answer the 'Think and Remember' questions at the end of the chapter. Read pages 241–247 and then do the 'Science and You' questions on page 248. Read pages 741–767 in the literature book. Make a list of all the words in bold print and define them. This completely numbs the students. They hate that busy work. They might do the work because it is so easy or because they need the grade for athletic eligibility or college admission, but textbook pages never inspire, motivate, challenge, or teach students. So many teachers seem to let the textbook do their job for them.

My other answer to your question is that there is very little review or supervision of teaching. The principal or an assistant principal visits classrooms to observe a teacher three times a year, every third year. Is there any other business or organization in this country where workers are evaluated based on so little information? Good teachers would like some ideas on how to do even better. Average or bad teachers need serious attention. We just are not set up or staffed to do that.

Boyle: Everything I'm hearing sounds very important. Ms. Woodford and Ms. Burlington are right. I'd like to add another idea. I talk to the students a lot. I hear one question from them more than any other. The question is "why?" Why do I have to take statistics, trigonometry, and calculus? Why do I have to take English class after English class when I already know how to read at a 12th-grade level and write good papers? Why do I need to take physics when nothing I'm ever going to do will use physics? Why do I need to take another class in U.S. history when I have had that subject so many times before in elementary and middle school? Those are important questions, and sometimes it is not easy to give a convincing answer.

For some students, school is just a requirement to finish, and then they can go do something they care about. You see that every day. Students who stay at school for sports practice, a club meeting, or for marching band seem to be really excited about those activities. In the classroom, do you see the same level of excitement? There are reasons for that. I know some coaches who put a lot more energy into coaching than into teaching. We sure make a big deal at school when a team is successful, but when students do great academic work, there is much less celebration. That must send the wrong message to students. If we celebrate football wins more than straight A grades, it must look like the purpose of school is to win football games. Students notice what we reward at school. I would ask that we always reward academic achievements more than we reward anything else.

This is a different topic, but we have to do more about safety at school and enforcing rules. I'm a teacher. My job is to teach. I'm all about getting each student to learn and learn. I think the purpose of teaching is to get every student to learn. It's hard to do my best work as a teacher if some students skip class, sneak outside to smoke, use vulgar language all day,

steal from other students, and vandalize the building. Can't we have surveillance cameras? Can't we have more school law enforcement officers to
constantly patrol the halls and the campus? Can't we get tougher with the
students who need to be sent to an alternative program?

Ashcroft: It's so amazing to hear all of these topics being discussed. I'm
in my third year of teaching health, and I coach the boys soccer team. I
came to this meeting today to ask that we find some way to get every student involved in a sport or club or other extracurricular activity. My experience is that those activities can mean a lot to students and can give them
a reason to care more about school.

I still think everyone should be in some activity, but, you know, the
classroom is the activity that everyone already is in. We've got to make the
classroom experience great for every student. My biggest concern is how
apathetic so many students are about their classes. Sure, some of the students are scholars, they learn, they study, they listen, they make great
grades. Even those students deserve better opportunities so they are able
to achieve all they can. So many students just go through the motions of
school. They go to class, sort of pay attention, do some work, study a little. Make C grades or D grades and never get out of that rut. It sounds
harsh, but one reason they just go through the motions at school may be
because so many of their teachers just go through the motions. You know,
textbook, worksheet, video, quiz, textbook, worksheet, video, test. Next
chapter; repeat the process. I can't imagine putting myself through that
routine. I would never expect 16-year-olds to get much out of that routine.
In my health classes we do health, experience health, think health, use
healthy ideas, and live healthy habits. The students love cars. There are a
lot of health issues that relate to cars, like safety and pollution. They love
food and sports and movies and money. There is so much health in food,
sports, movies, and money. My students get interested in health because
it is real health, not textbook health.

Johnson: Wonderful thoughts from everyone. I know you have work to
do and places to go, so let's finish our time together now with one topic.
Tell me, please, what you think the purpose of teaching is. Some of you
touched on that, but it really made me think, so let's take a closer look at
that. What's the purpose of teaching?

Burlington: It's interesting, isn't it? We don't talk about that much or at
all. We talk about school improvement plans or programs to prevent bul-
lying. We talk about achievement gaps or professional development programs, but we rarely ask ourselves what this is all about.

I would say that the purpose of teaching is to make sure that every student has the basics. If we do that, then the students can move on into more school, into a job, and into their adult life. I'm a big believer in the basics. If every student learns the basics, we've done our job.

Woodford: The years I've spent as a counselor have changed my thinking a little, maybe a lot, on questions like this. I deal with so many troubled students. Dysfunctional families. Students who take several strong medications daily at school. Students in serious psychological counseling outside of school. Students involved in drugs, in cults, in crime. What is the purpose of teaching for these students?

Then I deal with students who have questions about college, scholarships, college applications, test scores, and college tuition. What's the purpose of teaching for these students?

Of course we deal with 1,950 students in this high school each day. Is there one purpose of teaching for everyone? I guess there is, now that I think of it. Teaching has to give each student the experience that shows them how they can become everything they are capable of. I guess that is really optimistic, but I mean it. Teachers and students should have experiences in classrooms that result in each student seeing that through the process of learning, their lives can become more right now and always than they had realized it could be.

Boyle: Here's my answer: The purpose of teaching is to give everyone the opportunity to learn. We can't make everyone learn. We can't make every family insist that their children take school seriously. We can't solve every personal or societal problem that Ms. Woodford mentioned she and the other counselors deal with. We can give everyone the opportunity to learn. I'd say that is the purpose of teaching.

Ashcroft: In the summer I have another job. I work as assistant manager of a restaurant. The owner of the restaurant tells us to do everything necessary to make sure that every customer is 100% satisfied with their meal. I remember one family last summer. They had placed their order and it was slow to arrive. I quickly took them a plate of free and healthy appetizers. They loved it. So we spent $2 on food to satisfy five customers. It wasn't enough to say that sometimes service is slow. We had to satisfy the customer. If you think about satisfying the customer as your top priority, you do your job differently than if you think that each customer gets the good with the bad, sometimes service is good and sometimes service is bad. The restaurant owner insists that service is always great. The purpose of the restaurant is to fully satisfy every customer.

We don't always think like that at school. I know, we can't satisfy every student with pizza every day, no homework, and lots of free time. We can satisfy what students need and that is to completely learn every part of the curriculum in ways that are interesting, worth doing, meaningful, and real right now.

I had a professor in college who said the time-release formula of education does not motivate elementary school students to study and learn a lot just because they'll need to know all of this for middle school. We tell middle school students to study and learn a lot because they'll need to know all of this for high school. Then we'll tell high school students more of the same, 'Study and learn this because you'll need it in college and on the job.' College students are told to study and learn to prepare for graduate school or careers. Then people finally get their job, and they have to go to continuing education.

So I think the purpose of teaching is to make learning happen right now in ways that make the learning matter right now. How's that?

Johnson: That makes sense. It's great to be with all of you today. We'll keep this conversation going for a long time. I'm eager to work with you, the other teachers, and the students. Thanks again for your time and ideas.

As he reflected on what he had heard, it became obvious to Mr. Johnson that while four people do not provide total input of all perspectives across the faculty and staff, these four people had different ideas about the purpose of teaching. If any organization is not unified toward a common purpose, it automatically limits what it can be and what it can accomplish. If teachers are aiming in different directions, what goals are going to be reached? Mr. Johnson's new job will have many challenges and difficulties along with many possibilities. He realized that establishing and implementing an overall, fundamental purpose for the school could help direct all efforts toward vital goals. If the efforts were scattered toward multiple directions, the school would almost sabotage itself.

Mr. Johnson emailed the school's faculty and staff. He also worked through the language arts teachers to get student input. His request was direct: "In my visits so far, I've heard very important ideas about our school. One very essential question has come up. The most important work done at school is what teachers and students do in the classrooms. So, tell me please, what do you think the purpose of teaching is?"

Replies from educators came quickly via email:

"To develop potential."

"To cover all of the material."

"To prepare students for their careers."

"To develop lifelong learning skills."

"To prepare students for adult life."

"To show every student how to learn and how to succeed in school and in life."

"To get every student up to a basic level of literacy, math skills, and people skills."

"This may not be what you are looking for, but I've always thought that a teacher's job was to cover the curriculum so every student had some awareness of everything they were supposed to learn. Some learn it and some don't, but teachers are supposed to go over the entire curriculum with all students."

"To be honest, I never thought about the purpose of teaching. I know what the job of a teacher is. I know what I do when I am teaching. So, I'd say the purpose of teaching is to do the job of a teacher and that means to give every student an equal opportunity to learn."

"The purpose of teaching is to provide an equal opportunity for every student to learn the material we cover."

"I'd say that it is to make students think. Too often in school students just passively complete dull assignments or really awful busy work. I do everything I can to make students think."

"The purpose of teaching is to guide the student. I don't pound information into them and I don't entertain them. I don't reward them and I rarely have to punish a student. I tell them what they need to learn. I show them ways to learn it. They do the rest. Some do very well. Some do enough to get by. Others fail miserably. Still, I give everyone a chance and I'm willing to work with anyone who makes some effort. I never do the work for them."

"To prepare students for college or for jobs or for the military. Everything we do at school is to prepare students for their adult life responsibilities."

"My idea about the purpose of teaching has not changed in 23 years of teaching. Tell students what they are supposed to do. Supervise students as they do or do not do what I told them to do. Give grades based on the facts of who did what. I'm not here to motivate, counsel, or listen to excuses. I'm here to give them the chance to work and to experience the reality of the decisions they make."

"My purpose as a teacher is to be sure that students learn. It's like with my doctor. When I'm sick, I expect my doctor to do whatever it takes to get me well. So I expect myself to do whatever it takes to get students to learn. Sure, I follow policies and laws, but I'm allowed to try and try again with students, so that's what I do."

"The school buys the textbooks and all of the supplies that come with them. The school gives me the curriculum guide. I divide all of that into 175 days of school so we cover everything. Each year we are told to cover more, so I squeeze it all in somehow. That's what I'm required to do."

"Maybe the answer is to get test scores up. All of these new laws about education seem to be obsessed with test scores. No matter what else we do, if test scores are not up we get criticized. So I guess the purpose of teaching has become to increase test scores. I'm afraid that some students could get lost in the test score stampede, but test scores seem to control everything now."

"I know that teaching is supposed to emphasize that students learn the curriculum, but let's get real. Schools are not staffed to do that job in today's reality. The problems students bring to school or cause at school make learning difficult for everyone. Until we deal with everything—from parental neglect to the juvenile justice system sending offenders back to school instead of back to jail—how can we live up to our purpose and really teach?"

"The purpose of teaching once was to provide instruction for every student. Now it is to get the test scores up."

"The purpose of teaching is to absolutely maximize the learning results and achievement of every student."

"The purpose of teaching is to cause learning."

Mr. Johnson was given a summary of student input as provided by the chair of the language arts department who compiled student input from every language arts teacher. This had been a writing task in every language arts class designed as a two-minute thought-starter for the beginning of class. Some teachers reported that this had become the starting point for very lively and productive discussions in classes. These ideas came from students:

"Teachers are supposed to be sure we do our work and stay out of trouble."

"It's all about jobs, isn't it? I've always been told that to get a good job, you need a good education. So that means the purpose of teaching is to get us ready for our jobs."

"I had an elementary school teacher who told us over and over that her job was to make us good citizens in this society. I guess that's it."

"Get me ready for college. Make sure I can get in the best college and make sure I get a scholarship. High school is all about getting ready for college."

"My uncle is a teacher. I know what he tells me about his job. It is to make sure that every student learns everything he teaches. That sounds pretty much like a dream to me, but he says he gets those results. Most teachers I have don't think about teaching like my uncle does. They just put the work in front of us and tell us to get busy because it is due tomorrow or because the test is on Friday. I'd say my uncle is right, but realistically, most of my teachers just get by and expect most students to just get by."

"I have a great teacher this year. She's the best teacher ever. Before having her as a teacher I'd say that the purpose of teaching is to get every student to be quiet and do the busy work every day. Now I'd say that teachers are supposed to get us interested in learning. This teacher has me so excited about science. I love cars. I get to do car science. So teachers are supposed to show us why learning is worth it."

"Here's what I think. Teachers are supposed to teach in ways that get us interested in learning. That's the purpose, to get us excited about learning. If the teacher is excited about the subject, we'll get interested in it. Oh, it really helps if the teacher likes students. We can always tell who wants to teach and who is just there for a paycheck."

"I don't know. I don't care about the purpose of teaching. I don't care about the purpose of school. School is so boring. I'm going to drop out as soon as possible. Forget this. Who needs school? It's so boring and stupid. I hate school. Most students hate school. If they have friends or play sports, they like that. But school is so dumb. I'm getting out."

"It's to make us learn or maybe to make sure that we learn something. Maybe it's to try to make us learn."

"Ideally it is to motivate us to be the best we can be. Teachers are supposed to do exactly what coaches do—make us the best we can be."

"The whole purpose of teaching is to get students ready for the next part of their education or life. High school teachers always tell us to study and learn so we'll be ready for college. I guess the purpose of teaching is to get us ready for the teachers we'll have next year."

"The purpose of teaching is the same as the purpose of all school. It's to get us ready for a job or a career. It's that easy. Go to school and then get a job. The better the work teachers get you to do in school, the better the job you could get."

"Get me ready for college. Actually, get me ready for a great college. Be sure I get accepted to a great college and that I earn a scholarship— actually several scholarships."

"My mother is a teacher. I hear her talking about teaching all the time, so my ideas are borrowed from her. The most important job of any teacher is to really get to know the students. Students work harder for people who care about them. So, if you want us to learn, convince us that you really care about us."

"To give me an advantage. We're always told that to do well in life, you need to do well in school. Okay, be sure I do well in school so I have that advantage. I know you can't do the work for me, but you can give me some interesting work to do. Please make it interesting."

Mr. Johnson reflected on everything he had heard and read. He thought that no organization could reach its goals until the most important goal was identified as the organization's magnificent purpose, reason for being, heart and soul. Mr. Johnson knew that until there was a common sense of purpose, there would be a common bell-shaped curve distribution of student achievement and of faculty or staff career achievement and satisfaction. Mr. Johnson firmly believes that the proven methods of great teaching are the most important resources available to teachers. He firmly believes that the purpose of teaching is to cause learning. He had to face the reality that every person who walks into the school may have a different idea about the purposes of a school, teaching, and education.

Mr. Johnson allowed himself a few moments to remember earlier years in his career. He taught 11th-grade U.S. history, taught 12th-grade U.S.

government, and he coached the boys high school soccer team. He made
it very clear in his classroom that everyone would learn, and everyone did
learn. The soccer team worked at every practice and in every game to win.
Every soccer player had the same purpose—to win games. As principal of
a high school, how would Mr. Johnson establish a shared understanding of
and dedication to the purpose of the school, which is to cause learning.
Very little would be achieved if everyone moved in a different direction toward a different goal. If everyone worked relentlessly and single-mindedly
toward causing learning, the result would be high-quality learning by
everyone at school. If everyone worked toward one different item on an
endless list of different goals, school would be a failure. Mr. Johnson directed his thoughts toward ways to build a shared sense of purpose across
teachers, administrators, staff, students, and their families.

The principal, teacher, students, staff, parents/guardians, and community associated with most schools could likely have a range of answers
to the question "what is the purpose of teaching," similar to the range of
answers at Mr. Johnson's school. Is there a different question that could
provide more similarity in answers?

Do you want all of the students at your school to become skilled in
basketball?

- No, that is not a priority at our school.
- Sure, that is an activity they could always enjoy.
- Maybe, but that's up to what the P.E. teacher does.
- Well, there's nothing wrong with that, but it is not as important as
  math or reading.

Do you want all of the students at your school to be able to play a musical instrument?

- Our curriculum does include music for each student, but it does
  not mean that playing an instrument is required for everyone.
- That's a great idea. I've heard of research that shows how much
  better students can do in school if they learn how to play piano or
  some other instrument.
- No, we just don't have the time or money to make that happen. We
  have higher priorities including math and science.
- There's nothing wrong with that idea, but if a student has no inter-

est in playing a musical instrument, why force them? Playing an instrument is not a requirement for college or for jobs, so why would we make everyone do that?

What about these questions?

- Do you want all of your students to be able to read well? Yes.
- Do you want all of your students to be able to do math well? Yes.
- Do you want all of your students to be able to write various types of papers and to do other writing tasks? Yes.
- Do you want all of your students to succeed in school? Yes.
- Do you want all of your students to have an educational foundation for lifelong learning? Yes.
- Do you want all of the students at your school to learn? Yes!

The questions answered with a yes are about academic achievement of students. Therefore, the purpose of a school is to cause learning. What makes that happen? Results-driven teaching! Therefore, the purpose of teaching is to cause learning.

Some basic, fundamental, obvious questions must be asked to achieve consensus. Of course the administrators, teachers, students, staff, parents/guardians, and community associated with a school would say yes to the question, "Do you want all of the students at your school to learn?" Some questions within that question, such as "Do you want all of the students at your school to be able to read well?" would also get general support. There would be a range of thoughts on questions related to basketball skills or musical instrument skills.

Warning: Think about the school celebrations, the publicity, the attention associated with basketball and other sports or with concerts and marching bands. Those activities can be exciting, educational, meaningful, and fulfilling; however, if sports and music at school are given the most noticeable recognition, it will appear that athletics and music are the school's highest priorities. Continue sports and music. Continue to celebrate sports and music; however, the purpose of a school is to cause learning, so always celebrate, publicize, and emphasize academic learning above all else at school.

Schools exist because students need to learn. The biggest allocation of time at school is for students and teachers to be in classrooms. The biggest allocation in a school district budget is for teacher salaries. The biggest allocation of square feet in a school building is for classrooms. The purpose of school is to cause learning.

The action that is intended to cause learning is teaching. The purpose of teaching is to cause learning. The resulting standard, then, is "was learning caused?"

Many decisions are made at schools. How will certain funds for instructional materials be budgeted? How will the hours during the school day be distributed across classes and other activities? How will teachers be evaluated? When will there be an assembly, a field trip, a guest speaker, a test, a reading contest, or a spelling bee? How are the best decisions made? The best decisions are made when the option selected is most consistent with and supportive of the school's purpose, which is to cause learning.

Many decisions are made by teachers when they are at school and when they are doing work elsewhere that relates to school. How often will homework be assigned? What will the homework assignment be? When will a test be given? How many questions will be on the test? Will I create the test myself or just copy a test that came with the supplemental materials that came with the textbooks? What will we do in class tomorrow? What am I going to do about students who have a D or an F so far in class, and am I going to do anything? What am I going to do to challenge students who make A grades easily, or am I going to do anything? If they make an A grade, have I done all I was supposed to do? Am I going to make copies of textbook publisher–provided worksheets, or am I going to design instructional activities for my students?

For each of those questions and for other questions that a teacher could ask, the answer is found in the purpose of teaching. Do what causes learning. Do what causes the most learning, the best learning, the highest quantity and quality of learning by all students.

Results-driven teachers are devoted to causing learning. The ultimate result is not to hand out worksheets or protest, "Well, I gave everyone the worksheet. I told them to read pages 217–222 and then do the worksheet. We saw a video about this yesterday, and we covered the key vocabulary with the word search the day before. I don't know why some of the students aren't doing the work. I gave everyone the same chance."

That same chance did not cause learning. The measure of a teacher is whether you caused learning. The measure of a teacher is not whether you assigned pages to read and worksheets to complete.

Results-driven teachers are dedicated to getting results. Results-driven teaching is dedicated to getting the results of learning to occur in the mind of each student. If the job of teaching is understood as having the duty of, the responsibility for, and the wonderfully meaningful challenge of causing learning, then the job of teaching is done very differently than if teaching is understood as being a classroom clerk who distributes worksheets to fill in and who assigns pages to read merely so textbook questions can be answered.

Results-driven teaching fulfills the purpose of teaching. A results-driven teacher will find, create, borrow, invent, discover, or identify classroom instructional activities that cause each student to learn.

Understanding, believing in, and committing to being responsible for causing learning can lead a teacher to be a results-driven teacher. "I taught them; therefore, they learned" is the glorious achievement and sense of fulfillment awaiting any teacher who adopts the idea, ideal, standard, perspective, dedication, and job description of results-driven teaching. With this perspective about teaching, it is contradictory for someone to say, "I taught them, but they did not learn." If teaching happened, learning happened. If learning did not occur, what the adult did was not results-driven teaching. When a teacher is results-driven, that teacher will find a way to make the results happen. We now move to a more detailed consideration of the job description of a teacher in which the bottom line and the headline are to cause learning.

5

WHAT IS THE JOB DESCRIPTION OF A RESULTS-DRIVEN TEACHER?

To cause learning.

"Yes, I do have one more question," the 25-year-old candidate for a high school math teaching position said as the job interview neared its end. He asked, "During my work with an insurance company in the past three years, I was promoted twice. Each of the three jobs I had were very clearly explained in precise job description statements. Do you have a job description statement for this teaching position at your school?"

The members of the interviewing committee silently looked at the school's principal hoping that she could answer the question. Her reply was accurate: "No. We do have a very lengthy evaluation form instrument that is used to collect data when administrators visit classrooms to do formal observations. That form has 13 different categories of teacher competencies, with anywhere from 8 to 15 indicators under each category. If the category is about the teacher's use of questions, one indicator relates to using a variety of question methods. I'll give you a copy of the evaluation form instrument if that is of interest."

"Yes," the candidate said, "that is certainly of interest. But just to confirm, there is no job description that defines the job of math teacher and the results the math teacher is expected to achieve?"

The principal replied quickly, "Exactly right. We emphasize the teacher evaluation form instrument. I'm sure that will tell you everything you need to know. We certainly appreciate your time today. We'll make a decision about this teaching position within a week. You'll hear from us, but feel free to call for an update."

The candidate knew that he would not be offered the job. That would save him the task of turning down the job. He also hoped his next interview in a different school district would have a different ending. It did.

At the end of that meeting, the interviewer said, "You mentioned there was one more question you had. We've asked everything we need to. You've had several important questions to ask us throughout this interview. So, please, what else would you like to know?"

The candidate said, "Do you have a written job description for each teacher, including a written job description for the 9th- and 10th-grade algebra and geometry math position I've interviewed for?"

The interviewing committee members smiled. Everyone on the committee knew the answer. The principal looked at the math department chair, who was obviously eager to answer the question.

"Yes, we do. In fact, the math department led the way at our school to create the written job descriptions. We had meeting after meeting. We got input from teachers, students, parents, guardians, administrators, staff, and community members. The input always emphasized learning. So, the motto you saw in the front hall, in the office, on the wall of the conference room, on our school shirts, everywhere you look at this school, you see everyone's job description. Teachers, students, staff, principals, families, volunteers—we all have this job description: to cause learning."

The teaching position candidate and the interviewing committee knew they had a match. The prospective teacher expected himself to cause learning. The school was dedicated to causing learning. The entire school community is driven to, toward, and by results. Results-driven teaching causes learning. That is the job description. That is the ethical imperative. That is the requirement of the conscience. That is the top priority and the bottom line. That is the purpose, job, duty, and adventure. That is the meaningful, rewarding, and challenging reality. That is what results-driven teaching is, and that is who results-driven teachers are.

The purpose of teaching is to cause learning; therefore, the duty, responsibility, measure, and purpose of a teacher is to cause learning. The job description of a results-driven teacher and, ideally, of all teachers is to cause learning. It will be a glorious day when the terms "results-driven teacher" and "teacher" are synonymous.

The purpose of a school is to cause learning. Schools are established to be places where teaching happens, which means they are places where learning happens.

For educators who accept that their duty is to cause learning, the way they do their job is guided by that fundamental conviction—my job is to cause learning. Doing the job of teaching with the intention to find, create, and make ways to cause learning means doing the job of teaching differently than if you see that job as just giving everyone the opportunity to learn, or distributing textbooks and worksheets to everyone, or assigning work for students to do and collecting that work, day after day, with no interaction and no interpersonal involvement. How a person sees, perceives, understands, and measures his or her job duty impacts how that person does the job.

Societies have been convinced for centuries that it is efficient and effective for some adults to have significant duties in the education of children and teenagers. Although a small percentage of families do educate their children at home, the vast majority of people entrust schools and teachers with most of the academic education of children and teenagers. Schools are in the learning business. Learning at school is caused via effective teaching at schools. The purpose of teaching at school is to cause the intended learning. The purpose of a teacher is to cause the intended learning.

How is learning caused? How do teachers make learning happen in the mind of each student? Begin by understanding that "cause" is a much stronger verb than encourage, facilitate, make available, or support. Cause means to make it happen. There are excuses and explanations, problems and difficulties, low budgets and high frustrations, students who are scholars and students who are criminals, but the bottom-line purpose of teaching is to cause learning. The excuses do not change the purpose or duty of teaching. The problems do not change the purpose or duty of teaching.

To be honorably involved in teaching is to accept a whatever-it-takes approach, knowing that legal, professional, and ethical guidelines must be followed. Learning cannot be limited by excuses and problems. Learning cannot be sacrificed to the power of excuses and problems. Learning must be caused despite excuses and problems. How is this done?

There is good news. We know what works. We know what great teachers have done and are doing to cause learning. Sure, some new problems may require some new solutions, but someone in another classroom or at another school has already solved the problems facing other teachers, so ideas and success stories can be shared. We know what works.

Results-driven teaching is continually reinvented, although that does not mean that teaching today rejects all methods and instructional activities that have caused students to learn in the past and that can still cause students to very effectively learn today. Some teaching methods have worked for centuries and merit continued use when they are the best way to cause learning today. Some classroom activities have never worked very well, and although still in use—will prepackaged, generic, superficial, ordinary, ready-to-copy, time-killing, fill-in-the-blank worksheets ever go away?—should be discouraged and, let's get serious, should be discontinued.

Teaching the current students in a classroom today includes the fascinating adventure of discovering how to best teach today's students. To cause learning now with today's students includes identifying how they most effectively learn today's curriculum. Why squeeze the students in a classroom today into the same old odd-numbered math problems on page 63 that students have been squeezed into for years? Math is much bigger and more fascinating than any selection of odd-numbered problems can convey. Students are more capable and more intellectual than any selection of odd-numbered problems can reveal. Once an odd-numbered class or worksheet class ends, the students quickly escape the limitations of the odd-numbered problems and pointless worksheets to encounter real math as they discuss the cost of a new computer, the big crowds at a new movie, the statistics from a basketball game, the price of a school yearbook, or the money needed for an upcoming field trip.

Just as it helps a physician to know something about a patient and about the patient's current health condition to accurately diagnose and treat him or her, it helps a teacher to know something about students and their current knowledge conditions to accurately identify what needs to be learned and how it can best be learned. Some say, "But doctors see one patient at a time, and they have nurses to help." I know. Teachers work with groups of 25 or more students, and we do not have assistants to help us. But do not despair. We know what works. We can fascinate a group of 25 students. The dynamic interaction of teachers, students, a variety of teaching methods, a variety of instructional activities, and the vibrant collision of ideas can captivate the group. You saw your best teachers do that. You have done that yourself. Some of your colleagues do that. We know what works. Physicians consult colleagues and learn from colleagues. Teachers can do that also.

For the results-driven teacher who is dedicated to causing unlimited learning, the fascinating adventure of discovering how current students most effectively learn is a joyous, irresistible, rewarding part of the teaching duty and job description. To learn about students is an unlimited experience for a teacher who sees teaching as a daily encounter with a daily discovery of unlimited ideas, possibilities, opportunities, challenges, and surprises. A "teaching" career of doing the same routine day after day, year after year, worksheet after worksheet, textbook after textbook, is not a real teaching career. That person passed the time as students passed worksheets from person to person and then passed or did not pass each Friday's test, which was limited in purpose or benefit or real value. A classroom clerk can manage that mundane, repetitive process, and no real teacher would impose that mundane process on students or on himself or herself.

Please know that one benefit of results-driven teaching is rather selfish. The results-driven teacher has a much more vibrant, fascinating, meaningful, productive, enjoyable, interactive, human, and genuine career experience than any teacher whose one-size-fits-all, paint-by-numbers, generic, "I taught them, but they did not learn," endless worksheets approach rarely if ever produces any meaningful results for students or for the teacher.

The purpose of teaching is not to distribute textbooks annually, worksheets daily, and tests on Friday. The purpose of teaching is to cause learning. Learning is much more dynamic and vast than any repetitious routine. Teaching is a renewing work of innovation and new interaction. A teaching career is 30 new years, not 29 reruns of the first year. But the pessimists persistently proclaim, "Those students just will not sit down and listen. They never do their homework, and they refuse to write anything, so I just cover material by covering students with worksheets, and at least most of them stay under control."

Students commit themselves to what fascinates them, what is real to them, what connects with their wholesome knowledge, interests, talents, and life experiences. The purpose of teaching is not to cover material, and it is not to cover students with worksheets; rather, it is to cause learning that uncovers wisdom, insights, and discoveries.

Students take school seriously when school takes students seriously as real people who are living real lives right now. When teaching and learning are real—please note, worksheets are not real—students will commit themselves to results-driven learning. They already are committed to results-driven learning about their favorite sport, their new car, their part-time job, their volunteer work at a hospital, their church youth group, or other real parts of their real lives. School too often seems unreal to students. Making school real removes some of the limits that teachers and students place on themselves and on what they do in classrooms. Results-driven teachers nurture, challenge, intrigue, fascinate, correct, and inspire students to become results-driven students who expect themselves to learn and who require themselves to learn.

Since the purpose of teaching is to cause learning, will doing the activities that great teachers do make someone a great teacher who causes learning? That could take care of some parts of teaching that are quantifiable, measurable, scientific, precise, and observable. There is more to it, including the qualitative, artistic, creative, personal, interpersonal, human, and humane aspects, which are essential for results-driven teaching. Just as curriculum equals what is taught and how it is taught, so teaching has a "what" dimension and an equally important "how" dimension. The actions of great teaching combine with the interactions, especially the personal and interpersonal interactions, to help create the adventure of results-driven teaching and the experience of results-driven learning.

This consideration of the job description of teaching and of how to implement that job description does provide some specific ideas, actions, and methods; however, this consideration also raises some questions and ideas that require continuous reflection. We hope that students will think about their learning and the work they do as students. Similarly, teachers need to think about their teaching, how they are causing learning, or if they are causing learning.

There is no permanently perfect procedure that will work every day, forever, in every classroom to cause maximum learning by every student. Still, maximum learning can be caused every day by, of, for, and with each student. Some successful methods do carry over from day to day, from year to year, from generation to generation. Other parts of effective teaching must be created anew. Learning changes. People change. How to cause learning in the minds of people who change is an unlimited adventure, duty, and discovery.

Teaching must include what is needed today to cause the intended learning by today's students. With that perspective of the job of teaching, you will not be satisfied with limits, with routines that continue merely because they have always been done with the ordinary, superficial, one-size-fits-all approach. If you see the job of teaching as being a results-driven teacher who causes unlimited learning and who also gets to experience unlimited learning about students and about teaching, you do the job with an unlimited enthusiasm and you receive from the job unlimited rewards, along with occasional fatigue and frustrations. But the occasional problems are not the parts that define the wonderful, unlimited whole.

That is hard work. Other professions and other jobs must also constantly update to meet current realities and to fully develop current opportunities. Cars are not manufactured today as they were decades ago. Emergency rooms use new medical technologies. Shopping malls are renovated and updated. Teaching is not unique in needing to be current, but that need to remain current does impact the perception and job of a teacher.

If keeping with up with students, curriculum, and new ways to cause learning are personally inspirational and invigoratingly challenging to you, you and results-driven teaching are already a wonderful match. If when you and the students are together, learning is caused, achievements are produced, and progress is made, you and results-driven teaching are already a good team. You expect yourself to be a results-driven teacher and nothing less would be acceptable. Sure, you could be productive in other jobs, but in this one job as a teacher, your productivity is unique. What you and the students create, explore, plan, and learn together can be done nowhere else with no other people.

To be a teacher, you have to be where the students are and you have to do what it takes to cause students to learn. To be a results-driven teacher, you have to understand where the students are academically; then you interact with them, beginning where they are academically and leading them where they can go. That journey, like the human mind and the human imagination, is absolutely unlimited. To be elsewhere or to do other work is just unthinkable for results-driven teachers whose heart, soul, body, and mind thrive in the classroom with students.

If that does not describe you, do some deep thinking and some deeper soul searching. Learning is unlimited. Why deny yourself and your students a learning experience that is unlimited? Why go through ordinary routines and get ordinary results if you get any results at all? Think about the job of teaching as it is seen by results-driven teachers, and see yourself doing the job with that perspective, with that standard, and with that type of career experience. It is better for you and it certainly is better for your students.

The purpose of teaching—to cause learning—is best achieved by people who are highly motivated to teach, who are highly skilled in teaching, and who continually refine their skills. People have varied reasons to be in the teaching profession, such as (a) teaching is who I am, it is my calling; (b) teaching is what I eagerly do by choice; (c) teaching is what I willingly do; (d) teaching is what I just ended up doing; (e) teaching is what I fell back on when other plans did not work out; (f) I'm going to teach for a few years and then do something else; (g) I teach so I can coach a sport; (h) teaching is a job I would quit today if I had any options or other income; or (i) I have four years to go until I can retire, so I'll just ride out those years.

Students deserve the best possible learning experiences. Students deserve more than limited efforts from people counting the days until retirement, people counting the days until the next big game they coach, or people who fell back on teaching and whose classroom activities fall back on worksheets and textbooks.

Years ago I quit asking students who misbehaved and were sent to the office any "why" questions. I did not ask, "Why did you hit him?" or

"Why did you throw the paper wad back at her?" or "Why did you use such vulgar, crude, trash talk?" Instead I began asking, "What were you thinking when you hit him?" or "What were you thinking when you threw the paper wad back?" The answers have included, "I was getting even," "I got my revenge," "I was thinking that he better not look at me like that again," or "I wasn't thinking anything." As the student hears his or her statement, the next steps become very obvious, because the student hears his or her admission of a mistake in thinking that led to a mistake in behavior.

What are teachers thinking when they prepare lessons for students? Are teachers thinking of the unlimited learning that can occur if precisely designed learning activities are prepared with attention to what is to be learned, who is to learn, and how those students most effectively learn? What are teachers thinking when they make 150 copies of prepackaged, generic, superficial worksheets to give one copy to each student even though students are anything but prepackaged, generic, and superficial? Is the teacher really thinking that this worksheet is absolutely the best way to fully reach all proper learning goals for these students today? Is the teacher thinking that this is good enough? Or is the teacher not thinking about much at all, except: "Well, you know, we need to do something so I made copies of these worksheets, and that should be enough to get us through today."

Implementing the job description of results-driven teaching that emphasizes the purpose of teaching—to cause learning—does not require that teachers work seven days per week, 12 hours per day. Nor does results-driven teaching prevent teachers from fulfilling family duties, pursuing hobbies, spending time with friends, pursuing graduate school degrees, or engaging in other free time activities. In the teaching profession, in the processes of causing learning, there continues to be this compelling truth—we know what works.

Each day brings the possibility of a new truth—we can discover, create, and experience learning activities that work even better as teachers apply the uniqueness of each student and the uniqueness of each class of students to the learning adventure by making connections between what students know and what they need to know. By doing what works, results-driven teaching is efficient. Reteaching is less necessary, because more students experience more learning the first time.

Two ordinary worksheets—ordinary worksheet is probably redundant—will never make up for what one ordinary worksheet did not accomplish. Teachers who get on the revolving wheel of worksheets to make up for low scores on prior worksheets put in more time and have fewer satisfactions than results-driven teachers who spend some pleasant, creative time designing instructional activities that will actually get results.

The purpose of teaching transcends what any one teacher knows or can do; therefore, every teacher who seeks to cause the best and most learning by students must continue to learn from students, other teachers, scholars of education, and experts in other fields in which people must constantly learn through continuing education or training updates. Teachers must also continue to learn through reflection and research. The totality of teaching and the totality of learning create unlimited possibilities for teachers and for students. If there is more that can be learned, there is more teachers can do, and results-driven teachers will eagerly do more work for and with their students so everyone benefits.

The human mind has abilities beyond what has been identified, developed, or understood fully. If that sounds loftier than the daily tasks of teaching, perhaps the perspective of some educators, especially classroom clerks, on the daily tasks of teaching is too narrowly defined. They say, "But it's just addition. Certainly we can cover addition with worksheets. Addition is not some universal totality of learning is it?"

How sad. Teaching is not covering material; rather, teaching uncovers ideas, concepts, insights, questions, answers, knowledge, and wisdom. Worksheet addition is the narrowest, most limited, most superficial approach to addition. To explore addition can be to explore recipes, space travel, weather, money, sports, or other real parts of real life in which students have wholesome knowledge, interests, or talents. Addition that connects with real life is addition that is eagerly and successfully learned. For the teacher to see addition as a vast adventure enables the students to see learning at school as a vast adventure rather than as a series of mundane chores. Sometimes the mind of the student has within it the essential ingredients of results-driven learning if a teacher will make the human and the academic connections with that student and the student's mind. That type of academic and human connection will help cause learning. That will help fulfill and implement the purpose of teaching. That will match the job description of results-driven teaching.

There are people who protest, "But some students are so defiant. Some are so lazy. Some won't work. Some just do enough to get by. Some students disrupt class. Some students make every possible excuse, and their families let them get away with it. What can I do? Those students just are not interested in learning."

Maybe those students gave up on school after too many years of limited learning in classrooms where limited teaching was the norm. Those students are interested in themselves. Each student—barring some severe psychological malady—is quite interested in himself or herself. Appeal to that self-interest. Students learned before they came to school as five-year-olds. Students of all ages learn outside of school. Students learned before they come to your class. Find out how they learned. Find out what motivated them to learn. Find out about their wholesome knowledge, talents, and interests. Find out about them. Build upon those foundations for new connections, new learning, unlimited learning, results-driven learning.

When a teacher believes that the purpose of teaching is to cause learning, that teacher does the job of teaching differently than does a teacher who sees classroom work as covering material, assigning work from the textbook, handing out worksheets, and reruns of last year. When we fully embrace the unlimited learning, the unlimited achievements, and the unlimited satisfactions that results-driven teaching can cause, nothing else will be acceptable for our students or for us.

A reader could understandably have these thoughts: "Aren't there any details? The job description is 'to cause learning'. The concept of causing learning, the mind-set of causing learning, the perspective of teaching as causing learning, and the results-driven teaching standard of causing learning are honorable, comprehensible, and clear, but aren't there any details in the job description? Maybe some attention could be given to how much learning must be caused and how the learning is to be caused. Also, does everyone agree that this job description is right? Does everyone see the job of teacher in the same way? Do people in a school or in a school system have different perspectives about a teacher's job description?"

First, which of the following job descriptions would you prefer your children's teachers to abide by:

1. To cause learning
2. To encourage learning
3. To provide opportunities for learning
4. To distribute textbooks, give assignments from textbooks, pass out worksheets, show videos, and have multiple choice tests each Friday
5. To provide the same classroom activities day after day, year after year, so the curriculum is covered

Let's hope that parents and guardians would select option number one from the list above, because it would do the most good for their children and for all children. Another question emerges: "Cause means to make happen, but what exactly is the learning that is going to be caused?"

If a student remembers that the Declaration of Independence was proclaimed in 1776, has that person learned about the Declaration of Independence? Recall of one fact about a historical event does not equal learning about the historical event.

If a student can calculate the area of a circle by putting numbers into the formula for finding the area of a circle, has the student learned about finding area, about why the equation works and makes sense, about the concept of area, about how a circle's area is different from a circle's circumference, about how circumference and perimeter are similar, about the numerical relationship between radius and diameter, about the numerical relationship between circumference and diameter, about why March 14 (3/14) is sometimes called Pi Day? This breadth and depth of knowing has not been caused by the teacher and has not been experienced by a student if the classroom activities were designed to go no further than demonstrating a few examples on the board of $A = 3.14r^2$ and then assigning worksheets or textbook pages of more problems to complete using different numbers in the same formula.

Learning about the Declaration of Independence requires much more in quantity of information and much more in quality of knowledge than mere recall of the date 1776. Learning about mathematical properties of circles and about mathematical calculations related to circles requires much more in quantity of information and much more in quality of knowledge than mere recall of where to place certain numbers in a formula or equation.

The date 1776 can be remembered to answer a limited question, but that answer merely shows recall of a fact. That answer shows no comprehension of the ideas, the events, or the impact of the 1776 Declaration of Independence.

Has a student learned about the Declaration of Independence if what the student knows is limited to recall of one fact? No.

Has a student learned about the mathematics of a circle if what the student knows is limited to recall of how to place numbers into an equation and then do the calculations? No. Even if the calculations are correct mathematically, the recall of the equation does not equal full understanding of how and why the equation works, what the answer to the math problem really means or actually communicates, or why a certain calculation must be wrong just by glancing at an answer that makes no sense in relation to the concept of a circle's area.

Cause means to make happen. When results-driven teachers cause learning, what exactly are they causing? They are causing students to fully know, to know that they know, to know what they know, to know how they acquired this knowledge, and to know how to acquire infinitely more knowledge. Such objectives demand certain classroom activities that lesser objectives—such as to give every student the opportunity to temporarily recall minute bits of data—do not necessitate.

The teacher who understands that the job description is "to cause learning" accepts both parts of that job description: (a) to cause (b) learning. This is dramatically different from a teacher who accepts only one of the two parts. To cause recall of many bits of data means that a teacher will make that recall happen; however, recall of data is not learning. Teachers who understand their job description as "to give everyone the opportunity to learn" know that learning is much more, quantitatively and qualitatively, than mere recall of bits of information, yet they are simply going to give all students the generic opportunity to learn rather than making the honorable commitment to casing all students to fully learn.

A teacher's dedication to the job description of "to cause learning" leads that teacher to think differently about teaching and, from those results-driven thoughts, requires that teacher to work differently as a teacher who is results-driven, for whom the result of causing learning is the bottom line, the highest priority, and the overall purpose.

Now we can pursue the idea that different people within a school, within a school district or system, and within a community could have varying perspectives on the job description of a teacher. The words used to present these varying perspectives are not based on endless research across the listed groups; rather, these words are based on observations the author has made during 22 years of working in education. So the point is not to present irrefutable evidence; rather the point is to suggest that because different people have different perspectives on the job description of a teacher, productivity suffers and uncertainty is common. A range of job description perspectives, such as the following, permits a range of job performance levels: "I did what the school board members told us to do," "I did what the principal told us to do," and "I'm doing exactly what the superintendent talked about at the start of the school year." That range could be eliminated with one job description that is official, precise, and results-driven: to cause learning. Teachers would then do only that which causes learning. Every action in the classroom would have to support the goal of "to cause learning" or the action is not used. Instructional decision making is simplified. Evaluation of teaching effectiveness is more precise. We are not there yet as seen in the following.

The teacher's job description as seen by school district officials, including members of school boards, could include these perspectives: a teacher is responsible for complying with all applicable laws, policies, regulations, and professional standards to assure that properly established goals for all students are reached as the approved curriculum is implemented in all classes at all grade levels.

Principals could summarize a teacher's job description with this perspective: a teacher is responsible for providing experiences that will implement the established curriculum, so each student makes the expected progress each year. Teachers will complete all required duties in addition to classroom teaching.

Parents, guardians, and community members could have a perspective about the job description of a teacher with this emphasis: teachers will give my child the best possible learning experience based on thorough knowledge of my child's needs, strengths, background, and ambitions. Teachers will be sufficiently productive so that the community investment in education is matched with proper results.

This perspective might be what students think about a teacher's job description: teachers keep us under control. They make us work. They punish people who are bad. Sometimes they let us do neat stuff. Some of my teachers are really great at their work and I learn a lot. Others don't do much and we don't do much either in their classes. So I guess a teacher's job is to get us to work and to keep us under control.

What thoughts and perspectives could teachers offer about their job description? These ideas could be included: a teacher's job is to be the professor, nurse, doctor, psychologist, counselor, psychiatrist, social worker, inspiration, behavior expert, conflict resolution expert, paper grader, homework manager, parole officer, juvenile justice official, instructional specialist, semiparent, mentor, creator of solutions to educational problems or excuses, maker of accommodations for each student with any possible syndrome or disorder, maker of challenging experiences for every gifted or talented student, and source of constant encouragement to everyone.

It is possible that some teachers would say, "My job is to give everyone the opportunity to learn. Some students take the opportunity and other students waste it." Other teachers may go straight to this results-driven answer: "My job is to cause learning."

Let's be blunt. Average teaching will not get above-average results from below-average students. Ordinary teaching will not get extraordinary results from any students. Superior teaching can get superior results from all students.

In Kentucky, during the nearly two decades since the 1990 Kentucky Education Reform Act, the guiding principle has been that "all students can learn and at high levels." That goal is reached if all teachers teach at high levels of effectiveness, at high levels of causing learning, and at high levels of results-driven accomplishments.

Also in Kentucky, a four-level, tiered system is used to evaluate some work done by students. The levels are novice, apprentice, proficient, and distinguished. Novice or apprentice teaching will not create proficient or distinguished learning. Apprentice teaching will not get proficient work from any student.

Actions follow thoughts. When a person thinks that the purpose of teaching is to cause learning, that person takes the teaching actions necessary to cause learning. When a person thinks that the purpose of teaching is to put students through a very predictable, prepackaged, textbook-controlled, worksheet-dominated, video-filled, Friday test sequence, then the teacher and the students will exit that process very similar to how they entered. What is the point of maintaining the academic status quo?

Education reformers, education administrators, community activists, political leaders, and corporate executives occasionally gather for summit conferences about schools, education, teaching, students, and teachers. The conferences conclude with a press conference declaring that education is more important than ever, so new management, organizational, political, and community initiatives are needed. If schools would just get the right program and manage its implementation correctly, all would be well.

The people who attend such summit conferences are well intentioned; however, they need to be in classrooms instead of at mountaintop conference retreat centers. School happens in classrooms. If the goal is to leave no child behind, you do not calm your conscience with a new law; rather, you teach the children you are determined to not leave behind. If you are not willing to do that, then talk to and support the people who are doing that direct work with students. Mountaintop summits, press conferences, and think tank or interest group position papers do not cause Tasha and Shawn to learn more math, science, social studies, or language arts. Effectively teaching Tasha and Shawn causes them to learn.

Aside from the disconnect of school reality and the content of mountaintop summits, in the actual arena of classroom teaching, there is an unfortunate disconnect. Is every teacher connected to the perspective that a teacher's job description is to cause learning? No. What would happen if all teachers understood that their job duty was to cause learning? First, the actions taken within the classroom would be screened through the demanding filter of "Is what I am doing with my students right now the best way to cause the intended learning?" That standard would eliminate the unproductive activities that pass time in classrooms but that do little or nothing to cause learning.

How can students fully learn and how can schools fully succeed when the teachers at a school approach their work with a range of perspectives about the purpose of teaching and the resulting range of classroom activities?

A school principal could use a school district's evaluation form or classroom observation instrument and still not know if the teacher being observed was causing learning. Some of the desired actions may be seen—use of technology in the lesson, clearly stated objective for the lesson, precise closure to the lesson with a strong summary statement, a variety of questions asked by the teacher, student work displayed on classroom walls, posters about important test-taking verbs on the walls—but that does not confirm that learning was caused. Perhaps the multipage classroom observation instrument and the long list of desired actions to be checked could be less bureaucratic, less assembly line, less formulated, less procedural, less pedantic, and more human, more realistic, more directly related to evaluating if learning was caused rather than if certain, narrowly defined actions were observed.

What is to be done about the reality that within the profession of teaching, there is a vast range of perspectives about what teachers are to do, how they are to do it, and what results they are responsible for obtaining? Different answers would come from the groups that have various thoughts about the job description of a teacher. School board members may require more professional development for teachers, because they think a six-hour session can overpower years of habits. Those six hours have no possibility of reversing years or decades of habits, but the school board can be told that people attended the professional development program and that the required topics were given due emphasis by the well-known visiting guest speaker who was paid a lot of money and who left quickly to go speak somewhere else.

State legislators and governors may think that better educational results would certainly occur if teachers and students were in school for more days. Increasing the school year from 180 to 182 days could create headlines, but what real impact is likely from an increase of 1% in the time that teachers and students are together? Would 1% more time doing worksheets and watching videos do any good? Rather, 180 days of results-driven teaching would be far more effective than 182 days of ordinary classroom activities. While governors and state legislators can add days to a school year, they cannot easily change a teacher's perception of his or her job description. That changed perception would have much more impact on students than a state law that adds two instructional days to the school calendar.

Principals could decide to observe teachers in the classrooms more often to see what is occurring. Principals could require that teachers submit lesson plans weekly so administrators have an awareness of the stated objectives and activities in each classroom. Realistically, in a school of 40, 80, or 120 teachers, if a principal spent one hour in each classroom, that would be 40, 80, or 120 hours of time. How many classroom observations per year are sufficient? If three hours are deemed sufficient at a school of 80 teachers, and if each classroom observation is followed by a teacher and principal conference, the time required is simply not likely to be available, given all of the other "cannot wait and cannot delegate" duties of school administrators.

Those classroom observations are for a tiny portion of the time that any teacher is with students. Even with frequent, one-minute "walk-throughs" for a principal to simply scan the classroom, the true picture of what happens daily in that classroom is not fully measured. When satisfactory teaching means merely making sure that enough boxes on the observation form are checked during any principal's visit to the classroom, learning is not the bottom line; rather, the bottom line comprises compliance with procedural specifics and quantifiable actions.

Perhaps a school district has a central office employee whose job title is "curriculum and instruction coach" or the equivalent. The job title could be more formal: assistant superintendent for curriculum and instruction. The job title could even be longer: associate director for curriculum, instruction, professional development, human resources, and student successes. The job title could be ambiguous: supervisor of instruction. No matter the job title, the person is expected to improve the instructional effectiveness of teachers throughout the school district. Can this be done personally with direct, face-to-face interaction with every teacher in the school district? Imagine a school district of 15 schools and an average of 50 teachers at each school. Is it likely that one person will have meaningful interaction individually with 750 teachers in one school year? No. So the person seeks efficient ways to cover material with all teachers rather than cause learning about teaching with all teachers. The person visits each school twice in the year to speak at faculty meetings. The person visits each school once a month to observe in one or two classrooms and to meet with the principal. Despite this effort, very few teachers were given sufficient time, ideas, or interaction to significantly impact what the teacher does in the classroom, how the teacher does that work in the classroom, and why—with what motive, personal standard, or professional standard of performance—that teacher does the work in his or her classroom the way it is done.

As we find limits to the options available from governors, state legislators, school boards, school administrators, and school district bureaucracies, what is to be done? Do not abandon those options merely because they have limits to the results they can provide. Apply those options as effectively as possible, but be realistic about what can be achieved. Assuming that education's problems can be solved by extending the school year for two days is just not realistic, reasonable, or very logical. The isolated action of extending a school year by two more instructional days could bring some improvements, but that action alone is limited in what it will improve and in how much improvement it will provide or make possible.

Some combinations of actions could have a synergistic impact. An instructional coach at a school who spends a full day each semester in each teacher's classroom and who works closely with each teacher continuously to trade ideas, develop instructional activities, provide suggestions for test questions, and offer proven methods of teaching gifted and talented students while also effectively teaching underachieving students in the same classroom could be helpful; however, combining the longer school year, the instructional coach, and a complete revision in how the school provides professional development for teachers could create a dynamic that no single action alone can create.

Still, to touch the depth of the strongest motivation to effectively teach and to reach the height of the most admirable results-driven teaching, an appeal to the conscience, the integrity, and the ethics of educators is made. The Golden Rule tells us to treat other people the way we would like to be treated. The Golden Rule of results-driven teaching is (a) to teach every student the way you would have liked your teachers to have taught you and (b) the way you would like to be taught now.

Think of the very best teacher you ever had. You wished all of your teachers could be like that one best teacher. Now, teach your students so they think of you as you think of your best teacher. Results-driven teachers do that not for the praise from students, but because it is right, because students deserve it, and because it creates a much more rewarding teaching career.

Think of the best professional development program you have attended. It was not three hours of a scripted presentation by a guest lecturer. It was interactive, lively, real, applicable to your work immediately, challenging, interesting, composed of a variety of instructional activities, and personal. That is the way you like to be taught now. That is the way your students like to be taught now. That is the way results-driven teachers teach.

The sources of a commitment to be a results-driven teacher are a teacher's integrity, ethics, and honor. The heart, soul, and mind of a results-driven teacher create an instructional imperative to cause learning. When the heart, soul, and mind harmoniously insist on results, the actions that cause the results will follow.

The job description of results-driven teaching is to cause learning. The reason to accept that job description is that your heart, soul, mind, conscience, integrity, ethics, and honor will accept nothing less.

Average teaching does not get above-average results from below-average students. Average teaching does not get above-average results from average students. Average teaching has two results for students: (a) The status quo is maintained and students follow their habitual patterns of grade distribution, or (b) students do work equal to or less than they usually do. The third result is that the teacher's career is very ordinary and superficial, even if it was filled with tasks, chores, activities, and procedures that keep the person employed via minimally complying with the school district's employment contract and committing no actions that could result in being dismissed, fired, nonrenewed, or otherwise removed.

Average teaching may keep a person employed, but it does not provide meaningful career experiences for the teacher, and it never gets superior results from students.

Results-driven teaching keeps a person employed, but it also keeps that educator meaningfully rewarded through the priceless moments that fill each day with interactions with students to cause learning. Results-driven teaching does get above-average results from below-average students. Results-driven teaching does get outstanding results from average students. Results-driven teaching does get superior results from above-average students.

How does results-driven teaching accomplish all of this? In my books *Extreme Teaching*, *Extreme Learning*, and *Extreme Students*, hundreds of learning-causing instructional activities are shown; however, merely imitating those activities will not assure maximum academic success. I use the concepts, research basis, and fundamentals of the "extreme" approach in all of my teaching, but the actual activity I will use tomorrow to cause learning is based on what I know about how my current students learn, what I know about what they know, and what the curriculum tells me they must learn. I create the instructional activities that will apply that body of knowledge about teaching and about my students to cause learning. I am driven to and by results. I will cause learning. How? That will vary. Why? Because students deserve it, because my integrity demands it, because it is right, and because there is no other acceptable option if I am going to teach students the way I would want to be taught if I were the student. That is the results-driven teaching Golden Rule job performance standard I require of myself.

Political leaders, laws, policies, school boards, school districts, and school administrators have job descriptions or job performance standards for me. I eagerly surpass those. I insist on being more and better than any employer could ever demand of me. I insist on being a results-driven teacher. I insist on causing learning. Anything less is unacceptable.

We now move on to a consideration of what teaching is not. Results-driven teaching causes learning. What doesn't results-driven teaching do? Chapter 6 answers that question and explores related topics.

6

WHAT RESULTS-DRIVEN
TEACHING IS NOT

Results-driven teaching is not practicing psychiatry. I recently commented to a colleague, "Nothing we are doing with that student relates to education. It's all psychiatry, and we are not credentialed as psychiatrists."

The psychiatry reference is used as an example of a larger category of issues, impacting some children and teenagers, which schools are increasingly expected to address. This trend is counterproductive for at least two reasons. First, schools do have the resources to cause learning but do not have all the resources to fully correct psychiatric, psychological, relational, juvenile justice, family, physical health, criminal behavior, housing, clothing, food, or other noneducational issues that may occur in the lives of children and teenagers.

Second, the time and effort that school personnel spend on noneducational issues can be a distraction from educational work. Schools are not staffed to serve as health and human services agencies to address all possible problems, abnormalities, syndromes, disorders, illegalities, family issues, psychological concerns, psychiatric concerns, medication management, anger management, grief counseling, financial, sibling, transportation, daycare, nutritional, physical health, or behavioral issues that can occur in the lives of students.

When a family takes a child to a medical doctor, it is to resolve a physical health issue. The family does not say, "While we are here, could you teach her to read, get her some new clothes, watch her while we go to work, and provide meals?" Some families—along with some elected political leaders; some national, state, or local community activists; and some educational policymakers—do expect schools to teach the complete curriculum and think, "While he is at school, please correct his bad habits, control his anger, feed him two or three times, keep his weight under control, dispense his medication, make him obey you (he just will not follow our instructions at home), and supervise him until 6:00 P.M. when we get home from work and then transport him home."

The job of a results-driven teacher is not to be involved in providing every possible service needed by children and teenagers. The job of a results-driven teacher is to cause learning. Schools as organizations and teachers as professional workers in those organizations have the right and the reasons to insist that schools be seen, evaluated, and supported as places where learning is caused. Families, churches, other governmental agencies, the marketplace, other professionals, charity organizations, and community groups need to address the childhood and adolescent issues and opportunities that are noneducational while, whenever possible, endorsing and supporting the educational work of schools in a spirit of partnership. All of the issues and opportunities can be addressed by the totality of service providers from family to church, public library to public recreation/parks departments, volunteer groups who mentor teenagers to neighbors who have after-school child-watching or babysitting duties, health departments to social service agencies.

Results-driven teachers certainly care about the totality of issues impacting students but simply cannot resolve all of those issues. When teachers can concentrate on causing learning, it is increasingly likely that more and better learning can be caused. For this increased quantity of learning and improved quality of learning to be caused, we have established in prior chapters and in other books previously mentioned what results-driven teachers do. For now, we will consider in more detail what teaching in general is not and what results-driven teaching in particular is not.

Results-driven teaching is not a generic, one-size-fits-all, impersonal approach to designing and implementing instructional activities in school classrooms. Designing instructional activities means taking the careful precision of an architect who is expertly designing the detailed plan of a new building, such that the project manager and construction crew can exactly build the structure as the architect envisioned it. Architectural work includes a uniqueness for each project. The purpose of the building impacts the design of the building. If every office building designed by an architect is an exact duplicate of the first office building designed by that architect, the results would be very few people coming to that architect for their design work.

When a family begins the process of looking at houses with the intention of selling their house and moving to another home, they expect a realtor to provide very personal service. No family would be satisfied with generic, one-size-fits-all, impersonal real estate service from a realtor who says, "The house I will show you today is exactly at the local market's median price point and it has the exact average number of square feet of all houses in this county. No matter how many people are in your family now, this house is big enough without being too big and affordable for any family with the average income for this metropolitan area. This house has the community's most common floor plan. This house is good enough in every way without being great or bad in any way. Everything about this house is okay. I'm sure you will be pleased." The client would not be pleased. The realtor would not make a sale.

The successful real estate agent listens closely and completely as a client describes the requirements for a house that would satisfy the client's needs. The agent then searches the current real estate listings for properties that match the requirements. The agent obtains much printed information for the client and then takes the client on tours of several or many houses. With each tour comes a discussion of the merits of the house and the shortcomings of the house. In time, through a very personal, tailored, individualized process, the agent will help the client find the right house. The real estate agent is results driven and knows that the goal of selling houses is best reached by providing superior personal service to clients based on the unique real estate needs of each client. Results-driven teachers think and work with a similar approach.

Results-driven teaching is not a reliance on or a repetitious cycle of textbook chapters, worksheets, word searches, and prefabricated Friday

tests provided as supplementary materials with purchase of typically ordinary, yet very expensive, textbooks and copied at the last minute on
Friday morning while remarking, "Wow, the copy room sure is crowded
today. I hope I get these copies made in time for class."

The people who write textbooks for kindergarten through high school
do not know the students in any classroom, but more importantly, they
do not know the students in your classroom. You do know those students. You can design the instructional activities that will best cause the
intended learning. The textbook cannot do that for you. The worksheets
cannot cause learning. The word searches may fill minutes, but they
teach nothing. How does finding a word that is hidden within a large
collection of diversionary letters teach anything to anyone? An objection
might be, "But the students like the word searches. They really enjoy
marking the words they find?" How are those statements ample justification for using word searches? What do students know after the word
search that they did not know before doing the word search? The likely
answer is nothing; therefore, the word search is unacceptable because it
caused no learning. Results-driven teaching does what causes learning.

Results-driven teaching is not limited to or limited by textbooks,
worksheets, and word searches for many valid reasons. One of the most
compelling reasons is that of the 4,000 people I have interviewed or surveyed about the best teacher they ever had, no respondent has indicated
that their best teacher relied on textbooks, worksheets, and word
searches.

Another compelling reason to avoid the paint-by-numbers ordinari-
ness of textbooks, worksheets, and word searches is that these three resources present a small portion of what can be learned about any topic.
What is the justification for any use of word searches when there are so
many better classroom activities? Worksheets that a teacher designs for
the precise purpose of causing learning based on what the teacher
knows about her students and about what her students need to learn can
be effective. Generic, prepackaged, prefabricated worksheets that a
teacher does nothing more than make copies of will inspire little more
from students than to copy answers from the textbook or from each
other. There simply is no generic worksheet that can cause learning as
effectively as materials that a teacher personally designs and creates for
her students based on the teacher's knowledge of how those students

learn, what those students have learned, and what those students need to learn.

Textbooks can be used as one of many resources to help cause learning; however, the textbook cannot control the classroom. Teaching is not a sequence of telling the students on Monday to silently read section 1 of chapter 3 and then write complete sentence answers to the "Think and Remember" questions at the end of the section. Tuesday, Wednesday, and Thursday are dedicated to the same procedure with sections 2, 3, and 4 of chapter 3. On Friday the students take the publisher-provided test on chapter 3, and when they finish that they can do the publisher-provided, chapter 3 word search for extra credit.

What does a U.S. history textbook tell students about Abraham Lincoln when compared with the total quantity and quality of what is known about Abraham Lincoln? Some teachers think, "We're just teaching them the basics. All of the students are not going to be history majors in college. It's not my job to make them historians. What the textbook has is good enough. It's too much work to do more than that. Who has the time? There's so much we have to cover. I have to stay on schedule." Those thoughts tell you what teaching is not. Those thoughts—excuses, to be honest—are not what you want your child's teacher to think. Those thoughts violate the Golden Rule of results-driven teaching. Results-driven teaching is committed to results, not excuses.

Teaching is not based on fads. It is not enough to think, "We have read the report about four schools in Idaho where reading scores increased 7% with the new Destination Reading Education Achievement Management (DREAM) programs. We want that same dream for our students." Most fads in education are similar to dreams—they fade away and do not impact real life.

We know what works in classrooms. In the search for instructional materials, programs, systems, and activities that will improve student achievement, educational officials sometimes impose a fad on teachers, classrooms, and students. They might say, "One school district changed to a strict dress code, and discipline problems dropped 7%. Let's start a dress code," or "One school began using this new reading program, and test scores went way up. Let's get that program."

We know what works to cause learning, but what works today in my classroom to cause my current students to learn what they need to know may not be what works in your classroom tomorrow to cause your students to learn what they need to know. It is very beneficial for teachers to trade success stories, effective lesson plans, and homework project ideas that motivated superior work from students; however, each results-driven teacher must adjust every great idea so the idea is tailored to work in her classroom now with her students now to cause the intended learning now.

Resisting fads does not mean resisting change. All of the 8th-grade economics students I have taught during the past four years have earned a grade of A or B. The curriculum for the class has centered on 17 core content vocabulary terms that students must know, understand, recall, apply, analyze, make sense of, and master. The teaching activities change with each group of students so I can make connections between their wholesome knowledge, interests, talents, and what they need to know. For one class, results were outstanding when the comparative quality of doughnuts from local bakeries became a case study in economics. For another class, learning was caused using competition in the breakfast cereal business.

When a friend emailed me some information about an online resource for economics teachers, I gladly visited the website. It was obvious that the website was a mere worksheet put on the computer screen. I would never impose a generic worksheet—paper or electronic—on my students. I use technology when it is the best way to cause learning, not just because technology is innovating at an extraordinary pace. Some of the 1990s technology companies were quickly fading fads that went broke. I invest my time and effort plus the time and effort of my students to get the desired results. Fads do not get the desired results.

Teaching is not tolerance of excuses. Results-driven teaching resists the temptations to make excuses or to accept excuses. Teaching is very demanding work. Teachers are expected to accomplish more now than ever before. Teachers must contend with an array of societal changes that increase the complexity of working with teenagers and children. Teachers must contend with demands placed upon them by people who cannot do the job of a teacher but who are certain they can and should tell teachers what to do and how to do it. Still, teachers must create excuse-free zones in which they work and in which their students work.

Any moment spent on an excuse is time not spent getting results. Any effort spent on an excuse is work not devoted to getting results. Any tolerance of excuses from students is an invitation to the student to see what he can get away with rather than to see what he can accomplish. Excuses are one of the enemies of teaching. Results-driven teaching does not tolerate excuses. Perhaps the exact opposite of results-driven teaching is excuse-driven teaching, which truly would be more accurately labeled excuse-driven nonteaching.

Teaching is not ordinary, predictable, mundane, pedantic, or superficial. Why? Because learning is not ordinary, predictable, mundane, pedantic, or superficial. Learning is fascinating. Activities in classrooms at schools that arouse no new fascination from students or that connect with no existing fascinations of students are activities that contribute to teacher lethargy and student apathy.

Some events and activities at school are extraordinary, unpredictable, innovative, energetic, and profound. From a science class experiment to a math class celebration of sporting events by using sports statistics to create math problems, school activities can be lively, purposeful, productive, and motivating. Teaching is not ordinary because students are not ordinary, the childhood and teenage years are not ordinary, and real learning is not ordinary.

Teaching is not showing video after video. What happens when a teacher says to the students, "Today we'll watch the video that is a documentary about the voyages of Christopher Columbus to the New World. Of course, cameras did not exist in 1492, but Columbus kept a detailed diary and historians have other reliable sources, so the film is accurate. Take some notes and we'll discuss the video tomorrow." What happens? A few students pay attention. Some students pay a little attention, but their eyes and their thoughts wander away. Some students pay zero attention. The 44 minutes of the video include about two very interesting minutes that could have been used to punctuate a class activity or discussion about Columbus. Videos are passive, wordy, inefficient, and of very limited productivity for causing learning.

Teaching is not a steady sequence of fill-in-the-blank questions, followed by odd-numbered problems, followed by the end-of-the-chapter questions, followed by homework that is not graded or that is not returned for days or weeks. What happens to a student who endures day after day of that fill-in-the-blanks routine? The student begins to see school as a blank that is not worth filling in.

Teaching is not assigning homework just because the textbook has pages in it that could serve as homework or because the textbook came with supplemental teaching materials that can be copied and used for homework. Teaching uses homework to cause learning that otherwise could not be caused. Results-driven teachers create homework projects and assignments with the same unique, creative, personal touch they use to design classroom instructional activities. Most students will eagerly, or at least willingly, do homework that is fascinating, worthwhile, meaningful, challenging, and real. Some or many students will resist homework that is truly unproductive, excessive, pointless, and unnecessary.

Teaching is not assigning busy work. Teaching is not pretending that busy work contributes to education. Students know when they are being given insignificant tasks that just fill the time of a class period. Busy work examples include inane worksheets with questions, riddles, puzzles, and writing topics or arithmetic problems of embarrassing banality. Students deserve better, even if some of them willingly complete the busy work because it is so easy, because they need the grade, or because they go through these motions in unspoken agreement with teachers who use busy work, thinking, "You do not ask us to do much work. You give us a good grade, and we will behave in your classroom."

Teaching also is not enduring bureaucratic busy work. Some school districts and some schools have monthly faculty meetings or weekly committee meetings when there is nothing to do or to discuss. Email communication would have been sufficient. Some of the "We've always met monthly" meetings that educators impose on themselves are adult busy work that waste time and frustrate employees. Teachers deserve better even if they comply with the meeting schedule merely to avoid being questioned about why they missed the meeting.

Teaching is not working yourself to exhaustion and to illness. That sentence may surprise the reader who was beginning to think that results-driven teaching mandated 18-hour workdays throughout the year. Teaching is demanding work. Many hours of effort are required beyond the hours of classroom instruction, but an exhausted, ill teacher cannot be an effective results-driven teacher.

As I write this paragraph, it is Monday morning of my school district's spring vacation. We do not have school this week. This spring vacation is more welcome than any in my career. Why? I have worked in four different schools in my career so far. I have worked in marketing/advertising jobs with three large companies. The corporate jobs were very demanding, and being results-driven was the norm, the requirement, the minimally accepted standard at those companies. The corporate jobs had two dramatic differences versus teaching: (a) sufficient support staff and (b) occasional pauses in the workday, including a usually nonworking lunch with adequate time. Teachers do their own secretarial work and other support staff duties that many corporate employees can delegate to other workers. Teachers squeeze lunch into a few minutes that also may include phone calls to return or emails to check. Sure, many people in business jobs have continuous duties at a relentless pace throughout their workday; however, a workplace of adults is different in demands on your heart, mind, body, and soul from a workplace where children and teenagers are 90% of the population. This spring vacation will help remove accumulated fatigue that I should not have allowed to build up.

The best teacher is not the most exhausted teacher. The most fatigued teacher does not win the results-driven award. Teaching is not a sprint to exhaustion, fatigue, weariness, or illness. Teaching is that lovely combination of hard work that is so productive and meaningful, it creates more energy than it absorbs. Busy work energizes nobody. Learning energizes everyone involved in the learning. Teaching is not an endless series of "since you did so poorly on the last chapter's worksheets, on this chapter I'll double the number of worksheets and use a quiz from each section of the chapter." That is not teaching. That does not cause learning. That does not create a vibrant classroom community in which students and the teacher learn together, work together, think together, and build mutual commitments. The classroom community takes work, but it makes the work so worthwhile that the work does not feel like exhausting labor; rather, it feels like and is discovery, wonder, thought, and learning. Work that fascinates, inspires, and fulfills people is energy creating, not exhausting or sickening.

Teaching is not controlled by textbooks. What a student obtains from a textbook can be useful, but it is limited. What a student can experience through well-designed instructional activities that a results-driven teacher creates is unlimited. Yes, textbooks can be one resource, but beware of this warning signal: when a student asks a teacher about some task being done with a textbook and says, "What are they asking me to do?" the textbook's impact has gone too far. "They" do not teach your class. "They" do not know your students. The "they" question is a warning sign indicating that the desired classroom community—the we and the us of teacher and student—is declining toward an impersonal intruder's invasion of the generic.

Teaching is not learning or emailing or voice-mailing a message like this for a substitute teacher: "Just have them keep working on the chapter they started yesterday. They can read it quietly and answer all of the questions at the end of each section. Just call the office if you have any questions." Such messages guarantee a difficult day for the substitute teacher and an unproductive day for the students. Follow the Golden Rule for substitute teachers—leave all of the information, lesson plans, and instructional materials that you would expect a teacher to leave for you if you were the substitute teacher.

Teaching is not calling in sick when you are perfectly well or reasonably well and could come teach with no health risk to yourself or to other people. Saying, "But I just did not feel like coming to school today. I just, you know, gave myself a day off. I wasn't sick, just ready to take a day off," violates our Golden Rule of results-driven teaching. School districts build in many holidays, conference days, teacher professional development days, and vacations. Causing learning does not require doubling the amount of work or the pace and speed of work. Causing learning is a marathon run at a very managed pace so everyone in the class—teacher and student—successfully go the entire distance. Teaching requires showing up at school and doing the job unless actual illness or family emergency make that impossible.

Some teachers might complain, "Central office just keeps getting in the way. If those people ever did work at a school, they have completely forgotten what it is like. They must just sit in their offices and go to each other's meetings and look busy. They rarely see a student. They never teach a class. Maybe they could substitute teach occasionally. They would beg for mercy. I get so tired of people who can't do my job telling me how to do my job."

Despite those genuine frustrations, teaching is not blaming the central office or state education department educators and bureaucrats for the difficulties within the job of teaching. Teaching is not bureaucratic. Public education is within the bureaucratic maze of national, state, and local governments, as well as local school boards, but what happens in classrooms between teacher and student does not have to be bureaucratic.

Teaching is not blaming the system, lazy parents, confrontational guardians, uninformed politicians, unrealistic laws, fantasy-world policies, or loud and unreasonable community activists. Teaching is doing all you can with what you have where you are now. Teaching is not making excuses. Teaching is getting results.

Teaching is not giving students a free day. If the tax payers or tuition payers are financially supporting a school year of 180 instructional days, then there are already 185 days in the calendar year when students are not in school. Weekends, teacher conference days, holidays, and vacations provide ample free days for students.

Students might say, "Can't we have a free day? Other teachers give classes a free day." The answer is no. I have not been asked by students if they could have a free day for many years. They know what the answer would be. The taxpayers are paying me to teach, so I am going to teach. The students need to learn so I am going to teach. There is more to learn, so there is more to teach.

When patients go to a physician's office, they expect to be seen and treated. Imagine being told, "I'm sorry. We're taking a free day. The nurses and doctors are here, but they are not doing any work today. They decided to play games and watch movies because they have worked so hard recently. You may watch the movie with us if you would like."

Teaching is not taking students on unproductive, inefficient, waste-of-time, and waste-of-money field trips. With creative use of the Internet and websites with webcams or virtual tours, many traditional field trip destinations can be visited via a computer lab. The virtual field trips can prevent some common problems. Field trips can be a sequence of hurry-up-and-wait frustrations. Line up and wait for the bus. Hurry up and practice the bus evacuation drill. Line up and get your ticket to the museum. Hurry up and wait for the museum tour guide to show up. Hurry up and wait for everyone to get out of the museum gift shop. Line up and wait to use the restroom. Hurry up and wait for the bus to pick us up. The six-hour sequence of hurry up and wait included 90 minutes of visiting the museum and four and a half hours of processes, procedures, and transportation.

A museum does have artifacts, art, or other important displays, but the field trip there is often inefficient. Other field trips are not educational at all. The alleged math and science day at an amusement park is much more entertainment than it is algebraic calculations or physics equations. The math and science of a roller coaster can be studied without taking students to the amusement park. Websites, pictures, models, and software that enables a student to design a roller coaster all could be much more efficient and equally or more productive than the field trip. The motives might be based on good intentions like the following: "Some of our students just never get to travel anywhere." That does not necessarily require that a school must fill the void of travel experiences in the life of some students. Some teachers say, "Our students have worked hard. The trip is their reward." Rewards for hard work can be earned by students, but that does not necessitate a field trip. Some, many, or most field trips provide minimal educational results. Field trips should have to pass the "is this the best way to cause learning?" test instead of thinking, "It's been three months since our last field trip so let's go to that program we got the brochure about in the mail. It looked pretty good. It should be okay." Pretty good and okay are unacceptable.

Teaching is not wasting minutes at the start of class or at the end of class by saying, "I'll have everything ready soon, so everyone just keep the noise down and we'll start soon," or "Well, we have only two or three minutes left in class, and that is not enough time to start something else, so just get your books together and you can talk quietly. If anyone has a question about the homework assignment, you can come up and talk with me after that."

The preparation for class, the materials needed for class, and the planning required for class are done well before class begins. Instruction starts immediately when class time begins. Instruction continues until class time ends. A results-driven teacher always has a set of two- or three-minute activities to use when a short amount of time presents itself after a lesson is completed. From drills on essential vocabulary to supersized flash cards that help students master fundamentals, from a preview of tomorrow's lesson to a quick discussion that connects current events to classroom topics, there are productive uses of unexpected minutes. No coach permits a team to end a game when two minutes remain on the clock. No teacher should allow pockets of time to be lost. If a class meets 180 times in a school year and loses three minutes per day due to lost time at the beginning and the end of class, the lost time is 540 minutes or nine hours of instruction. That is unacceptable. Every minute counts, so fill every minute with meaningful learning.

Teaching is not gossiping about students. Teachers don't say, "Oh, did you hear what those two 6th graders did? Then their families came in and got all ugly about it. I heard that both of the 6th graders were involved in stealing a teacher's cell phone, and then they tried to steal another student's purse," or "I gave him the homework assignment to do over and then, the little criminal, he wads it up and throws it at me. I said, 'Fred, I'll file charges against you. Just like your brother.' We had to file changes against him."

Such comments are unprofessional, unproductive, unethical, and counterproductive. When topics about a student are discussed, the comments are based on facts, are directed toward accomplishing something good for the student, are heard only by the people who need to be involved, and are not vindictive. Teaching is not gossiping about students. Teaching is not editorial comments about students or their families. Teaching is not making comments, encouraging comments, or listening to comments that, if made about you or your family, would be offensive in terms of what was said, how it was said, to whom it was said, why it was said, or where it was said.

Teaching is not working harder to coach a sport or sponsoring a club/activity at school than you work to design and implement instructional activities for students in your classes. A coach who meticulously plans every minute of athletic practice but who generically assigns textbook pages to be read in class has his priorities upside down. A coach who energetically pushes every member on the sports team to run faster or work harder but who tolerates underachieving student performance in the classroom is inconsistent at best and unprofessional at worst.

Teaching is not supposed to be a job people get so they can coach a sport while the teaching duties get the time and attention that is left over after coaching is done expertly. This takes us to another application of the Golden Rule. Teach your students with the same standards, commitment, energy, and expertise as you coach your athletes. Never expect or demand more from or give more to your student athletes than your student scholars.

It is perfectly proper to set the highest imaginable standards for students who you coach. Be sure that you set the same highest imaginable standards for yourself and for your students in the classroom. Ideally, teaching is not the job you have to do or endure so you can coach. Ideally, you get superstar results in the classroom and in athletics, but the classroom is the priority. I know how excited and irrational people can get about sports. Teaching is about academic achievement. Sports can provide wholesome experiences, but sports are not the reason schools exist.

Teaching is not doing what your worst teacher did that you always hated. We are not referring to that teacher you disliked because she made you work so hard and then later in life you realized the benefits of her efforts. We are referring to the worst teacher you had and the worst part of the teaching.

Maybe it was the teacher who, on every Monday, showed a filmstrip to the class. This took minimal preparation time. This almost gave the teacher a three-day weekend. The filmstrips were old and had outdated information. "In the future, people will land on the moon," was part of the audio of a filmstrip shown long after astronauts returned from the moon. The filmstrips taught nothing. The filmstrips were a waste of time. Anyone who spoke a word during filmstrip time got in trouble. Monday after Monday of pointless filmstrips is at the top of your list of the worst work done by your worst teacher. Never let yourself do what that teacher did. Filmstrips are educational relics, but the current embodiment of the filmstrip mentality—a video every Monday, a DVD every Monday—is just as unacceptable.

We know what does not work in the classrooms. We know what results-driven teaching is not. We know what a results-driven teacher is, does, believes, requires, creates, expects, and causes. In the next chapter, we explore the sequel to what teaching is not. We now think about what a results-driven teacher is not.

7

WHAT A RESULTS-DRIVEN TEACHER IS NOT

A results-driven teacher is not employed in an easy job. A teacher is not hired to do work that can be simplified, programmed, scripted, or reduced to an unvarying formula.

A results-driven teacher is not a clerk who merely makes copies of materials purchased by the decision makers at a school so those copies can be distributed to students day after day.

A results-driven teacher is not a social worker. Teachers cannot or should not intervene in complex issues involving students or families that go beyond academic instruction, because the expertise of teachers does not include social work. A teacher is not a counselor who can resolve the complex emotional issues that children and teenagers face. Despite the best of intentions to be helpful, a teacher could unintentionally cause difficulties by getting involved in circumstances or issues that go beyond the teaching certification and expertise.

A results-driven teacher is not a psychologist who has detailed insights about every syndrome, disorder, or condition that can impact children or teenagers. Most teachers took some college classes or graduate classes in educational psychology, in human growth and development, or in related topics; however, those classes do not equal a specialized credential to practice as a psychologist.

A results-driven teacher is not a copier and distributor of worksheets and other generic, impersonal, superficial materials prepared by unknown, far-away publishing company employees who design typically generic materials to supplement typically ordinary textbooks.

A results-driven teacher is not a factory worker in an educational assembly line where school parts are added year after year until the kindergarten through high school process is completed. Education does not happen the way a product is manufactured in a factory. Teachers who truly teach do not perceive students as products, classrooms as parts of an assembly line, or schools as factories. Schools are not places where products are manufactured. Schools are places where human beings are educated.

A results-driven teacher is not a person who repeatedly assigns textbook pages to read and textbook "Think and Remember" questions that really do not inspire much thinking and that are rarely worth remembering.

A results-driven teacher is not an entertainer who expects the job to be fun and expects learning to always be fun for students. A teacher knows that serious work has to be done daily at school and that additional serious work is done outside of school to grade papers or prepare lessons. The work can be quite meaningful, very rewarding, extremely productive, and highly satisfying, but while some of the experiences can be enjoyable, fun is not the goal or the purpose.

A results-driven teacher is not someone who maintains an "if this is Friday, we have a test" routine because that weekly schedule is what has always been done. Teaching is not being stuck in any routine. Certainly some classroom rules are necessary and some classroom processes enhance efficiency, but a rigid schedule that serves the routine instead of the educational achievement of the students is a mistake. A teacher does not give a test every Friday just because it is Friday. A test is given when a test is the best way to teach. A test can do more than measure recall of facts and provide grades for the grade book or computer grade entry system. A test can measure student achievement, continue the teaching and learning endeavor, and measure the effectiveness of teaching.

A results-driven teacher is not resistant to spontaneous, unexpected, unplanned opportunities for learning that develop in a classroom. "Well, that's interesting, but we have to get back to the rest of the worksheet" is a comment that squashes the creativity, ideas, imagination, thinking, and involvement of the student who made the interesting observation. A teacher applies the student's interesting observation as a vibrant instructional resource to help cause the intended learning.

Imagine if, during a math class working on decimals and fractions, a student made this comment: "That's like the price of a gallon of gasoline. It's never an exact penny. It's always something point nine. I saw one gas station where the price was something and 9/10 cents. How do you get 9/10 of a penny?"

A results-driven teacher does not see that student's observation about decimals and fractions as a distraction from the lesson, as a theft of time that has been allocated for something else, or as interference with the teacher's routine. A teacher rejoices with such useful input from a student, makes that input a vibrant, effective resource for everyone in the class, and says something like, "Great question. Let's draw a sign on the front board that looks like a sign at a gas station. We'll put the price on it and include '949' after the decimal point. We'll make a second drawing like this to show .94 and 9/10 instead of a decimal, so we have both of the examples that Shawn mentioned. Now, do the math to calculate the cost of 10 gallons of gas. While you do, that I'll calculate the cost with the 9/10 left off or the 0.009 left off. We'll see what the difference is, and that could help us understand why the price includes the fraction of a penny." The teacher's objective for the class will be reached, but the spontaneously available path to the objective now becomes part of the journey. A results-driven teacher does not reject such gifts. A teacher opens those gifts, shares those gifts, and causes learning with those gifts.

A results-driven teacher is not aloof. A teacher does not have to be an expert on all of the favorite movies, music, television programs, video games, or fashion trends that captivate students. A teacher should be sufficiently informed about, aware of, and willing to be told more about these topics, because those interests of students could become classroom learning resources and because of the genuine rapport that can be established when teachers listen to students speak about their wholesome interests. The conversations and the topics must be within the wholesome category so proper professional standards are maintained. A teacher does not let a discussion of a currently popular movie consume an entire class period; rather, a teacher uses a minute or two

of discussion about the movie to intellectually warm up brains and cu-
riosities for the activity that day in class that deals with short stories.
What similarities or differences are there between a movie and a short
story? Could a short story become a movie?

A results-driven teacher is not distant. A teacher does not arrive at
school at the latest possible minute and leave school at the earliest possible minute. Nor is a teacher the first person to arrive at school and the
last person to leave school. A teacher is not seeking to stay employed by
doing the minimum amount of work that still passes any basic legal or
professional requirement. Nor is a teacher working endless hours. A
teacher is not distant; rather, a teacher is properly and genuinely involved with students, with colleagues, with learning, with school activities, and with the overall educational experience.

A results-driven teacher is not superhuman. A teacher cannot solve
every problem facing every child or teenager. A teacher can cause learning. By causing students to learn, a teacher is doing what he or she is
certified to do and is hired to do. The experiences that a teacher provides to students in the adventure of causing learning can have a ripple
effect that provides encouragement to troubled students, direction to
aimless students, motivation to failing students, challenge to gifted or
talented students, and goals or ambitions to all students. A teacher is not
a superhuman who can achieve the impossible. By being a great teacher,
a results-driven teacher, some parts of learning and of life that students
thought were of no benefit or thought were impossible now are seen as
beneficial and possible, within reach, and worth the effort to obtain.

A results-driven teacher is not lazy. Results-driven teachers do not
say, "Well, I know that some teachers do all of that fancy planning. They
talk about it at lunch sometimes. Pictures or very short videos they find
on the Internet get used in their classes for 10 or 15 seconds. Imagine
doing all of that work for just 10 seconds of use in a class. I've always
used the textbook. It has plenty of pictures in it. Why go to the trouble
to get more pictures and project them up on a screen when every student can quietly read the chapter, look at the photographs in the chapter, answer the questions in the chapter, and stay on schedule? We buy
the textbooks for good reasons, and I use the textbooks because they
cost a lot of money. Why waste that money by not using the books?"

Textbooking is not teaching. A results-driven teacher is not a text-booker. A results-driven teacher accepts the responsibility to cause learning. The totality of what can and should be learned goes far beyond what a textbook can include. Great teachers use a variety of teaching methods and activities. A person will never be a real teacher if the person is lazy. Real teaching does not and cannot emerge from a lazy approach to work. The best teacher you ever had was not lazy. To be the best teacher your current students have ever had, laziness is not an option. Results-driven teaching's Golden Rule applies again.

A results-driven teacher is not bureaucratic. They don't say, "Well, I know I said we would try that experiment again today and change one variable to see what happens, but we just don't have the time. It's Thursday and if we are going to be ready for the test tomorrow, we have some different material to cover today. I've double-checked the test that comes with the book for this chapter. There are some questions you will not know if we don't move on to the last section of the chapter today."

What could be done to make that situation much more human and much less bureaucratic? Say, "Great news. We can try that experiment again today. I've got almost everything set up at your lab stations. One person from each lab group will come up here to get the other supplies each team needs. First, let's discuss the lab the way we did it yesterday. Then we'll talk about the change we will make in one variable today. When you finish the experiment, we will analyze the results and see what was different from yesterday, if anything. Then we'll evaluate those results in terms of the new ideas and vocabulary that I had scheduled for today. Everything will fit together perfectly. More good news. Tomorrow's test will be me demonstrating the experiment both ways with the original variable and then with today's variable. I'll even film the work you do today so anyone who is absent can see that. On tomorrow's test, you will use the 10 science terms that go with this topic as you analyze the experiments. Any questions? Yes, Brian? What do you study for the test? Good question. The best way to study is to be very involved and to pay total attention to the lab you do today and then to our discussion about yesterday's lab and today's lab. So let's start now. Each lab group sends one scientist up to see me now to get the rest of your materials."

Notice the difference between the bureaucratic-driven example and the results-driven example. The teacher is absolutely in charge. The teacher is making some adjustments to enhance learning. The teacher is aware of and sensitive to time, schedules, learning objectives, lesson plans, and curriculum. The teacher is also sensitive to the human beings who are students in her classroom. She knows how her students learn. Bureaucrats and bureaucracies do not know students, do not work directly with students daily if at all, and can become policy-driven instead of results-driven. Teachers work within bureaucracies but do not have to become bureaucratic. Teachers are people who work in a people-driven job. A teacher is not a person whose adult years are spent vainly attempting to relive childhood or teenage years. They don't say, "The students are some of my best friends. I'd rather be with them than anyone else." Be careful. The students are children or are teenagers. You are the adult. It is wonderful when a cordial, friendly, symbiotic rapport is established between students and teachers, but that does not mean the teacher returns to childhood or to the teenage years. It means that the teacher genuinely interacts from an adult perspective with people who are in the childhood or teenage years of life.

Your students may say, "Come on. When you were 14 years old, didn't you ever forget to finish your homework? Just let me turn in the rest of it tomorrow." Your students may seek your sympathy or compassion by asking you to travel in time back to when you were their current age.

You should reply, "When I teach you about math, I do not teach you what I knew about math when I was 14 years old. I teach you everything I've learned about math that relates to the geometry class you have with me. What I learned in college and graduate school helps me teach you math. What I've learned throughout my teaching career helps me teach you math. I'm also going to teach you about time management and accepting responsibility. The homework is due today. You know that you can always do more homework than is assigned, so on the next homework project, be sure to do a lot of extra work, and that can help make up for the part you did not complete for today. As part of that extra work next time, be sure to include what you did not do this time."

A results-driven teacher is not quickly or easily angered. There are times when a teacher needs to express anger in a direct, straightforward, controlled, edited way. Please remember: not everything that comes into the brain should come out of the mouth. Remember also that some students are very skilled, experienced, expert shouters or yellers. They would be glad to get into a shouting match with you. Their idea is that shouting is easier than working, behaving, or listening. They also get to brag to their friends that they got in the last word with you.

I use the word "no" with students when I see misbehavior. I don't go into a long psychological evaluation of their misbehavior when all that is needed is the word "no." The tone and the volume will vary with the seriousness of the misbehavior. A student who cuts in line in front of other students may just need a stern glare and a moderate "no." A student who is about to shoot a rubber band at someone may need to hear "No!" If they say, as I extend my hand for them to give the rubber band to me, "But I was just playing" I might respond, "We don't have recess or a playground. This is a school. Give me the rubber band and any others you have. This is your one chance to prevent the problem and stay out of trouble." If they try to protest, I'll cut them off with, "This is your one chance." No debate or argument, just an emphatic repetitive order with a clear, certain, serious tone of voice and a rehearsed facial expression that Hollywood directors would pay for. That was a slight hint of approaching anger. "Comply now or else" is the clearly understood message.

If teachers yell at everyone about everything, their real, staged, or habitual anger has minimal impact. Anger is to be expressed selectively, not as the first option and always with control. Expressions of excessive anger change the emphasis from the mistake the student made to how the adult resolved the student's mistake.

A results-driven teacher is not endlessly patient. A teacher is not quickly impatient. A teacher's goal is results. If a teacher tries to use a different homework policy than the one just presented and uses the following incentives or options, what it being communicated? First, homework that is done completely, correctly, and early can earn full credit plus bonus points. Second, homework that is done completely, correctly, and on time can earn full credit. Third, homework that is done completely and correctly but late cannot earn full credit. The maximum amount of credit that can be earned if homework is one day late is 80%. The maximum amount of credit that can be earned if homework is two days late is 60%. Students learn that their grade is completely within their control. Students realize the time management benefits of being early or on time. Students realize the time mismanagement cost of being late.

A results-driven teacher does not accept excuses. A teacher does not make excuses. A teacher exemplifies the "results, not excuses" approach to school. A results-driven teacher doesn't say, "I meant to get those tests graded so I could return them to you today, but, well, I guess the time just got away from me. This is Friday. We took that test last Friday and you have another test today. I'll really try to get all the tests back to you next week, no later than Thursday since you'll have another test next Friday."

A results-driven teacher does not make excuses. A teacher gets results and says, "Welcome to the Monday morning episode of our social studies class. You had a test on Friday, and I'm returning those to you right now. Take a few moments and read everything I wrote on your paper. We'll discuss the test after everyone has a minute to read their paper. The grades were very impressive. Your essay answers were high quality. As we discuss the test, tell me of any grading error you think I made and I'll double-check that for you." Tests that are returned within one or two days of the students taking the test can be used as meaningful transitions from one topic to the next sequential topic. Tests returned one or two weeks after they were taken will garner little more than a quick glance at the grade by the students to whom the test is old news.

Results-driven teachers do not make excuses. Results-driven teachers find ways to overcome the obstacles that for other people become excuses like, "I know the physics professor from the college was supposed to visit our class today, but when I emailed her this morning, she said her calendar had the visit to our class for next Monday. Of course, we do not have school next Monday, so that just cannot work. I was so sure that we had everything scheduled for today." Results, not excuses. The results-driven teacher would have been in touch with the professor in person, by phone, and by email several times since the visit was first scheduled. The morning of the visit is not the first and only time to confirm plans.

To every problem, there is an equal and opposite solution. For every excuse, there is an equal and opposite action that can provide the intended result and nullify any need for an excuse.

A results-driven teacher is not absent on Monday or Friday, week after week. Results-driven teachers must be in school with students to get results. Students, teachers, staff members, and administrators resent the person whose absences from school are always on Monday or Friday and who is even more likely to be absent on a Monday if there was no school on Friday or on Friday if there is no school on Monday. Repeatedly creating three- or four-day weekends frustrates colleagues and tells students you are not fully dedicated to or serious about teaching, while increasing costs for your employer who must pay for a substitute teacher every time you are absent. There are also those Mondays or Fridays when a teacher skips school and no substitute teacher is available. The people at school who did come to work on the day probably will be asked to take turns teaching a class for the needlessly absent teacher.

Teachers who use sick days when there is no sickness are being dishonest. Teachers who use sick days when there is no sickness are not honoring their obligations to their employer, their students, or their profession. Results-driven teachers do not use sick days merely because it is a pretty spring day, and being inside a school all day is not inviting when you might be outside in the sunshine and fresh air. Teachers tell students to attend school, to not skip school. The power of example is stronger than the power of telling.

A teacher, the educator whom we are calling a results-driven teacher, does not claim, "I taught them, but they did not learn." This same teacher does not say, "The students should know that, we covered it twice." This teacher does not say, "I think the students are ready for the test. We went over everything."

Notice the verbs, "covered" and "went over." Those verbs are vague and provide no certainty of results. What happens in a classroom when information is covered, when math problems, the colonies, novels, the periodic table is covered? "Cover" could mean anything from watched a video about the colonies to quietly read a chapter of a novel and then answered questions about the novel.

When a student finishes his high school classes for a day and then goes to tennis practice, he might wonder what the team will work on at tennis practice, but he or she knows the team will work hard on tennis. Maybe they will work on serves. Maybe they will work on backhand shots. When tennis practice is over, it is unlikely that the coach or the players will say, "We covered serves and backhand shots today." It is much more likely that they will say, "We really worked hard on serves today. We made a lot of progress. Our serves today were much harder hit and much better placed." The verb is "work," as in "we worked on serves." Why settle for "covering" colonies in the U.S. history class instead of working in a comprehensive analysis of the emerging revolutionary fervor in the months that led to July 1776? Why merely cover the Declaration of Independence when the right amount of work directed into and through the right instructional activities would result in mastery of the people, places, events, and ideas of the Revolutionary War period?

A results-driven teacher does not cover material or go over information with students. A teacher causes students to learn. When a results-driven teacher teaches, the students learn. If students are taught, they learned. For our purposes, the word "teach" means to cause learning. When another person, not a results-driven teacher, covers material with students or goes over information with students, some students will retain some memory of some or all of the material and information. Other students will recall little or none of the material and information.

Students who are taught learn. They know, explain, apply, analyze, discover, learn, remember, and think.

Students whose school experiences consist mostly or entirely of "covering" and "going over" were not educated and were not taught. They were covered with worksheets, textbooks, and videos. They were given word searches and odd-numbered problems to go over. Results-driven teachers do not let that happen. Classroom clerks insist on that happening. The different perspectives on the job of teaching by results-driven teachers and classroom clerks is the difference between causing learning by each student and causing lost opportunities, wasted time, and limited achievement by each student.

A teacher never thinks that students who failed to complete one worksheet should be assigned two or three worksheets so they will realize how important it is to follow instructions. Why does a results-driven teacher not double or triple the worksheet requirement? Because the results-driven teacher does not use worksheets to begin with. Prepackaged, generic, superficial worksheets do not cause learning, so they are not used by results-driven teachers.

Would a results-driven teacher double or triple the amount of work required of a student who did not complete the original assignment? It's an interesting question that suggests another idea for managing homework. Tell students that the work is due on time, done completely and correctly; however, though late work is accepted up to two days after the due date, if you turn the work in one day late, there is an additional work requirement, and if you turn the work in two days late, there is a second additional work requirement. These additions would be part of the price students pay for being late. The additional work would be meaningful and worthwhile, but what it promises in quality of learning experience for the student, it also requires in quantity of work done by the student.

A results-driven teacher does not attempt to use current teenage jargon to sound in touch with and to be part of popular culture. It can be useful to be aware of the meaning behind currently popular words used by teenagers. It can be useful to know something about currently popular music, movies, television programs, on other popular entertainment. The usefulness of such knowledge can include showing students that academic connections can be made between their wholesome knowledge, talents, and interests and what they need to learn at school.

You might hear a student say something like, "We're going to that concert this Saturday night. It will be great. I heard it was sold out. Some people paid $500 for a ticket. Our tickets were $50, but this concert is worth it." Music teachers, economics teachers, math teachers, and others could use the concert as a source of classroom activities that make connections between what students know and what they need to know. Those teachers do not need to attend the concert. Those teachers do not need to listen to songs that the concert bands will play. Those teachers do not need to get a souvenir shirt from the concert. Those teachers just need to know enough to make connections between the wholesome knowledge, interests, and talents of students and what the students need to learn.

In addition to those academic connections, there can be some genuine human connections. A teacher can ask Shawn on Monday morning, "How was that concert you went to? I saw the newspaper story. It said there was a huge crowd." That conversation can build some human connections in addition to create more insights about possible academic connections. Shawn might reply, "It was so great. We yelled for hours. There were a lot of people there from this school. You'd be proud of me. I did not buy the concert t-shirt; $37 is just way too much money for one shirt."

A results-driven teacher is not satisfied if some students fail, some students barely pass, and some students do okay. A results-driven teacher should have done better if some students easily made A grades but had no real challenge.

For a results-driven teacher, it is unacceptable that some students fail or that some students barely pass. Academic failure at a school with a grading scale where 65% is the lowest passing grade means that a student made a grade between 64% and 0%. During a grading period, during a semester, or during any time that a grade is calculated, there are many indications that a student is doing low-quality work or that a student is sometimes doing no work. At the first indication of a student's academic problems, a results-driven teacher takes action. The teacher works directly with the student, the teacher calls and/or emails the parent or guardian of the student, and the teacher emails the student's other teachers to see what the student's grades are in other classes.

That may sound like a lot of work. How long does it take to talk to the student? How long does it take to call and/or email the student's family? How long does it take to email the student's other teachers? Each of those actions would take a few minutes, and each of those actions could help solve the problem. How long will it take and how difficult will it be to solve an academic problem that is allowed to worsen over months or years into an academic crisis? Early action is efficient and effective, as it helps solve a problem before it builds into a crisis.

A results-driven teacher is not satisfied if some students did okay, but should have done better. Okay means that a student made C grades, average grades. Where does average take anyone? What opportunities await the average student? Do any colleges eagerly seek C-average students? Do any employees prefer students who did average work in school? The results-driven teacher will take actions intended to move the C-average student out of the ordinary level up to the good or great level. The results-driven teacher could show that student exactly what would have to be done differently on homework, in class activities, on tests, and on projects to move up from C to B or A grades. The student might say, "That's all it takes? I can do that. I guess I'm just used to doing what I usually do. No big deal. I can make those changes." Some students get in the C habit. They stay in that habit until acted on by an outside force such as a results-driven teacher. Then an inside force takes over when the student experiences more success, starts making B or A grades, and expects nothing less than good or great from herself or himself.

A results-driven teacher is not satisfied if some students easily made A grades but had no real challenge. For some students, A grades come easily if they make the effort. Some students who could easily make all A grades grow weary of the uninspiring, never interesting, rarely challenging routine at school. When middle school is a rerun of elementary school, when high school is a rerun of middle school, some students just do enough to get by and get out. Other students make A grades, but the grade shows they did very well on what was required. The A grade does not indicate what the student could have learned or could have achieved if school had challenged the student to do more than what comes easily.

A results-driven teacher is as concerned about underachieving A students as about underachieving F, D, or C students. This teacher does not equate an A grade with complete success unless the student had to do his or her best work to earn the A. One of the education jargon terms in recent years has been "differentiated instruction." For people who are unfamiliar with education jargon, "differentiated instruction" usually means that teachers provide learning experiences, opportunities, and challenges that accurately match the current needs and abilities of each student. This idea is not new, although the current jargon may seem to indicate that. My 8th-grade U.S. history teacher differentiated instruction 40 years ago. He gave us a wide variety of choices. There were many activities and projects we could consider. Nothing was easy or simple. Everything related to the topic. Sometimes we selected activities we were skilled in, and other times we accepted his encouraging suggestion to try something new. The results were very impressive. When we made an A grade, we had earned it. Sometimes he required us to qualify for an A on a test by doing more pretest work in quantity or quality. You had to do certain projects to qualify for an A test grade. If you did only enough projects to qualify for a B test grade, but made an A score on the test, you still got a B on the test. Now people could debate the merits of that system, but it eliminated any easy A test grades, because you had to do more and better work prior to a test. That extra work helped prepare you to make an A on the test.

Results-driven teachers challenge students to whom an A grade could come easily. The challenge is real, meaningful, and personal. The student does not resent the challenge. A high school senior who is a great athlete can easily outperform 8th graders in basketball, but the senior is not interested in competing against 8th graders just to get an easy win. The senior is eager to compete against the best team to earn a challenging victory. Students who are in the classrooms of results-driven teachers welcome the challenging academic work that will mean an A was earned by stretching their mind into the frontier of new ideas, new thoughts, and new learning.

Personalized instruction is part of results-driven teaching rather than differentiated instruction. The term "personalized" is not a mere semantic change from differentiated. Results-driven teachers teach people personally, knowing the strengths, needs, personality, interests, knowledge, talents, and goals of a student. Does that require some time and work? Yes. Does that get results for students? Yes. Does that provide meaningful career experiences for teachers? Yes. The goal is not to differentiate instruction just to meet the bureaucracy's requirement for differentiation of instruction. The goal is to cause learning. To the extent that differentiated instruction causes learning, wonderful results confirm the worth of the differentiation. To the extent that the differentiation is personalized and based on what a results-driven teacher personally knows about the people in the classroom, the likelihood of wonderful results is enhanced. Personalizing includes differentiating, but can be much more because it is personal, human, real.

Results-driven teachers are not perfect and do not expect themselves to be perfect. Results-driven teachers are great at their work, yet they expect themselves to continually improve. Results-driven teachers do get to see their students do outstanding work, work that surpasses the state requirements, work that is sometimes perfect. As the following essay explains, results-driven teachers are motivated by the possibility of students doing outstanding work, superior work, perfect work.

MOTIVATED BY YOUR PERFECTION

"So what makes you work so hard? You know, every day in class you are so excited and everything. You never just give us busy work to do. Why do you work so hard?" the student asked. The student seemed to be sincerely curious about the topic, so I thought of the best way to honor this profound question with a meaningful answer.

I said, "I am motivated by the possibility of your perfection." The answer amazed the student and the answer satisfied me. I could not recall previously explaining my motivation to be a teacher, to be the best possible teacher I could be, to be the best possible teacher anyone could be, with the words, "I am motivated by the possibility of your perfection."

The student replied with a smile yet some perplexity. She said, "My perfection? You mean that your reason to work so hard is for me to be perfect? That's amazing. I figured you worked hard to earn more money or to win some award, but your answer really surprises me."

It was easy to agree with that. I said, "Well, it has always been true, but I have never heard myself use those words before. Still, I really am motivated by the possibility of you reaching academic achievements, learning, thinking, and knowing more and better than you ever have. My dream will begin to come true when you experience greatness as a student that goes beyond any amount or quality of learning that you have ever known. My dream is complete when you have moments of perfection by asking the most brilliant question, by gaining the most thorough insight, by reaching the most compelling conclusion, and by experiencing thinking that takes your brain into a new frontier of thought. So my motivation is you, your achievement, your progress, and eventually your moments of perfection."

The student had another urgent question and said, "But perfection? That's really hard to do. I've made a 100% grade before, so I guess that was perfect because nothing was wrong. I had an A+ on a paper recently, so that must mean it was perfect. Sometimes, I make a B or sometimes I just don't understand what we are doing in a class, but it eventually makes sense most times. Still, perfection all the time sounds really hard."

She was right. Perfection is really hard. The pursuit of perfection in a world, in a school, in a society where "good enough" is acceptable will raise questions. My thoughts turned to music, because I was once asked what my favorite music is. My answer was "The symphonies of Beethoven." The next question was "why?" and the answer was direct and certain: "Because they remind me of the possibility of perfection."

There is no limit to human thought. We can think of perfection. The thought can be the beginning of the pursuit. The pursuit can be the beginning of the first part of many necessary accomplishments that, when all parts are completed, lead to moments of absolute perfection.

"I am motivated by the possibility of your perfection." Why is that my motivation? Because I am a teacher, a results-driven teacher whose duty is to cause extreme learning in the lives of extreme students and whose greatest joy is when students mentally realize the possibility of their own perfection and then actually seek and achieve that perfection. Doing my teaching job with this concept, with this perspective, and with this intent means that I am surrounded each day by and involved each day in the pursuit of perfection. As that pursuit of perfection becomes achievement of perfections, the results are without limit. Even when perfection is not attained, more and better work is done because we sought perfection. Achieving 90% of perfection is better than 100% of okay or good.

The times when students reach perfection are built upon moments, hours, days, weeks, months, and years when teaching perfection has been pursued always and has been experienced with increasing frequency. Doing the best possible teaching for students and with students maximizes student achievement while also maximizing the career experience of teachers. Everyone wins.

I told the student, "I am motivated by your perfection and that motivation is good for both of us. Thanks very much for asking me about my motivation and for causing me to think anew about why I teach and how I teach." When we listen to students, when we see students as real people who are living real lives right now, when we learn with and from them, when we create classroom experiences that cause learning, when we create a classroom learning community, everyone learns together.

If you connect them they will learn. If you connect with them everyone learns together. If you touch their lives and their minds, students will learn. If you permit students to touch your life and your mind, you will learn. Such are the perfect joys of extreme teaching, of causing extreme learning, and of developing extreme students by being a results-driven teacher.

Before we leave this chapter, the reader's thoughts about "what a results-driven teacher is not" merit attention. On separate paper, please write your reflections on what a results-driven teacher is not.

The next chapter takes us into the thoughts, hopes, questions, ideas, ideals, concerns, confidence, and doubts of a college student who is considering or who is anticipating a teaching career. What does the college student who is preparing to be a teacher need to know now? That is the topic of chapter 8.

8

WHAT COLLEGE STUDENTS PREPARING TO BE RESULTS-DRIVEN TEACHERS NEED TO KNOW NOW

Ask a lot of people for a lot of advice. Here's an example. As a freshman in college in 1972 I asked two professors—one taught French and one taught Spanish—if there were any benefits to studying one language over the other. They politely and diplomatically told me that I should follow my preference, that either study would be worthwhile.

Many of my high school friends took French. My family, wisely, made me study Latin in high school. The choice of what international language to study in college was my decision. I selected French. I took seven classes of French in college. I am certified to teach French. I like the French language and I am glad to know it; however, I should have obtained much more advice in 1972 before selecting a language. Someone should have told me to look at a map of the world and identify where Spanish is spoken, then where French is spoken. Someone would have pointed out the emerging demographic changes in some parts of the United States as more cities had more Spanish-speaking residents.

The job opportunities at middle schools and high schools that would be available to me today if I were certified to teach Spanish now would be vast. The opportunities to use Spanish in daily conversations in the community would be success stories for me instead of regrets about opportunities missed.

Talk to people who work in schools. Get their advice on employment realities now and in the near future. If getting certified to teach U.S. history is your heart's desire, do that; however, add certification in math, science, Spanish, or technology so you are a more versatile employee. When you look for your first teaching job and there are no openings for a U.S. history teacher but there are many openings in math, science, Spanish, or technology, you will have much better competitive advantages in the marketplace.

I would like to teach math, but I am not certified to teach math in public schools. I have worked with many students through the years to help them understand math. That work is done individually or when I teach one class for a teacher who is arriving late or who is observing a colleague teach.

For me to become certified to teach math would involve several years of taking one or two math classes per semester in the evening. It would have been so much easier to have included those math classes in my college years, to have earned math certification 30 years ago when I was in college, and to have entered the teaching profession initially with that certification in addition to my certification in U.S. history, political science, and French.

You might protest, "But I'm no good in math. I have to take three math classes in college as a graduation requirement, but that is all for me. My major is English, and I'll be certified to teach high school English. That is the one subject I always have done best in. I'm sure I'll be able to find a high school job teaching English. Every high school has English teachers."

Right, and every high school has lots of English teachers who return year after year. When there is a job opening at Clinton High School for an English teacher, there will be several or many local residents who apply for the job and, via Internet, there may be many people who apply for the job who live throughout the state, country, or world. Give yourself all of the competitive advantages possible. Be able to show that knowledge of English and your ability to teach English are superior, but realize that other applicants for the job are going to present impressive skills, abilities, college transcripts, experiences with students, and related work experiences. What can you do for the potential employer that no other applicant can do?

Imagine telling a potential employer, "I am very eager to teach English. I know that the students at Clinton High School will master writing, grammar, literacy, and more in my classroom. I can do more for you. My teaching certification also includes math, grades 9–12, and computer science, grades 9–12. It was not easy getting those three certifications. I went to school each summer during college, and I worked each summer at our college's academic camp for middle school students and 9th graders. My emphasis was to get students caught up to their grade level in math and in reading using some very sophisticated and individualized computer programs."

The school administrator who hears you explain your experience and your career preparation has many reasons to put you at the top of the list for the teaching job at Clinton High School. You can do more for the school than many other applicants. The school administrator will evaluate you as a prospective teacher, but also has to evaluate you in relation to the school's total curriculum, faculty, staff, and students. Your versatility makes you stand out in a crowd of job applicants. Yes, your preference is to teach English; however, you have also gained and applied your ability teaching math or computer science applications. Perhaps the school also has a math position opening. Perhaps the principal is planning to add a technology/computer position and you would be perfect for that job when it is added to the faculty in one year. Give the school district, the school, the principal, the interviewing committee more reasons to select you than they have to select anyone else.

This chapter begins with the above career advice because of the few regrets I have about my teaching career, the regrets at the top of the list all relate to what I could have accomplished in college that would have been completed very efficiently then and that would have been beneficial to me for an entire career of three or four decades. Very early in your first semester of college, talk to professors in the teacher education program, and talk to professors in the academic areas where you will major, minor, concentrate, or otherwise take enough classes to be certified to teach. Find out what the minimum requirements are for being legally certified to teach a subject, but take more classes than the minimum because you intend to be a great teacher, a results-driven teacher.

Talk with teachers, principals, and school district administrators to get their advice and perspective. Ask them, "If you were a freshman in college, what would you want to know so you could be fully prepared to begin a teaching career four years later?" Also ask them what they have learned during their career. For example, very few college students state their career goal is to become the principal of a school or the superintendent of a school district. College students who are interested in a career in education usually say that they intend to become a teacher. After some years of teaching, they might get interested in school administration. In anticipation of possible opportunities or interests that may develop throughout a career in education, what should a college student do now and not do now? Career educators could offer helpful advice on that. Most people begin their career in education as teachers and complete their careers in education as teachers. Teaching is the best job and the most important job in the education profession because it is the job that puts you in direct contact with students all day, every day. Advice and perspective from experienced educators about how to manage a 30-year career in classroom teaching—with no venture into administration, supervision, counseling, specialists, or other education support roles—is helpful. You need to know what people who are already in your desired profession know. The earlier you know what they know, the more you can apply, test, confirm, revise, update, and benefit from their wisdom.

College is a marvelous time to read some books about educational philosophy, educational psychology, theories of learning, and emerging research in the field of human growth and development. Read those books. Ponder those concepts. Contemplate those theories. Reflect on those ideas. Create your personal educational philosophy. Read Plato's essay "Meno," and keep reading it throughout your career.

Now anticipate the moment when Tasha and Shawn are the first students to walk into your classroom on the first day of the first school year of your teaching career. Tasha and Shawn are real people living real lives right now. The educational philosophers and educational theorists whose books you read do not know Tasha and Shawn. Those philosophers and theorists will never meet Tasha or Shawn and will never teach Tasha and Shawn.

You just met Tasha and Shawn. In a few minutes, class will begin. Which philosophy or theory will most impress Tasha and Shawn? None. These two students will not be impressed by any educational philosophy or theory. They can be impressed with you and they can be fascinated with the instructional activities you provide for them. Certainly, your work may be impacted and inspired by philosophers and theorists, but the most significant impact and inspiration is this: How do I most effectively cause Tasha and Shawn to learn?

During the college years, as you study education in preparation for your teaching career, visit schools and watch the best teachers at those schools. Visit camps in the summer and watch the most effective camp counselors work with campers. Volunteer to help with the youth group or the Sunday school program at a church. Volunteer to be a tutor in an after-school program. When a college class requires that you observe 15 hours in a teacher's classroom, observe for 30 hours, going to two classrooms for 15 hours each. See what causes learning and what does not cause learning. See what fascinates students and what builds apathy, frustration, misbehavior, and failure in students.

I was recently given the glorious opportunity to speak with college students who are preparing for teaching careers. The 19 scholars and I thrived on a lively, practical, inspirational, honest exchange of ideas. As an answer to their interest in my philosophy of education I shared four statements: "We know what works. Students are real people living real lives right now. If you connect them, they will learn. If you connect with students, everyone learns together." End of philosophy, beginning of creating classroom instructional activities that cause learning taking advantage of (a) what is known about how great teachers do their jobs; (b) how willingly students do commit to learning that is real; (c) how productive teaching is that connects what students know—their wholesome knowledge, interests, and talents—with what they need to know; and (d) how productive and genuine the classroom community becomes when students realize that the teacher takes them and their input seriously.

So college students preparing for a career in teaching should read the profound thoughts of educational philosophers and learning theorists and debate the perennial and contemporary societal issues that schools confront. As you have that uniquely academic experience and contemplative journey that college can be, ask yourself this question often: When Tasha and Shawn are in my classroom, what do I do to cause learning? Tasha and Shawn will not learn because you have mastered philosophies and theories. Tasha and Shawn will learn as you implement effective instructional activities that the philosophies and theories may inspire but that your knowledge of Tasha and Shawn will much more importantly inspire. No matter how solidly researched or brilliantly reasoned, the philosophies and theories are generalized concepts. Tasha and Shawn are specific, individual students who are real people living real lives right now. You cannot philosophize or theorize Tasha and Shawn into learning. You can fascinate, intrigue, amaze, challenge, encourage, interact with, guide, correct, listen to, and demand high-quality work from them. You can connect what they know with what they need to learn and make their education real.

If you graduate from college at age 22 or 23 and immediately begin your teaching career, you will have the physical health and physical fitness benefits of being young. Teaching effectively is physically demanding and can be physically draining, so take great care of yourself. Getting up to teach classes Monday through Friday is quite different from getting up to attend college classes Monday through Friday. Be prepared for that change. The basics of staying physically healthy are vital—eat nutritiously, exercise daily, get enough sleep, and avoid anything harmful.

You remember that your family used to tell you, "It's a school night, so turn off the television, finish your homework, and get to sleep on time." You will return to that routine when you become a teacher. School nights will require very sensible time management, because there are papers to grade, lessons to plan and prepare, and grades to enter into the computer. And what about getting some exercise, stopping by the grocery store, returning phone calls and emails, plus getting to sleep at a reasonable hour? Some advice: spread out the tests and homework assignments. Early in my first year of teaching, I made a rookie mistake. All of my classes had a test one Friday. I created the tests, of course, so there were a variety of questions, including objective fill-in-the-blanks, short answers, one-paragraph answers, multiparagraph answers, and multiparagraph essays. The test was taken by 162 students, and I insisted on getting the tests back to them the next school day. I graded tests Friday night, all day Saturday, and all day Sunday. From then on, I staggered the schedule for tests and homework so the workload for me was balanced across the days instead of loaded heavily on some days.

Teaching absorbs your energy, yet effective teaching can also renew your energy as you cause learning. It is energizing to see Tasha make progress and to read Shawn's brilliant answer on a test. In your teaching methods and classroom activities, do what works to cause learning. Do not waste time and energy on activities that merely fill the time. The students and you will get no energy from superficial routines. Results-driven teaching is lively, creative, imaginative, demanding, productive, and rewarding. The price you pay is work. The reward you get is results. For all of that to happen, you need to be very healthy, so take great care of yourself.

Beware of possible illnesses, allergies, and other health problems that can occur as you are working in a building that is new to you. There can be materials in the building to which you are allergic, so be cautious. If your classroom has chalkboards, ask for them to be replaced with marker boards so you and the students do not have to breathe chalk dust. Some students at school are getting sick, are sick, or are getting over a sickness on any given day at school. You will be near students who are sick, so take every wise precaution—that means do what your mother and grandmother always told you about taking good care of your health. You remember their wisdom, so follow it.

Your heart will be touched when students achieve magnificently. Your heart will be broken when students cheat, defy, curse, steal, lie, give up, get suspended, get arrested, and drop out. Did your college classes tell you that there would be some days in your teaching career when you feel on top of the world and other days when you feel that the entire world is crushing down on top of you? What is to be done?

The most discouraging moment of your teaching career is not the one part that describes the entire whole. If a crime occurs at your school and you witness the crime, you could be subpoenaed to testify in court about what you saw. On a day when you would much rather be teaching, you are instead in a courtroom taking an oath to tell the truth and then answer questions as you sit in the witness stand. As disturbing and agonizing as the courtroom experience could be, it is not the one hour that defines your 30-year teaching career.

The most wonderful moment of your teaching career is also not the one part that describes the entire whole. A student who you taught years ago personally invites you to attend her high school graduation. At that lovely ceremony, the student who invited you is one of three high school seniors who will speak as part of the graduation program. As part of her speech, the student thanks you by name as the teacher who above all others is most responsible for her success in school, her graduation from high school, and her scholarship to an outstanding university. This graduation gives you a precious memory, but it is not the complete description of your career.

Your career will be a series of days, weeks, months, years, and decades in which what you teach and how you teach will describe the totality of your work. Your career is the sum of all the interactions you have with students, all the lessons planned, all the creative instructional activities you designed, and all the extra effort you invested in Tasha and Shawn. It is in the day-to-day moments of teaching, when you consistently cause learning, that you establish the parts that do accurately describe the whole of your career.

Know the subject or subjects that you will teach. Make outstanding grades in college. Your students will not benefit much from a teacher who made C grades in college, who skipped some classes in college, who delayed work until the night before a paper was due, and who prepared for tests the night before or the morning of instead of keeping up or keeping ahead of the syllabus.

What you will teach your students throughout your career is not limited to what you know when you graduate from college. Through graduate school, you will continue to learn about the subjects you teach, and you will continue to learn about teaching. Of equal or more importance is that you continue to read, to research, to reflect. Continue to be a student of teaching, a student of students throughout your career, and a student of the subjects you teach.

We know what works. Think of the best teachers you have had throughout your years of school, and use some of their teaching methods in presentations you make to your college classes and in work you do during a practicum or student teaching assignment as you continue your college work toward teacher certification. Keep in touch with those great teachers whose teaching so deeply impressed you. Talk to them now and throughout your career. Do not imitate them, but do borrow their most effective teaching methods and do apply their insights while also including your unique methods that cause learning.

You may hear your professors mention state, regional, or national conferences they attend or are invited to attend. These conferences are sponsored by education groups that may be organized around mutual interests related to a subject that is taught in school, related to a particular age group that is taught in school, or related to an ongoing or emerging issue impacting schools. Some conferences are sponsored by various community, corporate, political, or civic interest groups that seek to impact education. Beware of these conferences and be very demanding of any conference, workshop, or convention that you consider attending. You and your employer will spend time and money for you to attend these events. Throughout your career, there will be many of these events that you are told about and that some of your colleagues attend. Be very selective and be very demanding. Do not go to the January conference in San Diego just because the weather in San Diego in January is better than the January weather where you live.

There are books you can read and websites you can visit that give you many of the informational benefits of attending the conference. There are dissertations that you can read that give you the benefit, insight, and conclusions of each author's years of research. There are capable educators in your community now, and there will be capable educators in the schools where you teach who you can observe, talk with, learn from, and trade ideas with. You and these colleagues can create frequent conversations about teaching that will surpass in practicality and efficiency the trip to San Diego because no travel is involved and because you will discuss the reality at your school.

The education profession publishes hundreds of monthly and quarterly magazines about teaching, schools, students, and issues that impact education. Your school, your school district, your local library, or a college or university library will have these publications. Read them so you know what works in teaching according to the authors of the articles in those publications. Be sure that what you read and use allows you to answer the question: "If I use this idea, will it cause Tasha and Shawn to learn when they are in my classroom on Monday morning?"

One hour of lesson planning might be consumed in 10 minutes of classroom activity time. Plan more than you think will be needed.

One hour of lesson planning might create an activity that the students respond to so eagerly and productively that you extend this activity from one day of class to two or three days of class. The goal is to cause learning, not to rigidly adhere to a schedule. Keep in mind that you must cause learning of the entire curriculum assigned to you, so make days two and three of this extended adventure connect with more curriculum components than you originally planned. This way, the extra time accomplishes as much or more than you needed to complete over those days according to your original plan.

Coaches often have a collection of skill-developing drills that can be effectively used at any time. Teachers should have a similar collection of purposeful skill-building drills that can be used when a pocket of time appears. Imagine: Today's lesson plan went very well, but it went faster than you expected. There are eight minutes left in class. It's vocabulary skill drill time. Math problem superstar challenge time. Short story reading aloud time. Current events newspaper article analysis time. Multiplication table drill and practice time. Have meaningful, purposeful skill building drills ready to use whenever unexpected time appears. Update these drills to be current with the topics and the students you are teaching now, but applying previously mastered skills, ideas, and information is good mental exercise and is important confirmation for you that students remember what was studied earlier in the school year.

You have chosen teaching and/or teaching has chosen you. As a college student, you have many career options, and you have many choices of a college major or minor. At some point in your college years, you may question your plan to become a teacher. Maybe you have a summer job at a camp and something happens that discourages you, that makes you question whether working with children or teenagers is the best career for you. Do not let that one incident at camp have too much or too little impact on your thinking. Talk to the camp director. Talk to more experienced camp employees who can help you learn from the incident. Reflect on this camp experience, correct any mistake you made, and promise yourself to continually improve as you grow in the job.

Other college students may also question their career choice, their academic major, or their academic minor. Some college friends of yours may change their career goals and their fields of study. Colleges are prepared to guide students through these adventures of self-discovery. If you are in your heart, mind, body, and soul cut out to be a teacher, no other work will satisfy you. If the work you are to do in your career is with students, you have to be where the students are. Being true to that honest awareness of who you are is an essential element of living genuinely rather than pretending to live. It is quite tragic to realize at age 40 or 50 that a person never did the work that most mattered to him or her. Avoid that regret. You have heard life tell you to teach. People have told you that you would be a great teacher. You have watched your best teachers and realized that their work interested you more than any other job you know of. In your moments of sincere soul searching, you know that you are supposed to teach. Remember those truths when you encounter difficulties or challenges. Persist. Living the life you are supposed to live is worth it.

Yes, you will have to deal with students who misbehave. Students know what the penalty will be when they break rules or disobey instructions. Using any penalty, punishment, or disciplinary action that is less than what they know they deserve signals to them that you did not take their misconduct seriously. Disciplining a student does not end your opportunity to teach the student. The disciplinary action is how that student needs to be taught now. When that is resolved, you will return to academic instruction and a more cordial interaction with the student.

Some laws that impact education are very frustrating and some are just plain mistakes; however, until that law changes, you are obligated to follow it as it exists. The same is true for policies and regulations. More advice: Do all you can to prepare for your work in your classroom to maximize the achievements of students. For now, concentrate on doing all you can in the area over which you will have significant authority— what happens in your classroom. Keep a record of questions and concerns you have about policies, regulations, and laws. When the time is right, ask those questions and express those concerns. There will be opportunities in your career to serve on the groups that review policies or that offer perspective to lawmakers. Until then, learn, learn more, keep learning. Study, study more, keep studying. Think, think more, keep thinking. Have as many quality volunteer or paid experiences as you can fit into your schedule to work with children, teenagers, teachers, and other people who work closely with children and teenagers.

During your college years, add an extra dimension to each class you take. Silently evaluate the teaching that is being done. Ask yourself what the professor's objectives are for the course and what the particular objective is for each day's class. Notice the different teaching methods, activities, styles, and dynamics used by various instructors, assistant professors, and professors.

Now, take this several steps further. Reflect on your years in high school, middle school, and elementary school. Think of your teachers, how they taught, what was most impressive and effective, what was most ordinary and ineffective. Think of clubs or sports you were involved in during those school years. What did the best club sponsors or athletic coaches do to make the experiences beneficial?

Reflect on summer camps you attended, church youth group events, scouting activities, local recreational leagues, or other experiences in your childhood and teenage years where an adult worked with you in ways that enabled you to learn now about how that adult taught. To the extent possible, talk with these people from your childhood and teenage years to better understand how they perceived their work. What perceptions did your best teachers, camp counselor, coaches, and mentors have about their work that led them to do their work in such effective ways? What perceptions did the other people have that permitted them to be satisfied with less effective ways?

How a person perceives his or her job impacts how that person does the job. Few jobs require greatness, but within each job is the opportunity to do the work in a great way. To become a results-driven teacher, you must first understand that a teacher can, should, and must require himself or herself to get results, the most important of which is to cause learning.

Notice the vast resources within your life experiences, memories, thoughts, mind, and brain. There is no limit on human thought, so think limitlessly, learn with unlimited mental range, and in so doing, continue you preparation to be a results-driven teacher by requiring yourself to be a results-driven student.

For readers who are in college, what else would you like to know about a career in teaching? Make your list of everything else you would like to know. Write that list now and then go get the answers, insights, information, wisdom, advice, and guidance you seek.

For readers who have completed college, what else would you suggest needs to be known by college students who are preparing for a teaching career? Make your list of everything else you would like those college students to know, and then write an article for a professional education journal, visit a college class, invite local college students to your classroom, and create new professional partnerships.

From what college students who are preparing for a teaching career need to know, we now move in the next chapter to a consideration of what teachers who will stay in teaching for an entire career need to know, anticipate, be ready for, and impact.

9

WHAT RESULTS-DRIVEN TEACHERS WHO WILL STAY IN THIS PROFESSION NEED TO KNOW

As results-driven teachers continue their careers, the duties will become more demanding. The demands will become more difficult. The difficulties will become more complicated. The complications will become more urgent. The urgencies will become more frustrating. The frustrations will become more numerous.

Amid that escalating and expanding storm, results-driven teachers will continue to cause learning. Why? Because students need to learn and deserve to learn, and because results-driven teachers will always find ways to intrigue, fascinate, encourage, challenge, nurture, involve, and inspire students. How? Using some time-tested teaching methods that have worked since Socrates, using connections between what students know and what students need to learn, using already successful ideas, and using ideas and resources that have not been created yet.

Throughout your teaching career, national, state, and local governments will continue to expect more and more from schools. The authorities in those political offices could not do the school work, the social reform work, the social services work that they direct educators and schools to do. Those same political authorities may not provide sufficient authority or adequate resources to educators to accomplish the expanding and demanding list of duties assigned to schools. That is frustrating, but it is likely to continue to be the reality.

The history of American public education includes significant reform efforts every few decades or more often. Throughout your career, you will see your school district initiate many new programs, policies, procedures, and professional development efforts to increase student achievement. Some of those initiatives will be fully implemented and will be evaluated as successful. Some of those initiatives will be abandoned prior to complete implementation because a new superintendent and/or new members elected to a school board reversed an earlier decision. Despite the comings and goings of these changes in your school district, you will still have many opportunities throughout each day to educate your students in the "promised land" of the classroom where political leaders, school district officials, or school board members rarely visit. Those people deal with laws, policies, regulations, programs, grants, and other bureaucratic creations. You must abide by the laws, policies, regulations, grant requirements, and chain-of-command directives; however, those do not completely control how you teach your students, how you interact with your students, how you challenge, encourage, motivate, involve and fascinate your students. So fill out the forms required by the bureaucracy on time, completely, and accurately. Attend and helpfully participate in faculty meetings, professional development programs, and other required gatherings. Then go cause learning in the lives of Tasha and Shawn.

You may decide to get involved quite actively on a committee at your school. Your school may have a decision-making or policy-making council that has authority over some topics at the school. You may seek a position on that council or you may work with colleagues to create recommendations for that council to consider. Your school district may occasionally seek teachers to participate on a policy review task force, and your involvement with one of those groups that creates recommendations for the school board could be of interest to you. The department of education in your state may seek email input on various topics or may seek teachers to serve on advisory boards, and that work may be worth your time.

The best use of your time throughout your teaching career will be designing and implementing instructional activities that cause students to learn. That will be true in the first year of a teaching career and in the final year of a teaching career.

Results-driven teachers can anticipate much debate over laws such as No Child Left Behind. Future presidents and members of the U.S. Congress will debate that law, revise that law, consider occasional requests to repeal that law, argue about funding for that law, evaluate testing methods used by states and schools to show compliance with that law, question whether that law violates the wording and/or the intent of the Tenth Amendment to the U.S. Constitution, and confront the political philosophy and motive of the federal government increasing its role in education at the state and local levels. Some decisions related to the No Child Left Behind law or other laws will be very significant, so express your thoughts to members of the U.S. Congress, but direct most of your time, energy, effort, attention, and concern to your students. You can cause your students to learn much more than you can cause members of the U.S. Congress to learn, for at least two reasons. First, you are face-to-face with your students daily. Second, members of Congress are given input from many constituents who have varying and opposing opinions, so the time a member of Congress can spend with you or considering your ideas is quite limited. The time that you and your students spend together is abundant and can be as productive as you make it.

Some very difficult new societal trends will emerge or some complex existing societal trends may move from complex to chaotic. More grandparents will rear students whose parent is or whose parents are in prison, subject to a court order to have no contact, unfit to rear children, unwilling to rear children, deceased, addicted to drugs, or otherwise not involved. What happens to those children or teenagers when their grandparent can no longer rear them? What impact will this have on your classroom as this demographic trend increases? You and your colleagues may need to lobby for a school social worker to be added to the support staff at your school.

Budgets will get tighter. One reason is that between the years of 1981 and 2006, the national debt of the United States increased from $1 trillion to over $8 trillion. That debt continues to grow at an alarming rate that cannot continue endlessly. State and local governments increasingly face budget difficulties. Taxpayers are pushed and pulled by every level of government that faces budget challenges. Education will be one of many public expenditures that will compete for available tax dollars or available bonding dollars. You can anticipate that financial problems will increasingly impact educational decision making during your career.

What do these budget problems mean to a results-driven teacher who is very skilled, respected, favorably evaluated, known as a superior teacher, and successfully completing her eighth or eighteenth year of teaching? It could mean that the school where you work now may not be the school where you will work next year. If a school district has to reduce its payroll and not rehire some teachers, your status as a tenured teacher may keep you as a school district employee, but may necessitate placing you at a different school. You will miss colleagues from the old school, yet you can be a results-driven teacher at the new school as a different Tasha and Shawn enter your classroom on the first day of school.

As budgets get tighter, you will be asked to accomplish more with less. How is that done? Ideas. The power of ideas is more productive than the power of purchased instructional materials. It costs absolutely nothing in financial terms to assign my 8th-grade economics students their choice of designing a new sports arena, designing a new sporting goods retail store, or designing a new sports television network. The students did superior work on the homework project, and everyone learned a lot. The creativity, innovativeness, and work ethic of a results-driven teacher can always produce more learning than the instructional materials might produce.

Throughout the career of a results-driven teacher, some of your colleagues in teaching will do outstanding work. You will be honored to know them, eager to learn from them, and thankful to know them. You will work with other people who do their job very poorly, who are unnecessarily absent often, who complain about everything, and whose students try to get out of their class as often as that educator tries to get out of school. The administrators of your school are the people to deal with such personnel issues. If another teacher's work or lack of work impacts your effectiveness—for example, the teacher is absent often and never leaves anything for the substitute teacher so the classroom, which is adjacent to yours, is quite loud on every day there is a substitute teacher—you could speak with that colleague first. If the problem continues, you could notify the school administrator with a statement of facts, but with no editorial comment. In most cases, you will still be able to very effectively teach your students even amid the frustration that comes with an underachieving colleague.

On the encouraging side, some students will accomplish more than any students in earlier generations accomplished. It will be a joy to teach these young scholars, to learn with them, to learn about them, and to learn from them.

Some high school students are ready to graduate after three years of high school. Some results-driven teachers will get to invent new learning opportunities that make their senior year of high school an unprecedented learning experience. College classes taken for dual high school and college credit, independent research studies done under the guidance of a results-driven high school teacher, work/study co-op ventures with local employers, and distance learning using new Internet capabilities are emerging experiences that some high school students benefit from now and that more high school students can benefit from in the future. These intellectual and innovative experiences can provide much satisfaction for a teacher and much learning for students.

During your career, it is possible that some classes, which in a prior generation were taught only in high school, will be taught in middle school. From geometry to computer science, from vocational training to video production, educational experiences once reserved for high school students may expand to middle schools. This can create new career opportunities for middle school teachers with the proper credentials.

Throughout your career, you can anticipate that each year will bring more new stories about how poorly students in the United States compete with students from other countries in math, science, and literacy. Elementary school teachers can expect that each of these reports will create new urgency to find some system, program, or grant-funded initiative that will guarantee that all elementary school students are at or are above grade level in math, science, and reading by the end of the 5th grade. The accuracy of the studies may not matter. A bad headline may require action to address the perception that students in the United States simply do not measure up to students worldwide.

These will be times in your career when your school or your school district introduces a new program, a new class, a new process. You will think, "I remember when we tried that 10 years ago. It wasn't a bad idea then, but it got replaced. Maybe it will work better now or maybe it will be given a better chance this time." Some education innovations are revisions of something done years ago. You can safely anticipate that some ideas will get recycled whether they deserve it or not.

Throughout your career as a results-driven teacher, you will hear colleagues speak of an earlier time when teachers were respected, rules were obeyed, instructions were followed, homework was done, and families were involved in the school and were supportive of teachers. How likely is it that there was once a golden generation of perfectly cooperative students who each had perfectly reasonable parents/guardians? Despite the problems caused by some students and ignored by some families, a results-driven teacher can, throughout a teaching career, have the respect of students and colleagues, get compliance about rules and instructions from students, have students willingly complete and proudly turn in homework, and secure the involvement of parents/guardians.

On the other hand, reality says that some students will violate the most serious school rules. These students will be suspended from school, perhaps for the maximum time allowed. Some of these students could be expelled from school. In the school district and state where I work, a school administrator may suspend a student for a maximum of 10 days. A school board may expel a student, based on a school administrator's recommendation and all available evidence, for a maximum of one year. If a teacher is involved in any way—victim, witness, informant—with situations such as these, it can be very discouraging, but it need not defeat you. Most students do what they are supposed to do most of the time. Find hope in that and build upon that.

Beyond violation of school rules, some misbehavior at school is also criminal misconduct. Some students will commit crimes at school and/or in the community. These students may be processed through the juvenile justice system and then returned to school as they await trial. They may be educated, temporarily as they await trial or as an order of the court, in a juvenile justice facility or at an alternative school. Their presence at school is a potential threat to your health and safety along with the health and safety of everyone else at school.

In the interest of the health and safety of students and adults at school, it seems reasonable for teachers to increasingly insist on more alternative education programs for students who cannot or will not cooperate and succeed at a regular school. The potential for a serious crime to occur at school during your career is real, so you have every right to insist on more school law enforcement officers, more surveillance cameras, and more electronic screening devices including metal detectors.

On a more hopeful and encouraging topic, throughout your career, you can confidently expect that students will eagerly respond to learning activities that are real; that connect with their wholesome knowledge, talents, and interests; that take into account the fact that you treat students as real people who are living real lives right now.

I began teaching 26 years ago at the age of 26. Throughout those decades of working with high school and middle school students, some truths have emerged that, I am certain, will remain true throughout the remainder of my career. I would suggest that the following 10 conclusions will be valid for the career of any educator in the near future and, perhaps, forever.

First, there is no limit to the good that can occur when you listen very closely to students. In the hallways, in the cafeteria, in the classroom, at school athletic or musical or theater events, before the first class of the day, and when you happen to see each other in public. Listening is powerful in many ways, one being that it helps you get ideas about the wholesome knowledge, interests, and talents of students. For example, you become aware of a movie that is popular with students. You do some research to find out how much it costs to make the movie and how much business in ticket sales the movie has done so far. Those numbers become the basis for some math problems that fascinate the students and that cause them to learn math.

Second, students are real people who are living real lives right now. Make school connect to their real lives right now. Take advantage of the power of now, the power of relevance, the power of connecting with parts of life that students are already motivated by and committed to. What better case study could a high school social studies teacher use to demonstrate how a bill becomes a law and how citizens can express their ideas than with a state government proposal to increase the requirements for teenagers before they can earn a driver's license?

Third, students will always need teachers who touch the lives of students. Results-driven teachers require themselves to impact very significantly and very positively the academic life of each student. As results-driven teachers cause students to learn math, science, language arts, social studies, and many other subjects, they also cause students to learn how to learn, think, listen, express ideas, manage time, correct mistakes, and reach goals. They cause students to learn about the value of hard work and the self. They also cause students to learn that they are cared about and that their life matters to someone who, before this school year began, they had never met.

Fourth, there will be students who cause problems, get in trouble, and disrupt classes. There will be students who never cause problems, never get in trouble, make wonderful contributions to classes, and are absolutely exemplary. There will be students who are still wavering between good and bad, right and wrong, success or failure. There will be underachievers, overachievers, students who are satisfied with barely passing, students who drop out, and students who earn full scholarships. Results-driven teachers can make a difference for good in the lives of individual students in each of these categories. The need for that difference to be made will be true as long as schools exist.

Fifth, schools will be expected to do more, achieve more, correct more, teach more, feed more, supervise after school more, dispense health care and medication more, intervene with family situations more, and reduce dropouts or failures more. Our society is facing increasing problems, complications, and the lingering aftermath of prior mistakes. Schools will be asked to correct much of that which impacts children and teenagers. Insist that schools be schools, not full-service social impact agencies. The workload will increase. Be prepared. Be very good to heart, mind, body, and soul.

Sixth, we know what works in teaching and we will always know what works, even as we add to what works. To say that we know what works is to say that we know how to cause learning. We know what our best teachers did to cause us to learn. We know what we do with our students that causes them to learn. We can ask colleagues what is working best in their classrooms with their students. We can read the books, journals, dissertations, and websites to identify more examples of highly effective teaching. We can ask our students what experiences at school cause the most and the best learning. As new ideas emerge, new technologies are invented, and new research is published, we can keep up with innovations that help us cause learning.

Seventh, some old ideas, methods, or fads will occasionally be recycled. Education sometimes has a pendulum factor. School districts might provide vocational preparation experiences for middle school students, and then decide that that age group is too young for vocational preparation. Some years later, a suggestion might be made that some 11–14-year-olds could benefit from vocational preparation experiences, so it is tried again. The new curriculum may emphasize currently emerging vocations for which there is high demand or may follow a traditional approach, such as industrial arts, with carpentry projects being made by students. Some ideas in education come, go, and come back. It is wise to ask, before the idea comes back, if this idea is the best way to accomplish current goals.

Eighth, schools will increasingly be expected to deal with complicated psychiatric and/or psychological disorders that students experience. Schools will increasingly be expected to provide early morning supervision, instruction, or enrichment before the school day, after the school day, during some school vacations, and during summer. Staffing and budgeting these extended programs will be very difficult, but society will increasingly assign these tasks to schools. Educators would be well advised to insist that schools be schools—places where the top priority is causing learning—and resist efforts to make schools into 365-day-a-year, social service centers, in which the educational programs become a lower priority.

Ninth, society will continue to expect that schools resolve all issues of academic failure, underperformance, or inadequate performance as measured against standards. All schools will be expected to get all students up to a certain measured minimal level of academic achievement. That is an honorable ideal to pursue, but it does raise issues. For example, some students achieve great athletic success on school sports teams, but schools are not expected or required to get every student up to a minimum standard of physical fitness or athletic achievement. There are legitimate reasons ranging from health factors to family preferences, yet while accepting that there is a range of physical achievement across students, there is no acknowledgment that there could be a range of academic achievement across the student population that schools can impact only to a certain extent. Society will continue to insist that schools get every student up to a certain elevated level of academic achievement. Certainly, a bell-shaped curve of academic achievement throughout the student population is unacceptable; however, in search of the impossible, schools should not be criticized for attaining the possible.

Tenth, the search for quick fixes will continue. This search continues because it never succeeds. Avoid the unproductive teaching fads that race through boards of education, schools, classrooms, education conferences or conventions, professional development programs, or education journals. We know what works, so resist anything that cannot work. Do what works.

The reader may have additional thoughts about what will likely be confronted and experienced by results-driven teachers throughout their careers. On a separate paper, please add your ideas to the list of 10 already provided.

I've heard students say, "We never do much in that class," "The teacher usually lets us talk or listen to music if we finish our work," "He never gives us any homework," "The teacher said he would be right back. He told us to just wait for him," "My grade has come up in that class, but the teacher is three weeks behind on grading papers and putting the grades in the computer," "We watch a lot of videos in that class. It's really easy, but we get bored sometimes," and "She does the same thing every day. Problems on the overhead. Problems on the board. Problems to do out of the book. We never do anything else. I knew more math before this class than I know now."

Those real comments from students are heard far too often about far too many experiences in far too many schools. I have worked at four schools, and at each school I have heard students offer such evaluations as those above. The students were right. I have taught graduate school education classes for 13 years, and one theme from the students in those classes is their frustration with colleagues at their schools. That frustration is based on the minimal effort they see from some teachers. They say, "Why am I working so hard to do so much for these students when other teachers—some of whom get paid more than I do—do so little? Can't the principal do something? Is there anything I can do?"

There is every reason to believe that results-driven teachers who will stay in this profession will continue to notice some colleagues who do very little work, yet who maintain employment. It is possible that teachers at a school, if the school governance structure permits, could propose policies that are designed and intended to impact instructional practices. Some teachers will surpass those policies, and some teachers will work up to the requirements of the policy, but do no more and no less. Other teachers will ignore the policy or defy it. Enforcement of the policy will be the duty of a school administrator.

What is a results-driven teacher who will stay in this profession to do about the frustration that comes with the reality that some of their colleagues are not results-driven and give no indication that they will consider trying to become a results-driven teacher? One answer is to be the most effective results-driven teacher you can be in your classroom. Do all you can where you are with the responsibilities you have, the opportunities you have, and the resources you can get. Offer your ideas to school administrators. Participate on school committees that evaluate policies and practices at school. Contribute ideas to school district committees, task forces, and surveys. Concentrate on your teaching. The biggest and most important difference you can make in this profession is by causing learning within the mind of each student you teach. That will continue to be true throughout your career.

In the graduate school class on curriculum that I have taught to six groups of students, the culminating project in class touches our hearts, minds, and souls. Early in the semester the students, almost all of whom are currently teaching a grade between kindergarten and high school, tell us about the best teacher they ever had. The accounts are always of a person who, despite the terminology used, was a results-driven teacher. The students describe these teachers by saying, "He made me learn," "She never gave up on me," "He always encouraged me," "She took a real interest in me," "She made us want to learn," "He challenged us to do our best. We never wanted to let him down," "He listened to me," "She called my family to tell them about my good work," "She came to our games and other events," "He made learning real. He connected the subject to us and our interests," "She never let people get behind. Everyone had to keep up. Some of us got to do a lot more, but everyone had to master the requirements and then some extra."

Later in the semester, the graduate students write a paper that is based on interviews with five adults who are asked what they remember from their kindergarten through high school experience. The most common answer is a wonderful memory of an individual teacher who touched the person's life during the school years. The memory is usually more on how the teacher taught and how the teacher interacted with students than the actual academic content of the class; yet, the "how" of teaching certainly did impact the success students had in mastering the "what" that was taught.

The semester concludes with each student making a presentation to the class about his or her best teacher. The goal of the presentation is to enable everyone in the class to fully understand and to temporarily experience what it was like to have been in the classroom of the best teacher each student had. Without fail, the stories, the presentations, the memories, and the souvenirs evoke smiles, joy, tears, thanks, and wisdom. Some people bring papers, projects, report cards, or other items from that great teacher's classroom. These items have been kept and cherished for many years, in some cases for decades. Here's a composite example of part of a great teacher presentation:

"I will always remember my 6th-grade math teacher. I hated math. I did so badly in math. My older brother and my older sister were perfect students. Most teachers would always tell me wonderful stories about Shawn and Tasha. They expected me to be exactly like my brother and my sister. I thought that was unfair.

"So I get to sixth grade, and Ms. Hunter is my math teacher. She never said anything to me about my brother or my sister. I liked that. One day she asked everyone in class to write a list of our favorite things—movies, games, sports, and food. A few days later, we started seeing math problems and math activities that related to all of our favorite things. My favorite food has always been raisins. One day Ms. Hunter gave me a box of raisins in class. She had me show it to everyone. We each guessed how many raisins were in the little box. Then she gave a little box of raisins to each student. Everyone counted the raisins in their box. Very few boxes had exactly the same number. We did all kinds of math calculations about those numbers. What I remember is how proud I felt because math finally made sense to me. I know it seems strange, but this little empty raisin box is the one Ms. Hunter gave me 18 years ago. I keep it as a reminder of what a great teacher does to really teach, to really touch a life. I just hope that I always do for my students what Ms. Hunter did for me. So, here's a little box of raisins for each of you. Please take a minute and count your raisins. Then we'll talk about everything we could do in math and in other classes with this raisin information."

The presentations are about teachers who were results-driven teachers long before that term was used in this book or in other ways. Those presentations are about educators who required themselves to be results-driven teachers, whose understanding of their job was to get results and especially to cause learning, whose perception of teaching went far beyond what their employer required. The best teachers have been results-driven teachers not by requirements of a printed job description but by the requirements of their personal ethics, integrity, standards, and job description. Great teachers have always been results-driven teachers. Great teachers now are teachers who drive themselves to get results. The future will be the same. People who students will evaluate as the best teacher they had will be educators who are results-driven teachers.

For educators who will stay in this profession, there are many discouraging or difficult trends in society, families, and the lives of students that add to the complexity of teaching and the overall complications of working in a school. There is hope. Despite the difficulties of today and the increasing complexities that are emerging, students need to be in the classrooms of, under the guidance of, and recipients of encouragement from results-driven teachers. Students must be participants in meaningful, challenging, real learning with results-driven teachers.

The word "teacher" communicates the idea of a person who teaches. To teach means to cause learning. The result of teaching is that learning was caused. Students have always needed to learn and students will always need to learn. For educators who commit to doing whatever it takes within legal, ethical, and professional boundaries to cause learning, a career in this profession offers the opportunity to do work that matters, touches lives, and is fulfilling, rewarding, exhausting, and meaningful. The only teachers needed in education now and in the future are results-driven teachers. Following that example and living up to that standard could be the most important, most effective, most efficient, simplest, lowest costing, most revolutionary, most human, and most enduring educational reform ever. To be a participant in that reform is within the reach of every educator who will do throughout their career what results-driven teachers do. For now, the terms "teacher" and "results-driven teacher" are two different categories. Imagine the vast student achievement when the word teacher includes the perception, perspective, work ethic, standard, and bottom line of being results-driven. At that point, the term results-driven teacher would not be needed, because teacher would mean an educator who gets results, who causes learning. Such dreams must become reality. Any reality does include some problems, but to every problem, there is an equal and opposite solution.

With that thought in mind, we consider in the next chapter how to cope and thrive amid the frustrations and possibilities facing every results-driven teacher.

10

WONDERFUL POSSIBILITIES AND REALISTIC FRUSTRATIONS— HOW TO THRIVE AND COPE

A results-driven teacher takes meticulous care of his or her heart, mind, body, and soul. There are elements of optimism, faith, and hope within results-driven teachers. We are confident that despite the difficulties and the complexities of educating students in kindergarten through high school, we can and we will cause learning. There also must be elements of realism, practicality, and facts within results-driven teachers.

It is realistic, practical, and factual to acknowledge that eight classroom-based hours daily of direct interaction with groups of 25 or so students takes a toll on the human heart, mind, body, and soul. With papers to be graded, lessons to be planned, grades to be entered in the computer, reports to compile, meetings to attend, and professional development programs to attend, a conscientious teacher easily can have 15–20 hours of work weekly beyond the 40 classroom hours. The work at school is done with little or no support staff—teachers do not have secretaries or assistants. The work at school is done with few pauses. If a teacher does have a class period daily or occasionally for planning purposes, the results-driven teacher uses that time to work, not to pause.

When a marathon runner completes that 26-mile run, there can be a combination of invigoration and exhaustion. The invigoration is provided by the joy, satisfaction, achievement, and result: the goal was reached and the finish line crossed. The exhaustion is the reality of the physical, emotional, mental, and spiritual effort required to complete the action of running 26 miles. Successful marathon runners, while training for, participating in, and recovering from the event, must take great care of heart, mind, body, and soul. Marathon runners face wonderful possibilities and realistic frustrations. They must learn how to cope amid very challenging realities so they can create and thrive in wonderful possibilities.

Results-driven teachers and marathon runners have much in common. The same would be true for results-driven teachers and anyone who persistently and successfully pursues and reaches a very demanding, honorable, meaningful goal. Such pursuits and successes are filled with wonderful possibilities and with realistic frustrations. Achievement is experienced by people who learn how to cope amid challenge and who learn how to thrive amid opportunities.

Teaching will break your heart. This does not occur all day, every day, but it is certain to happen occasionally. When a student is killed in a car accident, it breaks your heart. When a student and his family lose all their possessions in a house fire, it breaks your heart. When a student gets arrested for bringing a gun to school, it breaks your heart. When a student of high ability does little or no work and then drops out of school, it breaks your heart. When a student is involved with drugs, it breaks your heart. When a student's family is so negligent that the student is removed from home, it breaks your heart.

A results-driven teacher is not immune to heartbreak. Your relentless determination to cause learning does not separate you from the reality of evil, anguish, immorality, illegality, abuse, or crime that students endure, create, live with, impose on others, bring upon themselves, or have imposed on them by friends, family, or strangers.

But teaching will fill your heart with love and joy, exuberance and contentment as you cause learning, inspire superior work, motivate students, learn from students, master new skills as a teacher, and make a difference in lives.

A results-driven teacher must cope with the heartbreaks. There are at least two useful ways. First, seek the involvement of colleagues, agencies, programs, mentors, and other experts as resources. No one results-driven teacher can resolve every human difficulty faced by all his or her students. Results that results-driven teachers obtain in partnership with other capable, dedicated, ethical, professional, people are beneficial to students. Some complex issues faced by some students must be delegated completely to other experts—some who work in a school system and others who work elsewhere. A colleague and I once discussed issues we were attempting to resolve with students, and we said, "Psychiatry. These issues are not educational, they are psychiatric. Our preparation to be educators did not include psychiatry." Results-driven teachers who defer to experts to resolve issues that are beyond the credentials of a teacher are wisely realistic.

Second, repair the damage when heartbreak hits. The pace of working at a school does not permit a mental health pause in the midst of a continuous action day. An 8th-grade economics class I taught recently had four students whose comments in our class discussion were becoming silly, personal, and counterproductive in direct violation of the requirement that everything in class must be G-rated, legal, and ethical. I said, "Everyone will now practice being quiet and under control for one minute." That was my way of restoring proper self-control and classroom control. Two of the four prior offenders laughed. I immediately called another teacher with whom I have a reciprocal time-out plan. The two students were given work to take with them to the other classroom. They contritely complied, but the misbehavior frustrated me and was on my mind for several days. I expect my students to become as results-driven as I am. Their misbehavior offended, annoyed, disappointed, and embarrassed me. While far short of heartbreak, the situation was still draining some emotional energy from me.

My immediate solution to the disappointment was to increase my energy level with the other students for the rest of the class period. We were very productive. They were very cooperative. Results were abundant. I reflected about the misbehavior and concluded that there were some procedural improvements I could make in the class with this group of students. On our most recent test, the class average was 98% with every student earning an A or B grade. We were getting results, but we could do better. I decided to channel my frustration and disappointment with the two students into energetic action that corrected their errors and that inspired my reflection, so changes in that class, which could prevent similar problems, would be made. To every problem, there is an equal and opposite solution. For the results-driven teacher, that aphorism is encouraging while still being realistic. There will be problems, but they can become the reason to create a solution and improvement that otherwise would not have been imagined.

Part of taking care of the heart is to absolutely embrace and savor the moments of joy, to create moments of achievement, and to vigorously celebrate accomplishments. I recently spoke at an education conference where each person attending was given a satchel. I had no use for this modified briefcase, but it was polite to accept the gift. A student told me that his binder had broken. He was quite concerned about how he would organize, manage, maintain, and find all of his materials. The simple solution was to give him the satchel. He grinned, rejoiced, and expressed appreciation repeatedly. He spoke to me after school to again say thank you. He walked out of school with the confidence of a corporate chief executive officer whose company just set new records for sales, profits, and stock price. There will always be problems, disappointments, frustrations, and heartbreak. Joys will not always just happen, so results-driven teachers create moments of joy in ways as human, humane, and simple as giving a student a pride-creating satchel that otherwise would have sat in a corner unused.

How does a results-driven teacher take care of his or her mind? Is this different from taking care of the emotions, disappointments, sadness, and joy? Here's one similarity for starters. Moments of joy can be created. Classroom activities that create moments of mental exuberance, professional activities that provide mental exercise, reading books that expand knowledge, and personal reflection that brings new insights can be very beneficial for the mind. Those experiences can be designed, created, manufactured, and caused. They may be too rare and insufficient to recharge the mental batteries if they are waited on to appear without intentional effort.

Why does a results-driven teacher need to take good care of his or her mind? Isn't teaching a sufficient mental activity to adequately energize and exercise the mind? Results-driven teaching is a mentally vibrant experience for the students and for the teacher; however, after a day of causing learning in the minds of students, a results-driven teacher may need to refresh, renew, and nourish his or her mind. How is that done? The best answer will need to be personalized for each results-driven teacher, but the following possibilities are good options.

Take a walk outdoors and think as you walk. The thinking part is essential. Sure, the walking is physically beneficial, especially if you maintain an aggressive pace and a lively stride. Still, keep the mind very active as you walk. Ask yourself questions and evaluate various answers. Reflect upon the successes and the difficulties of the day with emphasis on what caused the successes and on what caused the difficulties. Knowing the cause of a success can help create more successes. Knowing the cause of problems or failures can help minimize or prevent them in the future.

Feed the mind the wisdom of the ages and the most recent intellectual discoveries. Continue to learn about the subjects you teach. Continue to learn about how to teach. Read about potential hobbies—if you always wanted to learn to cook, read about cooking. The idea is to continuously exercise, develop, and provoke the mind, to take the mind on a new journey of thoughts that it has never experienced before but will soon go beyond.

There will be times when the mind of a results-driven teacher faces this reality—lack of knowledge. A student could ask an informational question such as, "How much gasoline can be refined from one barrel of oil?" to which the teacher does not know the answer. Printed or electronic resources can provide the answer. Perhaps the student is given the challenge and the responsibility to research the answer to the perplexing question so the student, the teacher, and the class can be informed and can learn together.

Lack of knowledge can occur with more complex situations. What does a school do to effectively educate a 15-year-old 8th grader who is failing 8th grade, who is truant, who is court involved, whose family is dysfunctional, whose father is in jail, whose family was just evicted from an apartment, and whose natural artistic talent is almost superhuman, but is of no interest to the student to use, develop, or apply toward a career? Did any one educator have sufficient career preparation to know what to do to resolve the issues facing that student? Did most teachers anticipate that they would have students who are in the midst of such circumstances? Who are the experts and what are the resources available to address these circumstances? What role can or should schools play in those circumstances that, although impacting how the student does at school, are not educational in nature or in origin? As results-driven teachers face such issues, new knowledge may be needed. What the mind currently knows and is aware of may not be enough to address the issues.

The mind of a results-driven teacher will need to grow in awareness and expertise throughout the teaching career. The teaching you do and the students who you teach are continually in motion. What you teach, how you teach, and which students you teach are different each year of your career. Accept that dynamism. Expand your mind's knowledge and ability to keep up with that dynamism, to learn from it, and to make it work.

A results-driven teacher expects and needs his or her body to be at peak performance each day. How is this done? In teaching, we know what works. In physical health and in physical fitness, we know what works. There are no mysteries, surprises, or secrets to attaining, maintaining, and improving physical health. Eat proper amounts of nutritious foods at the right times daily. Get exercise every day with sufficient endurance, and demand that your heart and your lungs are pushed. Get enough sleep daily. Drink ample water daily. Avoid tobacco, avoid drugs, and limit sugar.

There are many excellent books about physical exercise. There are very effective exercise programs that are taught through classes at fitness centers. Read those books and do what they recommend. Take those classes and get in the habit of daily exercise. You and a family member or friend can exercise together if that is helpful, encouraging, and practical for you. The experts on physical exercise and on nutrition eagerly share their insights and expertise via their books, classes, and other communication or instruction. Benefit from their knowledge.

Results-driven teachers need to take great care of heart, mind, body, and soul. The ideas above refer to care of the heart, mind, and body. What does the soul have to do with teaching? How can the soul of a results-driven teacher be nurtured, renewed, and supported?

Let's establish a common understanding of soul, especially as it relates to results-driven teachers. In theological terms, the soul can be understood in many ways depending on the religion, traditions, teachings, philosophy, or dogma of any particular system of belief. When considering the soul of a results-driven teacher, we are thinking of that system of beliefs, convictions, meaning, and purpose that the teacher brings to the job of teaching. The source of that system of beliefs may be entirely or partially based on a major religion, philosophy, science, psychological construct, particular religious writer, philosopher, church, or organization, or may be purely individual. Our point here is not to debate the truth or error of a person's deepest held belief system's origin but rather to reflect upon the importance of and the potential impact of lifelong development of a system of beliefs, convictions, meaning, and purpose.

How does a results-driven teacher nurture his or her soul as it relates to the job of teaching? Change the question with the above explanation of soul and possible answers may become more apparent. How does a results-driven teacher nurture his or her system of beliefs, convictions, meaning, or purpose as that system relates to the job of teaching?

What about beliefs? What do you believe about the job of teaching? A results-driven teacher believes that his or her duty is to cause each student to learn. This belief is the inspiration and standard for doing the job of a teacher in the ways that cause learning for, with, in, and by all students.

Acknowledging what you believe about teaching, students, learning, and school can be the starting point of analyzing the source, worthiness, impact, and practicality of those beliefs, as well as the integrity and honor revealed through those beliefs, whether those beliefs have changed during your career, and whether those beliefs need to be revised now.

Here's an example. One source for my belief that as a teacher I must be a results-driven teacher, meaning that I must cause each student to learn, is the time I have spent working in advertising and marketing for three large companies. Those companies insisted on results. My work ethic was established through employers who absolutely insisted on results.

Another source for my belief that it is a teacher's duty, obligation, purpose, and responsibility to cause learning is that I expect people who teach me to cause me to learn. I teach my students so learning is caused, just as I expected people who were my teachers to cause me to learn. That idea comes from the Christian standard of "do unto others as you would have them do unto you." This is what was mentioned earlier as the Golden Rule for results-driven teachers.

Consider convictions. What are the most deeply held beliefs that you have about teaching? What certain convictions do you find at the absolute core of your conscience that reveal the essential truths about teaching as you understand truth?

I have always believed in the depth of a certain conviction that Socratic questioning is an effective way to cause learning. With each class of students, I will vary the questions to build upon their strengths or knowledge, interests or talents. The commonality is a Socratic questioning approach. My conviction about Socratic questioning is based on reading Plato's "Meno" many times to understand that quintessential presentation of the Socratic approach. My conviction about Socratic questioning is based also on 22 years of seeing that approach cause learning with my students in middle school, high school, college, and graduate school classes. My conviction about the Socratic method is further supported by many of the superior teachers I had who used that method so effectively.

How does a results-driven teacher develop, strengthen, challenge, and nurture his or her convictions? Identify them, know their origin, evaluate their merit, evaluate what actions those convictions impel you to take, and determine how honorable, ethical, and beneficial those convictions are.

Also consider meaning. What does it mean to you to be a teacher? What personal meaning do you find in doing the work of teaching? How meaningful is it to you to work directly with students in classrooms? What explains the life-affirming, life-changing depth of meaning that some educators find in and through teaching?

For me, teaching is unsurpassed in meaning because teaching is the work I do best and care about most. When I have done jobs other than teaching, I often wondered what it would be like right then to be teaching at that moment. When I teach, I do not wonder what it would be like to be doing any other job at that moment because teaching is the one and only job I know of that renews my mind, energizes my body, nurtures my heart, and stirs my soul.

Yes, there are times when teaching has the opposite impact. Teaching can perplex the mind, exhaust the body, break the heart, and agonize the soul. The times when teaching has those impacts are not the parts that define the whole. Those unfortunate parts are not to be ignored or denied; however, they are not to be allowed to control.

A results-driven teacher can have more control over his or her job than it might appear to some educators who continually bemoan the increasing list of problems and the increasing list of tasks added annually to the job. As long as a teacher has the authority to control what happens in his or her classroom, that teacher has an enviable level of authority, autonomy, freedom, and trust.

Even as governments expand their regulatory involvement in what students are to learn, results-driven teachers continue to prize their professional freedom to decide how learning will be caused. It is through how they cause learning, interact with students, design lessons, create fascinating homework projects, encourage students, and discipline students that results-driven teaching and results-driven teachers most effectively touch the lives of students.

It is time for the reader to ask the question that has been simmering during this chapter: "Keen, what's teaching got to do with health of heart, mind, body, and soul? Why consider emotional, mental, physical, and spiritual health and well-being as part of the results-driven teaching concept?"

Good question. First, I gladly defer to experts on those categories of health and well-being for detailed, expert guidance. Second, a results-driven teacher draws from many resources including her or his own heart, mind, body, and soul. Third, there are situations that occur in schools that can temporarily reduce or deplete the vitality and the health of heart, mind, body, and soul. That vitality and health must be restored so more serious health conditions do not develop and so devotion to the job does not decline. Fourth, to maximize the results of the wonderful possibilities within teaching and to effectively cope with the realistic frustrations within teaching, superior health and fitness of heart, mind, body, and soul are very useful strengths, resources, and assets.

What are some of the wonderful possibilities that can occur in the career of a results-driven teacher? Throughout history, right now and most likely forever in the future, results-driven teachers will have the opportunity during each moment of each school day to cause learning, to touch lives, to make a difference. There are some more specific possibilities that may vary depending on unique goals of the school where you work or depending on areas of emphasis that school districts, local governments, state governments, the national government, or community groups are advocating or opposing. Some of the possibilities follow.

Some middle school students can easily, successfully, and willingly complete the middle school curriculum in two school years instead of the common three-year time period allocated to middle schools. These students could master the curriculum of 6th, 7th, and 8th grades in two years. That creates wonderful possibilities for a hybrid third year that could include some middle school advanced work and some initial high school work. That creates a wonderful possibility for moving directly into high school one year ahead of schedule—yes, social maturity can be a question, issue, or concern; however, experts in the areas of accelerated learning and in gifted and talented education can provide the needed guidance.

In places where middle school is already two years, perhaps 7th and 8th grades, some students from elementary school, who have mastered the 6th-grade elementary school curriculum early, could move to middle school one year ahead of schedule. Again, social maturity will be a factor to consider.

The total kindergarten through 8th-grade curriculum and process need not require nine years for each student. Imagine the wonderful possibility of "grade 8 ½." A student in that grade has completely mastered the elementary and the middle school curricula, but for a variety of reasons, it is agreed that going to high school right after completing 7th grade is not advisable. Grade 8 ½ could be a combination of discovery, inquiry, research, projects, self-paced computer instruction, group work with other students in grade 8 ½, some high school classes taught online or via a variety of independent study, much reading, community education experiences, and community/school service work. A similar possibility exists to create grade 5 ½ for an elementary school student who has mastered the kindergarten through 5th-grade curriculum, but for whom advancing to middle school is not advisable right after fourth grade.

More high school students will increasingly blend their senior year of high school with their freshman year of college or with technical/vocation training that previously required and awaited graduation from high school. There are many explanations for what makes this type of wonderful possibility needed by more high school students. One reason is that in recent decades, some classes that were typically taught only in high schools have been taught in middle school. When a middle school student successfully completes geometry in 8th grade, the high school math sequence is impacted because by the junior and senior year of high school, that student is ready for math classes that, until recently, were more commonly taught in college only.

For results-driven teachers who work in high schools, there are many important possibilities to be explored with the range of innovations that stretch from preventing 9th-grade failures to maximizing new opportunities for 12th graders. As innovative as some ideas may seem, a review of the history of education in this country will find references to grades 13 and 14 in some schools many decades, if not a century, ago. Learn about and learn from those historical precedents, but do not be limited by them as you help create the wonderful possibilities that are needed by students now.

One teacher might say, "If only they could learn how to repair cars or build houses. They would work on that. They would take that seriously. We could include math and science so easily. They would read about cars. They could study the history of houses, architecture, and communities. We could include endless technology. Some of these 7th graders just are not going to make it through year after year of the typical classes they have to take."

That is a realistic frustration of a 7th-grade teacher who is attempting to get a 14-year-old to find the lowest common factor of a set of numbers. The student did not do the math last year in 7th grade and he is not doing it now, but when he helped his father and his uncle with a new roof they put on their house, he did the math, he did the work, and he set the pace for the entire work crew. If that 7th grader could take vocational education classes at school, could develop his roofing skills, could acquire additional construction knowledge and skill, he would have a different perspective toward, attitude about, and commitment to school. He could also become a results-driven student.

The teacher's realistic frustration with the student is matched by the student's realistic frustration with school. Certainly these matching frustrations suggest that a wonderful possibility is waiting to be championed by results-driven teachers who (a) make their instruction real by connecting learning with the wholesome knowledge, talents, and interests of students and (b) advocate for school experiences such as vocational education programs for middle school students.

When students are organized by age, there is a variety of achievement levels. If all eight-year-olds are together, the variety, the range of academic accomplishments will be broad.

When students are organized by academic accomplishments, there is a variety of ages. If all students who read at the 4th-grade level are together, the range of ages will be broad.

What's an elementary school to do given the above realities? What wonderful possibilities exist or can be created to cope with the realistic frustrations? There could be more productive groupings for elementary schools than kindergarten through 5th grade or 6th grade. If there are reasons against or barriers to creating a kindergarten through 2nd-grade school and a 3rd-grade through 5th- or 6th-grade school, then within a school building some variations could be considered and tried.

Another realistic frustration is when teenagers—illiterate, low functioning, far behind grade level, court involved, or fully capable, actually on grade level, actually on schedule to graduate from high school—drop out of high school. How does a results-driven teacher cope with this situation? How do you help that student thrive in school?

There is not a one-size-fits-all answer. The ideal before-school program may work with some students. A unique combination of classes and a job could work for other students. A social worker–teacher–law enforcement officer trio could work with these students. Alternative educational programs at an altogether different school could be helpful for some students. One adult who spends five caring minutes with the student at the start of each day might be all it takes. There are enough success stories in education to confirm that from each realistic frustration can come a wonderful opportunity to cause learning, to touch a life.

There probably will always be media stories about private schools versus public schools. This is a false battle, although the news stories create real frustrations. Many legal rights and protections guaranteed to students, faculty, and staff in public schools do not always exist in private schools. Private schools select who is accepted into the school and who stays at the school. Public schools accept and work with every student who may legally attend.

Many if not most private schools are not able to, are not organized to, and do not expect themselves to provide the totality of educational services that public schools offer. Private schools with a religious affiliation obviously serve a purpose that tax-supported schools cannot serve. Resist this debate about public versus private. Thrive where you are.

One part of the public and private debate is vouchers, the use of tax money for attendance at private schools. Our society does not use transportation vouchers. If you ride public transportation, there is probably some tax support or subsidy of that. Our society does not give you a voucher to help pay for a car if you select private transportation over public transportation. A public park is supported in part with tax dollars. If someone joins the private swim club rather than use the tax-supported swimming pool at the public park, that person has no reason to expect a country club voucher. The final warning on this topic is to private schools. If you seek to maintain your private status and nature, resist the temptation of public tax money. Where public tax dollars go, you also find policies, regulations, regulators, and rules.

Teenage or younger criminals need new institutions that are hybrid jails/schools. Teachers can help point out this need and can endorse this idea. Creating these new facilities may be politically complicated, so beware of the time it may require and of the new frustrations that political and bureaucratic endeavors include. You may prefer or need to let someone else lead on this topic, but do offer leaders your perspective and offer your perspective persistently.

School boards and other governmental bodies will expect you to do the nearly impossible right now and the absolutely impossible next year. Each task the school board expects you to complete may be quite possible, but the always increasing list of tasks may have reached the nearly impossible level. Communicate reality to school board members. Work with colleagues, perhaps on a school committee or on a school district committee, to create realistic recommendations for the school board. Let them know that you eagerly accept responsibility for getting learning results, and show by the results you get that your standards equal or surpass theirs. Let them know that, from your unique vantage point of the classroom, you have essential insight about what is needed to make those results happen. Be ready to answer the question "What do you need from us to get the desired results from you students?" Express appreciation when that support is actually provided. Ask questions when that support is delayed or denied.

It is frustrating when a student is failing your class but is doing very well in another class. The student has shown the ability to succeed and is missing the wonderful possibilities of additional success. Results-driven teachers can create these wonderful possibilities by finding out what is causing the success in the other class and by bringing as much of those causes of success into other classrooms where that student is not doing as well.

On a separate paper, write some of the realistic frustrations that you encounter in your work as an educator, as well as some of the wonderful possibilities that you have identified, that you are working on, and that you dream of in your work as an educator. In addition, consider how one of those wonderful possibilities could help you address, impact, or resolve one of the realistic frustrations.

Let's add another thought about perspective, because an essential—in truth, the fundamental—characteristic of a results-driven teacher is the perspective toward the job of teaching. Because a results-driven teacher perceives the job of a teacher as getting results and, above all, causing learning, that person does the job of a teacher in ways that get results.

Teaching is not a to-do list job for a results-driven teacher any more than rearing a child is a to-do list job for a conscientious, devoted, loving parent. That parent simply cannot say, "Well, I loved my child this morning. I fixed her a good breakfast and I gave her a ride to school. I can mark loving my child off today's to-do list." Rearing the child is a continuous duty of, adventure for, and blessing for a conscientious, devoted, loving, parent. There are times when the parent and child are face-to-face, and there are times when they are at separate places, but the parenting is perpetual.

There are times when a results-driven teacher is face-to-face, brain-to-brain, mind-to-mind, idea-to-idea, question-to-answer with students. There are other times when the results-driven teacher and students are in separate places; however, the results-driven teacher's thinking about teaching, extra effort to cause learning, and dedication of time toward teaching are continuing.

This certainly is not to say that a results-driven teacher is a workaholic. This is to say that results-driven teachers have a perspective about teaching and about themselves that intricately includes teaching as a vital part of the definition of self. For results-driven teachers, causing learning is an expression of who we are, what we are, and why we are. Despite the current and future frustrations, results-driven teachers confidently, persistently, and effectively continue to teach in pursuit and frequent fulfillment of wonderful possibilities, such as the following preview:

"Welcome to Wilson High School. You are the class of 2018. When you complete your three years here, you will be fully prepared for college, career, the military, vocational training, plus other duties as adults, family members, and citizens. As you know, high school used to be four years long, and some of you in selective, extended high school programs may use that option, but most of you will be ready to graduate in three years.

"Let's watch this preview of the next three years that await you at Wilson. The last part of this vicarious video is interactive, so be ready to get up and move. You will be surrounded with video images that, as you know, appear without use of any screens. This technology uses portal immersion laser lumination systems to create visual images. So watch, please, as a member of the class of 2015 takes you on a video virtual tour of the next three years. When you hear the traditional high school graduation music being played, please stand up and walk in place. You will be convinced visually that you are walking across a stage getting your high school diploma."

For people who work in schools during the next 10, 20, or 30 years, there will be amazing applications of emerging and yet-to-be-invented technologies. The books students once carried in bulky backpacks may be on discs, may be downloaded onto handheld receivers, or may be transmitted via currently unknown methods. More classrooms may be increasingly paperless, with computers of all sizes and electronic communication replacing papers to distribute or collect. Perhaps books and discs or downloads will peacefully coexist. There will be many wonderful possibilities with new technological resources. There will be new frustrations as the new technologies work, then do not work, do not make sense, then make sense, are not user-friendly, then are user-friendly.

Students will still come to school bringing their hopes and their hurts, their dreams and their difficulties, their successes and their failures, their family strengths and their family troubles. Teachers and students will gather in classrooms. Each desk may be Internet ready. Each classroom may be a collection of electronic wonders.

Each classroom will also be a collection of human beings with a wide array of abilities, strengths, needs, problems, achievements, and possibilities. Whether from a book or from a screen, students will need to master reading, writing, math, and much more. Whether a book, a screen, or both are used, the essential factor will still be the interaction between teacher, student, ideas, and learning.

The world, nation, states, and cities will be more crowded and more competitive. Demographic trends and decades of money mismanagement will bring severe financial issues to governments that went so far in debt earlier or that delayed so many urgent expenses that financial problems forced severe actions. Other societal concerns—divorce, crime, poverty, illegal immigration, diseases, terrorism, juvenile crime, job outsourcing, and more—will continue.

Amid all of the challenges of the years ahead, results-driven teachers will still be able to cause learning with, by, and for students. The future in general and the future of education in particular each hold as many wonderful possibilities as realistic frustrations, problems, and crises. The future and the present moment have this in common—there is no limit on how much learning can be caused. Results-driven teachers now and forever can and will cause learning.

A few days ago a former student visited me at school. He was there to tell me that he would be involved in the youth Sunday worship service at his church. He invited me to attend. Because of his invitation one year ago, I attended his youth Sunday service. I will do that again. He will appreciate my attendance. He will be pleased with the time and effort an educator invested in him. I will hear important thoughts from the teenagers who present their beliefs through songs and skits, through prayers and mini-sermons. I will learn as much as I teach, probably more. My only required action is to be there. This is easy, yet this is one more wonderful possibility that is irresistible and quite simple. In this case, all I have to do is show up. What learning will I cause? The student will know that I care about the real life that he is living right now.

In two weeks I will attend a piano recital of a 7th-grade scholar whose email and later in-person invitation greatly pleased me. I attended his recital a year ago, and we had wonderful discussions about it. Youth Sunday church services and piano recitals are possible topics of conversations that begin with the following: "Hi. Any plans for the weekend?" as a student leaves school on Friday afternoon. Sometimes the wonderful possibilities emerge from a very simple, human, friendly encounter. The learning that is caused may create lifelong memories. More and more graduate school students of mine emphasize that the best teacher they ever had seemed to always be there, to always show up, to attend the school events, to attend the events outside of school, and to continuously expand the foundation for results-driven teaching by being there, by showing up, by putting concern and interest into actions that children and teenagers not only notice and appreciate, but respond to in ways that bring new energy, new commitments, and new possibilities back to the classroom.

The wonderful possibilities for and the realistic frustrations of teaching intersect at school. What is a school? Is it a place where anything and everything that impacts or involves children and teenagers becomes part of the responsibility of the school? If that concept of a school is allowed to replace the concept of a school as a place of learning, will some wonderful possibilities be compromised and some new frustrations be added? Results-driven teachers are encouraged, if not warned, to vigorously defend the purpose of a school as a place where learning is caused, not as a place where all social services potentially needed by children and teenagers are provided, managed, or communicated.

The purpose of a school is to cause learning. The highest priority learning commonly includes academic areas such as math, science, language arts, social studies, and other fundamentals. The learning can include vocational training, computer skills, fine arts, home economics, health, physical education, driver's education, and much more. Additional learning can come from extracurricular activities such as clubs, marching band, athletics, or other student organizations that schools provide or endorse.

The purpose of a school is to cause learning, but that purpose is not to cause every possible bit of learning about every possible topic or skill, interest, or need. Priorities must be established so actions are directed toward known, specific, measurable, achievable, school-compatible goals. Every group that would like to include its message, subject, agenda, and curriculum in the school curriculum cannot be allowed to do that.

Schools are not and should not be 24-hour-a-day, social service agencies. The "schoolness" of school can get lost if more and more people see school as the place where everything from meals to clothing, health care to psychiatric or psychological counseling services, daycare to summer activities are provided, while students also go to class and do school work. Just because people ages 5–18 attend school does not mean that schools must be the comprehensive agency through which every possible need of that age group is addressed. Schools are at their best when relentlessly and precisely concentrating on doing the work of educating, of causing learning. When that highest priority of schools is diluted by an endless list of well-intended social engineering, social services, or other endeavors, the purpose of a school can become vague. Vague goals are not reached. An organization that attempts to become everything to everyone can become of little or no help to anyone. For the wonderful possibilities of learning to be fulfilled, the realistic frustrations of excessive, peripheral tasks must be avoided.

Imagine that it is a late Friday afternoon. School dismissed an hour ago. The emails have been answered. Grades have been entered in the computer and the paper grade book. Student work to be graded this weekend is well organized in files that are in the briefcase. You have caused much learning this week. You have thrived on making many wonderful possibilities become real achievements. You have coped with, endured, and resolved the realistic frustrations of the week. The energetic momentum of the week has stopped and you realize that you are weary. Go home and relax. Play, exercise, watch a movie, take a nap, walk the dog, cook your favorite meal. Listen to soothing music. Enjoy activities with your family. Take good care of your heart, mind, body, and soul so you can cause more learning on Monday morning when Tasha and Shawn, two wonderful possibilities, enter your classroom.

With Monday morning in mind, and with Tasha and Shawn also in mind, in the next chapter we consider some case studies about school, teachers, students, causing learning, and being results-driven.

⓫

CASE STUDIES AND PROFILES—
RESULTS-DRIVEN
TEACHING IN ACTION

"When do we get to do another project?" the student asked; his question was completely sincere and was, for the teacher, completely unexpected. The teacher, Jason Prather, instantly realized that the 11th-grade math student was asking for more work. The only problem was that with eight school days left in the school year, Mr. Prather had not planned another homework project for his math students. How could Mr. Prather properly honor the student's very worthy question?

Thinking very quickly, Mr. Prather decided to include the student's thinking as part of the answer to the student's own question. This results-driven math teacher replied, "Soon. What did you have in mind?"

The student, Brian Roberts, said quite earnestly, "Well, I'm really interested in roller coasters. I know we have to do math, but there must be some math in roller coasters." Before Mr. Prather could reply another student raised her hand, so Julie was called on.

Julie eagerly said, "I'm really interested in fashion. It has math in it. The prices of clothes or the money designers make. I'd like to do some project about fashion."

The faces in the classroom were lighting up. The eyes were glowing. The minds were very lively. Whitney was called on next and said, "I'm a good cook, but I'd like to know more about cooking. Can I do a math project on cooking?" She seemed ready to begin working immediately. Mr. Prather realized that Whitney, along with Brian and Julie, were saying, "Please let us do more work. Please let us learn more. Please let us get more results."

Mr. Prather had an idea and said, "Great suggestions. Let's make this work. Everyone write down a topic you would like to do a math project on. You heard what Brian, Julie, and Whitney are interested in. Write down two or three of your G-rated, legal, ethical interests." Everyone smiled. Mr. Prather insisted that the standard of G-rated, legal, and ethical was always taught, followed, and reinforced.

Now it was time for a lightning round. Each student answers the same question. Sometimes a lightning round is designed to confirm that everyone in the class knows the correct answer. "Who was president of the United States during the Civil War?" is a question for a social studies class. The teacher makes direct contact visually with each successive student as one student after another replies "Lincoln." In 20 seconds or so, every student has participated and the teacher has had direct interactive contact with each student. This form of a lightning round can ignite some thinking as a student silently wonders, "It's Lincoln. I know it's Lincoln. But why is the teacher still calling on people if she already heard the right answer?"

Mr. Prather will use a lightning round this time to get a different answer from each student. He says, "Okay, this can work. Roller coasters, fashion, and cooking are interests that three of you have. We can create a math project that will work with those interests and with other hobbies. So everyone think of a G-rated, legal, ethical interest of yours or hobby of yours that you would like to do a math project about. Think silently for the next 10 seconds, and then we'll hear from everyone taking turns."

Ten seconds of silent indoor thinking was a common activity in Mr. Prather's classroom. The brain can create new ideas in very little time when given the opportunity to seriously think. The lightning round began as Mr. Prather called on Suzanne. Each student knew the sequence to follow, so the student sitting behind Suzanne was next and then the sequence continued through the rows of desks in the classroom.

"Chocolate."

"College."

"Basketball."

"Space travel."

"Track and field."

"Fashion."

"Criminal investigations."

"Cars."

"Soccer."

"Bicycles."

"Triathlons."

"Camping."

"Travel."

"Global warming."

"Chess."

"Politics."

"Roller coasters."

"Sailing."

"Reading."

"Tennis."

"Television broadcasting."

"Cooking."

"Paying for the prom."

"Getting a job."

"Paying for college."

Mr. Prather smiled as he heard the topics and as he imagined the learning results that could occur by exploring the connections between those topics and algebra, geometry, arithmetic, math. What especially fascinated Mr. Prather was that the students were creatively and eagerly using their brains in ways that would lead them to use, exercise, develop, and challenge their minds.

Mr. Prather's students knew the difference between their brain and their mind. As Mr. Prather had explained to them, "The brain adds one plus one to get two. The mind explains and applies the idea, concept, process, meaning, and use of addition." The brain is the foundation of the mind. Information and thoughts in the brain become building blocks for mental construction work done by the mind.

The brain and mind symbiosis was very important to Mr. Prather, as was the importance of taking each student beyond the procedural functions of the brain into the unlimited results that the mind can imagine and that the student can achieve.

Mr. Prather had an idea. His mind was racing through details of a way that each student could explore the topic he or she had mentioned. He said, "How's this sound? You each create a magazine. I'll give you the requirements such as front cover, back cover, table of contents, letters to the editor, number of articles, number of advertisements, overall length, connections to math, use of pictures, and how much of the magazine must be your original writing or drawing. The topic of the magazine is the topic you just mentioned unless you have already thought of something more fascinating to you. Does this make sense? Will this work?"

Several students smiled their yes answer. A few others nodded their heads to show yes. There were no complaints of "when will we ever need to know this?" or "why do we have to do this?" The teacher is in charge, yet the teacher and the students are working together to create a challenging, fascinating, learning-causing, intellectual activity that will get results. The students will use their brains to do the functional, procedural, action parts of the project. The students will use their minds as they develop the concept, the mental picture, the idea of, the ideal of, and then the design and plan for their project. The students and Mr. Prather know that the results will be outstanding, and learning will be caused. The classroom community of mutually supportive and appreciative members will thrive. The teacher and the students will learn from, with, and for each other and for themselves individually. Each project will have much math within it and will have creativity, art, writing, investments of time, and pride of accomplishment. The students will be driven toward superior results and will achieve superior results. Their brains and their minds will thrive.

The mind of a results-driven teacher understands teaching as being much more than a brain activity. Of course, results-driven teachers seek to impact the brain of each student, but that is merely the beginning of the learning adventure when a student is taught by a results-driven teacher. Results-driven teaching and learning brings new information into the brains of each student in ways that leads to new thoughts emerging from the minds of each student.

It is common to hear someone say, "I changed my mind." It is quite uncommon to hear anyone say, "I changed my brain." The difference in those two statements transcends semantics. If a person who did not know that Abraham Lincoln was born in Kentucky is informed of that historical fact, his or her brain can record that bit of information in the memory. Being aware of Lincoln's birthplace does not change anyone's mind about how Lincoln did the job of president of the United States.

A person could read biographies of Lincoln, read biographies of other noteworthy Americans of the 1830–1865 era, read books that thoroughly analyze events of 1830–1865, take a class in U.S. history, hear lectures on Lincoln, visit a museum display about Lincoln, read the verbatim texts of Lincoln's speeches and debates, attend historical re-enactments of events from the Lincoln era, and then think deeply about all of those sources of information, ideas, and insight. The result could be a different perspective about Lincoln than what was thought prior to the new learning. A person might change his or her mind about Lincoln because of a profound educational experience that impacted thinking, not that merely added another bit of information to be recalled.

Results-driven teaching fills the brain in order to fulfill the mind. Filling the brain does not mean reaching a capacity level beyond which the brain cannot accept, absorb, receive, or recall more information. Filling the brain does mean that educational activities are designed for, provided for, and experienced by students so the mental content within the brain, the reservoir of information, is always expanding in quantity, quality, depth, and complexity. From these continually expanding and deepening intellectual resources within the brain, there can emerge continually more accurate, insightful, profound, wise, meaningful, and reasoned thinking.

Once, when one teacher was absent from school, I agreed to teach her class for one period. I joined the group of polite, scholarly, cordial 8th graders, and we began a lively discussion of economics. We began with what was then current economics data: the stock market was down over 1% the previous day, the price of gold increased the day before to a 25-year high, the price of gasoline had recently increased 25 cents per gallon in our community, and interest rates had just been increased again to levels not seen for several years. They asked probing questions. Their brains had absorbed new information that had intrigued, provoked, activated, and energized their minds.

One young scholar was especially fascinated with the recent and rapid increase in the price of gold. Her question was from her mind: "What's it mean?" Our discussion deepened and widened as we went from brain information to mind thinking, reasoning, analyzing, and learning.

The only teaching tools I had used were the catalyst of connection and the force of fascination. I knew that all of these students were highly successful in math. They found the potentially puzzling intricacies of numbers to be compelling mental challenges that took their minds from curiosity to contemplation to conclusion. The financial statistics I presented connected with their knowledge of math and led them to do much more than calculate percentage changes in prices; rather, the statistics helped them make sense out of the numbers, to find meaning in and from the numbers, to think thoughts they had never pondered before. I was filling their brains so they could fulfill their minds. The statistics I presented connected with their skills in math and their eagerness to use math for more than numerical calculation. They used math to gain insight, understanding, wisdom, and learning. The numbers and the related ideas fascinated these students such that their minds became the driving force in our work. My resolve to be their results-driven teacher energized their resolve to be results-driven students. Everyone learned. Everyone experienced results.

Let's use math as an example. To cover math means to go over math with emphasis on short-term recall of bits of information. In a classroom where the educator covers math with students, the outcome likely will be that some students recall some of the facts about math. Some students will pass the test that measures recall. Other students will fail that test. Few if any students will fully master math if the classroom activity only minimally expands the number of facts in the brain and is unlikely to energize thoughts from the mind.

The results-driven teacher has an understanding of teaching that is significantly different from a "cover the content" educator. Covering material is what classroom clerks do. Causing learning is what results-driven teachers do. Causing unlimited learning is what the best results-driven teachers do.

How can a teacher cause unlimited learning? Doesn't the learning stop when the bell rings and class ends? The learning does not have to stop then. Students who have learned, for example, that gold's price reached a 25-year high can make sense out of that new price and understand what that new price means internationally, nationally, locally, and personally. They will have experienced a fulfillment of their mind that prepares them for, creates hunger for, compels them to seek, and is satisfied only by more, deeper learning. Those students will continue to think, read, wonder, ask, and learn more about the topics we explored after our time together ended. Our time together was limited. The learning caused during and after that time together is unlimited because their minds are sufficiently aroused now to accept no limit on learning about these topics. They will continue to find ways to properly feed and fill their brains so they can fulfill their minds and, in so doing, fulfill life's most magnificent hopes, dreams, duties, adventures, challenges, and callings.

For out next case study, we will listen to the thoughts of a results-driven teacher, Katie Fletcher, as she drives home from school. Katie is talking to herself, but we get to listen:

"That's it. I've had enough. Why does some 15-year-old future criminal think it is okay to yell and tell me to get out of her face? Being anywhere near her face is the last place I would ever want to be. How am I supposed to deal with that student? Is she going to do the French homework I assigned? Is she going home to yell at adults there? Are there any sensible adults at her home or does everyone in her life yell at each other?

"I have to quit this job. I still think I'm a great teacher. I know French, the language, the culture, everything. I really know it. So many of these students just will not work. They get in the way of everyone else who is willing to work and who is eager to learn.

"Then there was the other awful incident. I can still see the blood. It was awful. That 16-year-old thug pushed the other student and tripped him. Bang. As he fell, his head hit the edge of the door and blood was everywhere. I called 911. They came and took the victim to the hospital. He will recover from the injury, but I will never recover from what happened next. The criminal was not arrested. The police and juvenile justice system seem to think that misbehavior at school is a crime only if it is the most severe felony. The same type of assault resulting in a 911 call anywhere else would mean the thug is arrested. Oh, no, we can't do that at school.

"Here's the worst part. Because no weapon was involved and the victim is going to heal, the criminal gets to come back to school. Who is he going to bloody up next? He's in that federal government category of students who can be suspended from school for only 10 days each year. He had already been suspended for eight days before this assault. Who can teach in a school system where crime is not punished?

"I have to quit. It breaks my heart, but I have no choice. I've tried and tried. I've done everything I can. The good students deserve better. The incorrigible students need to be removed and educated or given job training or rehabilitated or all of that in some tightly confined place.

"Why did it come to this? I always wanted to teach. I always intended to be the teacher who amazed and inspired students. Something went wrong. I think I know what went wrong.

"Schools just have not kept up with the times. The stores where I shop have more security than schools do. Stores take actions to prevent or prosecute theft of a $20 shirt more than schools take action to prevent or prosecute misbehavior or crime at school. The school district officials have their comfortable and safe offices. Schools are not as comfortable or safe, but the officials don't take us seriously when we ask for surveillance cameras, metal detectors, law enforcement officers in schools, and more alternative education or rehabilitation programs for incorrigible students.

"It's like schools are still organized for 1960, but it's not 1960 anymore. I've heard teachers who have worked here for 25 years say that the school has the same administrative staff structure as it did decades ago, but there are more and more administrators at central office. What do those people do? They need to believe us when we say that reality in schools today is not what it was in 1960, 1970, or 1980. There are some serious problems that need new solutions. How can I teach French in a school where juvenile criminals are arrested on Saturday, released on Sunday, and heard bragging in school about beating the system on Monday?

"Well, I quit. We are asked to do too much, and we are given inadequate resources or support. They say, 'Hi, Ms. Fletcher. This is Frank. He just got out of juvenile detention. Please teach him French.' Frank assaulted two people. Frank stole from them. Frank is a repeat offender. Bonjour, Frank. Get real. Maybe Frank needs to go to the school district's central office or to the governor's mansion or to the White House for school. The people in those places seem to think that teaching Frank is very easy, so let's give them the opportunity to work with Frank. They would not last a day.

"How can I keep coming to work in such as unhealthy atmosphere? My safety is at risk. My teaching is undermined. Good students are cheated by a system that surrounds them with thugs. I'd love to teach. It was always my dream job. This is not the job I expected. It is not the job it should be. I quit."

Katie is telling the truth about serious incidents, trends, and problems. Katie is also honestly expressing her frustrations and fears, her disappointments and despair, her fading dreams and determination.

Katie's appeal to school district officials and to political leaders to fully realize the current facts about school is genuine and based on reality. Will those officials and leaders get serious about identifying and dealing with the realities at schools? Will they act in time to impact Katie's decision?

What is the results-driven teaching reply to Katie's thoughts? First, the reply is not one of unfounded rationalization or magical optimism that would tell Katie, "Oh, it's not so bad. The students don't mean any harm. It will get better." Second, the reply is not "All jobs have problems. It may not be any better if you change jobs." Katie's concern is the unique set of unresolved problems in her current job, not the fact that every job has some problems. Third, the reply would not be critical and tell Katie, "Get tough. Don't let them get you down." Toughness is needed by the school district and by political leaders. Katie is plenty tough, but the toughness of one teacher is not sufficient to match the impact of perplexing social problems that some students bring with them to school. Katie sincerely longs to teach, but she cannot be a one-person police force or social services agency and still teach. She believes that her job is to cause learning, not to rehabilitate juvenile offenders. She is a great teacher, but she is convinced that she is being asked to do more than effective instruction can do.

What is the results-driven teaching reply to Katie? It would be as follows:

"First, Katie, please give yourself credit. Because you are a results-driven teacher, you perceive teaching and school differently than people who just go through the motions, who never expect much of themselves, their students, or their school. The realities at school that concern and frustrate you are genuine. You would like to see those realities addressed. Other people just default to an approach of getting by, getting through, getting out at the end of a school day, a school year, or a school career.

"Second, please pull the alarm. If you were the one and only person who realized that the school building was actually on fire, you would need to pull the fire alarm to warn everyone, to protect everyone, and to notify the emergency experts at the fire department to come immediately.

"The school you care about so deeply has brain-threatening, mind-threatening, health- and safety-threatening, student achievement–threatening, and teacher achievement–threatening conditions that have the seriousness of a fire, but not the noticeable immediacy of a fire emergency. Pull the alarm. There is no academic achievement alarm switch to pull that is comparable to a fire alarm, but there are options that can be activated. Work through your school and school district chain of command to inform everyone directly, diplomatically, honestly, and thoroughly of the realities at school. Persist and insist. Be sure to continue getting superior results in your classroom. That helps confirm the validity of your other concerns. You are not a faculty lounge complainer. You are a results-driven teacher who is asking a school system to take the necessary and realistic actions to be a results-driven organization.

"Third, please remember that while teaching has many frustrations, it can also be the source of many unique rewards. To be a teacher means to be where the students are. You could succeed in your next job if you do leave teaching; however, that success will not be in the arena of causing learning in the brains, minds, and lives of students. Before you leave teaching, before you leave this school and this school district, ask what options exist or could be created here. You know that wonderful achievement occurs in your results-driven classroom. Now, please consider ways that you could guide your school into becoming a results-driven school and your school district into becoming a results-driven school district."

Our next case study features a variety of high school teachers who are at different points on the teaching spectrum. They range from results-driven teachers to excuse-driven classroom clerks. We listen to their discussions at a meeting of their school's curriculum and instruction committee. The participants are listed below:

- Grace Covington, 22 years of teaching social studies
- Celeste Hamilton, first year of teaching math
- Matthew Howard, six years of teaching physical education
- John Mitchell, 18 years of teaching science
- Andrew Phoenix, 10 years of teaching Spanish

Covington: We have only one topic on the agenda today, but it is really important, so let's get started. Thanks for being here. Okay, the topic is this: Is our school using the best possible teaching methods? The school board and superintendent are asking every principal to have a group at each school study and evaluate this topic. So what do you think? Are we using the best possible teaching methods?

Hamilton: I'm using every teaching method I learned in college. Of course, I finished college only one year ago, so this is my first year of teaching. I use a lot of technology in my classroom, from graphing calculators to PowerPoint presentations. I even use old-fashioned methods like flash cards, but those helped some of the algebra students and geometry students. If there are better teaching methods, I'm open to using them because some of my students struggle with math no matter what I do.

Howard: My classes are physical education. We play a lot of games and sports. We exercise a lot. We measure our progress. We read about exercise and we do some projects, like invent new games. I once gave them a baseball bat, a volleyball, and six orange marker cones. Their job was to invent games to play using that equipment. They were very creative. So I do the best I know how, and I'm always looking for better ideas.

Mitchell: I've taught science classes for 18 years. This has been the best year ever. I'll admit I pretty much did the same thing year after year for 10 years or so. Books, worksheets, videos, and multiple-choice tests. Then I started coaching soccer at our school. I kept explaining soccer skills using science words. Well, some soccer players started talking in class about how science was making them better soccer players. Force and motion, gravity, and Newton's laws made sense to them now. So I always look for ways to connect sports and other real-life activities to science.

Phoenix: I've been here 10 years. Every few years a new group of school board members or a new superintendent gives the principals some directive or order like this one about the best teaching methods. So we have committee meetings, take surveys, write a report, and send it to the school board. Usually we never hear anything until a few years later, and we do it all again. We could just take our school's report from four or five years ago and update it a little. I use the teaching methods that keep my students under control. They behave, so I guess that means I am using the best teaching method I could use.

Covington: I've taught social studies for 22 years. I never use teaching methods that I've been told were bad. It does concern me that some students fail my classes every year. But other students do very well in my classes. I give everyone the same opportunity to read the book, do the homework, take the tests, even complete extra credit. Everyone could make an A grade, but not everyone does. Is there a better way to teach than what I do? How would we determine what the best way to teach is? Is there one best way or are there many ways that can work?

Howard: We talk about questions like that in the graduate school class I'm taking. The topic is curriculum. The professor defines curriculum as what we teach and how we teach it. That's a new idea to me. I always thought that curriculum meant all of the subjects taught at school. We did a research project for class. We each interviewed five adults about what they remember from their kindergarten through high school experiences at school. The results were amazing. The strongest memories were not of classes or of subjects. The strongest memories were of teachers, what they did, and how they did it. People remember people and the experiences they shared. So I'm doing more and more in my classes to create experiences where the students and I interact. I don't stand and watch them play soccer; I get out there and play. I can interact personally with each student in each class that way. It seems to work as a motivation to students and it sure helps me know how each student is doing. They would still play soccer if I stood and watched, but it seems to matter a lot that I get involved. How I teach now—using personal interaction with the students—makes them learn what I teach, like soccer, so much better.

Phoenix: Well, let's be careful. Let's not pick one teaching method and say everyone has to use only that.

Hamilton: Hey, if you know of a great teaching method, tell me. I don't have to be required to use it. I'll eagerly use anything that works.

Covington: Good point. There are many teaching methods that work, and there are other methods that never work very well or at all. So we could have a list of many teaching methods that teachers are free to use and a list that are not to be used because everyone knows they never work.

Mitchell: That work has already been done. There are many good research studies that have been published about great teaching. Don't you remember those books our principal encouraged us to read two or three years ago about four characteristics of very effective teachers?

Phoenix: I remember. I wrote those characteristics in Spanish and made a poster. I'll share the English version with you. Very effective teachers— the author called them "extreme teachers"—have four characteristics. First, they use a variety of teaching activities, methods, and techniques. Second, they are enthusiastic about teaching, about students, and about learning. Third, they challenge their students. Fourth, they connect what is being learned now with the real lives that students are living now. It makes sense and it's easy to remember. It's not easy to do at first, but it works and it gets easier the more you use it. Hey, if our principal had us read those books a few years ago, why are we having this meeting to discuss the same topic again? Just like I told you. Here we go again.

Covington: Let's be more hopeful. I do remember those books. Mr. Howard, your idea of having students create new games is one way to make a real-life connection. Children and teenagers do invent games. Plus, you were challenging them to think. When you play soccer with them, it shows your enthusiasm and it adds to the variety of teaching methods. Maybe we're already using the best teaching methods.

Hamilton: I have a unique advantage as a first-year teacher. I've been required to observe 10 teachers in our school this year as part of my first-year professional growth plan. I'm sorry, but I almost went to sleep in a few classrooms. Some teachers here are all worksheets, all the time. Other teachers are fantastic. The results from one classroom to another are all over the place. So not everyone at this school is using the best possible teaching methods based on what I saw.

Covington: What do we do next? The principal needs some recommendation from us.

Howard: Could we ask every teacher to send us a one-paragraph email describing or listing the teaching methods they use? We could compile those and then evaluate that big list versus those four characteristics of very effective teachers. That would at least be a start.

Covington: If that is agreeable, I'll send the email tomorrow to all teachers and ask for their reply within three days. I'll put the total list together and email that to all of you next week. Then we can create our report and our recommendations. Thanks for your help today.

What is missing from that committee discussion? Take a minute and reflect. You are right. The committee is going to evaluate current teaching methods versus highly effective teaching methods, but the committee also needs to have information about results.

Doing what highly effective teachers do is very important. Doing what highly effective teachers do and getting highly successful results is vital. The best teachers use only the best teaching methods, but continually make adjustments based on how much and how well students are doing. Use only the teaching methods that work, but "that work" is confirmed by the results you are getting. If Mr. Howard's students did not learn about physical education when they created a new game, Mr. Howard needed to make adjustments to cause learning. He shouldn't say, "But it's a new activity. I'm supposed to use a variety of activities." Results rule. A variety that does not cause learning is an unproductive variety. Vary the activity until learning is caused, until the result of causing learning happens.

Consider this conversation between a principal and a teacher as our final case study:

Cook: Mr. Sutherland, your lesson plans for this month show little or no concentration on the approved curriculum for 9th-grade language arts. Please explain this.

Sutherland: Well, I just thought those big literature books were so overwhelming that we would begin with a few weeks of fun activities to get off to a good start. I know that the sports section of the newspaper is not classic literature, but it is interesting. We want our students to read, don't we?

Cook: We also want our teachers to teach in the most effective ways, don't we? Mr. Sutherland, change the lesson plans. Of course, a variety of reading materials can be used. Compare and contrast a sports article with a classic short story. Your lessons show no evidence of how you will evaluate student work or what the objectives for each day are, and they also don't show much more than a few weeks of random newspaper reading. I know it is the football season and your coaching duties take time, but your first job is to teach effectively. I'll visit your class during the next several days to see the great work we both know you can do. Get the revised lesson plans for this week to me by tomorrow and for the rest of the month by Friday. By the way, that book of football plays you assign your team to learn is about as big as a literature book, but you find ways to get the entire team to learn it. Maybe there are some teaching ideas you can borrow from your coaching. Certainly, you need to expect as strong a work ethic from your students as you do from your athletes. You should expect the same performance from your teaching as you do from your coaching.

With everything you now know about the concept, work, perspective, idea, and ideal of results-driven teaching, reflect upon these questions:

1. How could Mr. Sutherland have prevented these problems and concerns?
2. What is the most important issue in this case study?
3. What should Mr. Sutherland include in his improved lesson plans?
4. What else does Ms. Cook need to do to resolve this?
5. What was Mr. Sutherland thinking when he submitted such superficial lesson plans?

How people think about, understand, and perceive their job significantly impacts what they do in that job and how they do that job. Results-driven teaching goes far beyond the requirements of any educator's job description or job performance evaluation form. The standards for results-driven teaching come from the conscience, the integrity, the heart, the soul, and the mind.

Students benefit in unlimited, lifelong ways when they are taught by results-driven teachers. Those results-driven students commit to filling their brains so they can fulfill their minds throughout a very fulfilling life.

Results-driven teachers have career experiences that fill their days and years with rewarding moments. Results-driven teaching blesses results-driven teachers with experiences that fill their brains so they can fulfill their minds, hearts, and souls throughout very fulfilling lives.

There are teachers who give students some opportunity for some learning and there are results-driven teachers who cause every student to experience significant, profound, worthwhile learning. When the word "teacher" and the work of teaching are synonymous with "results-driven teacher" and results-driven teaching, victory can be declared, but even then the victory must be maintained by an insistence on results.